Language Behavior in Therapy Groups

LANGUAGE BEHAVIOR IN THERAPY GROUPS

Ruth Wodak

Translated by
Andrew Smith

UNIVERSITY OF CALIFORNIA PRESS
Berkeley • Los Angeles • London

University of California Press
Berkeley and Los Angeles, California

University of California Press, Ltd.
London, England

Copyright © 1986 by The Regents of the University of California

Library of Congress Cataloging in Publication Data

Wodak, Ruth, 1950–
    Language behavior in therapy groups.

    Translation of: Das Wort in der Gruppe.
    Includes bibliographies and index.
    1. Group psychotherapy.   2. Interpersonal
communication—Therapeutic use.   I. Title.
[1. Communication.   2. Psychotherapy, Group.
WM 430 W838w]
RC488.W5813   1985   616.89'152   84–28005
ISBN 0-520-05201-3

Printed in the United States of America

1   2   3   4   5   6   7   8   9

To the memory of my father,
Dr. Walter Wodak

Contents

6: The self-assessment of patients and therapists 256

SCHEMATA

Preface

*"Yes, I must say, because now I no longer have the feeling that
I am all alone. Of course, I have my children, but I don't talk to
them, and nobody listens to me; and, I mean, you have the feeling
[in the group] that not only do you have problems yourself, but
that the others also have them"* (text 17, session 12, patient 10).

These words concisely convey the opinion of the patients of a
therapy group about the sense and effect of therapeutic discourse.
To what extent is it possible to offer assistance by means of therapeutic communication, or therapeutic discourse, in cases in which
everyday communication fails? What is the explanation for the
particular effect of therapeutic discourse and the therapeutic setting?

This book is based on an interest in the mechanisms of interaction
and communication, in the practical relationships between human
beings and institutionally controlled and secured communication.
It is, above all, an analysis of "disturbed" communication and an
opportunity of restoring "disrupted speech games" that allows one
insight into the intrinsic dimensions of human behavior.

Interdisciplinary research in the field of linguistics and psychotherapy is an obvious choice for the study of the aforementioned
questions: on the one hand, it moves at a fundamental theoretical
level (description and explanation of communicative phenomena
in therapeutic discourse, elaboration of integrative theories), and
on the other, this undertaking resonates with a pretension to practical relevance. This is where an explicit sociolinguistic and psycholinguistic analysis can open up new horizons for psychiatric
work, for communication between doctor and patient.

Chapters 1 and 2 indicate the theoretical and methodological
framework used to describe and explain adequately the phenomenon of therapeutic discourse: this is done with the aid of a pragmatic linguistic theory, the "three-level model" of therapeutic
communication (2.3). The empirical longitudinal study of a therapy
group is used to verify the hypotheses produced. At the same time,

the development and application of new psycholinguistic, text-linguistic, and sociolinguistic methods make possible an explicit understanding of the communicative processes involved (chapters 3–6). The results obtained regarding class- and sex-specific speech behavior and therapeutic effects stem from the qualitative and quantitative analysis of a textual corpus that gives objective insight into prejudiced social phenomena while providing a basis for the formulation of linguistic theories that hitherto have had to be oriented mainly toward explorative studies.

For the first time the effects of class and sex on communicative behavior have been examined within an interdisciplinary framework (2.4). To this purpose it proved necessary to develop a text-linguistic model for the category of problem presentation in group therapy, which is taken up in section 3.9. The category chart that was specially produced for the present investigation reflects an interdisciplinary approach that combines text-linguistic, psychoanalytical, sociopsychological, interactional sociological, and socio- and psycholinguistic categories and concepts (3.10).

Apart from the theoretical approach, the aim was to present as well the most vivid impression possible of the Vienna Crisis Intervention Center, the members of the group, and the therapeutic processes. Over and above the fundamental theoretical aspect, empirical investigations of this nature offer an insight into marginal social areas. Accordingly, this book will have achieved its object if it is regarded as a contribution to the humanization of personal relationships in our society.

At this point I should particularly like to thank Prof. W. U. Dressler and Prof. H. Strotzka for their help and attention. At the same time, I am deeply indebted to Dr. A. Becker, Dr. H. Leupold-Löwenthal, and Dr. O. E. Pfeiffer for their advice and discussion of particular problems.

Also, I want to stress my gratitude to Prof. Aaron V. Cicourel who made many very important comments and helped to edit the manuscript for translation. Without his help and support this book would not exist in English. In a few cases, where revisions were made, the theoretical position is updated.

I cannot sufficiently express my gratitude to the team of the Vienna Crisis Intervention Center and to the patients whom I had the opportunity of observing, for their cooperation and support.

I am also grateful to E. Scheiblauer and K. Zolles for their technical assistance in the production of a manuscript and in the computer analysis of data.

Finally, I should like to express my thanks to my mother, Dr. E. Wodak, and to my husband, Gunther Engel, M.A., for their kindness and emotional reserve during the production of the manuscript, a time often fraught with difficulties.

R. W.

Vienna
May 1980
and September 1984

1

Interdisciplinary Research: Psychotherapy and Linguistics— Psycholinguistics

I certainly exceed the conventional meaning of the word when I postulate the interest of the linguist in psychoanalysis. In this context language means not merely the expression of thoughts in words, but also the language of gestures and every other form of expression of mental activity, such as writing. It can then be asserted that the constructions of psychoanalysis are first of all translations from a manner of expression strange to us to one familiar with our way of thinking. (Freud 1976b, VIII:403)

We do not mean, incidentally, to despise the word. It is, of course, a powerful instrument, it is the means by which we proclaim our feelings to one another, the way in which we can influence others. Words can do immeasurable good and inflict terrible injuries. Of course, in the beginning was the deed, the word came later; in some circumstances it was cultural progress when the deed was moderated to the word. But nevertheless, the word was originally sorcery, a magic act, and it has still retained much of its original power. (Freud 1976d, XIV:214)

1.1. Introduction

At a time when linguistics as we know it today did not yet exist, these two statements of Freud summarized in an extremely compact form the purpose of interdisciplinary research, as well as the possible object of a fringe area such as psycholinguistics.

Language and speech behavior, in the broader sense of these terms as interpreted by Freud and not merely as a postulate of pragmatics and more recent linguistic theories, are an inalienable part of interaction and communication. It is not therefore surprising that speech and speech behavior play an important role in the therapy of disturbed communication and interaction.

Freud considered language relevant in several respects: on the one hand as an intersubjective means of mutual communication, for the expression of thoughts, feelings, and desires, and on the other as an instrument for the therapist's work, the therapist being regarded as a translator, as a mediator between private experiences unique to each individual and the colloquial connotations used in human communication. After all, the linguist assumes an important role, as he has the opportunity of explicating and objectifying these processes from the sphere of intuition, coincidence, and the individual and unique event and thus making it possible to reconstruct them.

Interdisciplinary research is regarded as desirable and worthwhile, a situation otherwise than what has been and often is still the case (for academic and sociological reasons) when scientists are unreceptive to intrusions from neighboring disciplines.

The fact, however, that Freud not only dealt a great deal theoretically with language in its function within and for therapy, but also that he developed a very personal, almost erotic, relationship to it is apparent from his work. We are not only confronted with a gigantic opus, but we see that there is an essential difference between it and other scientific works, as it is not written exclusively in scientific jargon (making it inaccessible to the layman) (Muschg 1975). On the contrary, Freud played with language: He was an artist, a novelist and author who had developed a feeling for the nuances and subtleties of language. No one other than a man to whom language itself was of great importance could have noticed how many meanings and connotations are associated with words, sentences, and texts—in other words, what is concealed behind verbal language.

From a historical point of view, the period in Vienna around the turn of the century and in the twenties appears to have been conducive to the study of language. Apart from Freud, we also find Hofmannsthal (1951:711), Kraus (1976), Schnitzler (1978:7 ff.), and finally Wittgenstein (1967) (Janik and Toulmin 1973). Wittgenstein in particular made language and its nuances and vagueness a central theme in his theory of language games. The tradition of Freud and Wittgenstein lives on today, both in modern philosophy and in linguistics (1.2.3, 2.3).

We can, therefore, trace a continuity that extends from these personalities and their ideas to the Frankfurt school (Habermas 1977) (1.2.6), and more recent trends in psychotherapy and research into disturbed communication (Watzlawick et al. 1972) (1.2.5). These recent trends include approaches in pragmatics, psycholinguistics, and sociolinguistics (2.4), linguistic philosophy, and cognitive psychology (3.9). From a scientific perspective, this development has not always been linear (Litowitz and Litowitz 1977:419 ff.). Apart from world political events, ideologies, and philosophies, many sectors of social science have been shaped by other theoretical approaches. I am thinking primarily of structuralism and behavioristic psychology (Skinner 1938), as well as of the development of systems theory and cybernetics (Parsons 1951), which strove to divide the world and its intrinsic aspects into clear, unambiguous functions and autonomous systems; there was thus no longer room for language in its diversity.

In the social sciences there was at the same time a search for new methods of quantification under the influence of the natural sciences. All kinds of qualitative research were disapproved (Filstead 1971). Today these extremes of opinion have been moderated, and there is room for compromise and reconciliation in theoretical and methodical spheres. Thus it is that qualitative methods again have a place, even in linguistics and the fields associated with it (3.5). Such terms as *textual understanding* and associated terminology have become quite commonplace; it is therefore certainly no accident that academic interest in psychoanalysis has grown, as the hermeneutic method is an inalienable part of the theory and practice of psychoanalysis (Soeffner 1979).

At the same time, psychotherapeutic research also strives to elaborate methods of objectification, methods that exceed the limits of individual case studies (Graupe 1975; Remplein 1977). At first glance, even the present investigation apparently contains contradictory trends in that it uses both quantitative and qualitative devices (4.5), sociological concepts (directed at the analysis of society) (2.4), psychotherapeutic concepts (directed at an understanding of the individual) (2.3.4, 4.4) and linguistic concepts (directed at the classification of a text) (3.9). Against the aforementioned background, however, it is obvious that these different approaches supplement—and do not preclude—one another.

As language and speech behavior are an intersubjective means of communication between humans, psychic processes manifest themselves linguistically (1.2.5), and similarly, therapy takes primarily the form of verbal communication, and in many cases processes of change can be detected in alterations of speech behavior.

An approach using linguistics and its subdisciplines is thus not only justified but desirable and important. The systematical and explicit analysis of therapeutic communication serves to objectify our understanding of the therapeutic procedure and thus contributes to psychiatric and psychoanalytical practice, as well as to fundamental linguistic, sociolinguistic, and psycholinguistic research. New dimensions are opened up, and such research gives us insight into the processes of communication, textual planning, and textual understanding. A new perspective emerges, one that gives us a better approximation of "meaning" and "understanding."

It is by no means my intention to provide a comprehensive historical review of the aspects that the two sciences and their taxonomies, methods, and theories have in common: this is the subject of a separate paper (Litowitz and Litowitz 1977). On the contrary, I consider it important to apply and report on the concepts and investigations that are of relevance to my own research, in other words, approaches dealing with disturbed communication and its therapy (1.2, 1.3). In the process, I shall only touch on "purely" psychotherapeutic concepts to the extent that they are of importance to the present investigation (2.2.3). In accordance with this intention, I shall not be concerned with definitions and terminological criticism; nor am I interested in the different ways in which the term *symbol* has ever been used. This is not a linguistic critique of the meaning of the terms *word, sentence,* or *text* in psychoanalysis, nor is it a scientific debate of the comparative value of the hermeneutic concept or other approaches.[1] Much of this has already been done, starting with Meringer's conflict with Freud over the validity of two approaches to the explanation of linguistic parapraxes (speech errors) (Meringer and Mayer 1895; Meringer 1923). It is not my intention to delimit scientific fields one from another but to use the concepts from other disciplines which offer a better understanding of linguistic, sociolinguistic, and psycholinguistic phenomena than would be possible by insisting on a "single" scientific concept. In this connection, it is easy to repudiate the charge of eclecticism: under no circumstances are individual terms and methods used without prior examination of their theoretical status.

Scientific and theoretical considerations make it impossible to integrate two or more sciences as an alternative concept. Each science divides its subject matter in a unique manner according to its own forms of validity, concepts, and methods. No one science, therefore, can definitively be reduced to another. Saying that psychic processes are the cause of linguistic phenomena (or vice versa) is also inappropriate (Zetterberg 1962). Relationships are established, but their direction cannot be ascertained. The problem is to find the most precise explanation and description possible of therapeutic communication (in this case, group communication) without having to specify the "origin" of the approaches used or without having to delimit one from the other. As a result of the integration of various methods, taxonomies, and theories, qualitatively new approaches (2.3, 3.9) and new instruments (4, 5.4, 5.5) are inevitably produced in any new discipline, for example, the interdisciplinary field of psychotherapy and linguistics. This methodological phenomenon will be referred to below in connection with the reciprocal mutual dynamics and influence between the object of investigation and the development of methods and theories (Kamlah and Lorenzen 1967; Krüger 1978).

1.2. Psychotherapy and linguistics
1.2.1. Common aspects

Dream texts and linguistic parapraxes (Freud 1973a, IV:61 ff.) are phenomena that have frequently attracted the attention of linguists (Fromkin 1973) and that have made psychotherapists (among them Lorenzer 1973 and Goeppert and Goeppert 1973) aware that an explicit linguistic analysis was called for. I do not wish to make further reference to these model examples, however, but will deal instead with communication and language in the therapeutic situation itself.

Yet the accommodating model examples do exhibit significant characteristics of therapeutic communication, such as diversity of meanings, which in many cases are strongly controlled by the unconscious. In the following pages it therefore seems expedient to consider several psychoanalytically oriented approaches that—in contrast to the earlier neurological approach—include language as an essential factor. We shall be interested not so much in concepts that interpret language taxonomically and descriptively out of context (i.e., that are influenced by structural paradigms) as in those incorporating situation, life history, and sociological context. These include schizophrenia research, which is strongly oriented toward communication theory (Leodolter 1975c, Wodak-Leodolter 1978b), the psychoanalytical school that continues the tradition of the Frankfurt school (Lorenzer 1973), the metatheoretical approach of

Habermas (1977), and finally, individual approaches, such as Jappe (1971) or Lacan (1958), which, although structural, nevertheless establish essential conditions for interdisciplinary research.

1.2.2. The development of Freud's linguistic concept: G. Jappe

"Freud's teaching is an etymology of psychic manifestations" (Abraham 1969:323). This pointed statement by Abraham represents a major aspect of psychoanalysis because it is a reference to the dynamics of psychic processes and thus to the nature of speech as a process. It also expresses an obsession with "the word." Etymology, in the sense generally understood by the linguist, deals with the origins and development of isolated words.[2]

Etymology is the point of departure of Jappe's attempt to follow the development of fundamental psychoanalytical terms and concepts with an emphasis on the description of Freud's linguistic concept (Jappe 1971). She convincingly illustrates how Freud's concept became embroiled with a psychology that had already been outgrown (Jappe 1971:90). "Our work consists of detailed evidence of the extent to which such a theory [linguistic theory] is lacking, what there is in its place, and the points of view from which an outline of this theory is apparent" (Jappe 1971:xiii).

The concept of verbalization and the conception of the basic rule proffer themselves as points of departure. Freud, Fliess (1949), and Balkányi (1964) adhere to a very narrow meaning of *verbalization*, that is, the formulation of psychic manifestations in words, in perceptible speech acts. They fail, however, to consider the affective and motivational components, the revival and recollection of repressed ideas and scenes.

Similarly, the "basic rule" was initially defined as an invitation to associative speech. Even A. Freud viewed the therapeutic situation as a "struggle to adhere to the basic rule" (A. Freud 1964:15). The linguistic concept had to be differentiated by means of analyzing the silence that occurred during therapeutic communication (Cremerius 1969:94 ff.): Everything that takes place in the therapeutic situation (which also includes silence) is communication. This corresponds to Watzlawick's axiom of the "impossibility of not communicating" (Flader and Grodzicki 1978; Watzlawick et al. 1972:50 ff.).

Increased importance is also attached to the interactive aspect of communication (between doctor and patient). Finally, it is assumed that it is precisely the affective factors that are an inherent part of verbalization and that must be integrated into the speech concept.

Without wishing to retrace here the development of psychoanalytical concepts in detail (Jappe [1971] has done this exceedingly well with reference to the aspects essential to linguistics), I find it necessary to point out the gap that exists between the analysis of linguistic parapraxes and dream texts by Freud (Freud 1973*a*, IV) and the recently acquired insights that have just been formulated. The technique of word association can be reconstructed using Freud's example of parapraxis analysis that has since become famous (see Freud's "signorelli" example, 1973*a*, IV:9). Although here, too, verbal recollection is linked to scenes, he does not draw the conclusion of including the context, the entire "language game" in his theoretical considerations. What remains is purely a phenomenological analysis of language (Jappe 1971:19).

The analysis of dream texts leads to the development of the theoretical concept of primary and secondary processes and of the schemata of regression and restitution and finally, to a differentiation between "conscious" and "unconscious" (Freud 1976*a*, II/III); the central role of language, however, remains unconsidered. "The word" is assigned to the conscious level, to conceptually organized thinking (Rapaport 1965:694 ff.). The conception of objects, conversely, is attributed to the unconscious, to instinctively organized thinking (Jappe 1971:68). Yet the fact that even conceptions of objects, and even the earliest stages of cognitive developments are at least connected with preliminary stages of symbolic organization has become general knowledge in psychology and psycholinguistics ever since Piaget (1969), at the latest.

> The problematical aspect of a situation, the paradigm of which we represented as the work of Charlotte Balkányi, results from the fact on the one hand that the relationship of language and consciousness is a central theme of psychoanalysis and has started to be appreciated as such particularly in recent times, and that, on the other, this relationship has been formulated by Freud in a terminology that originates in a way of thinking that has largely been superceded in psychology. (Jappe 1971:90)

This spell has been broken by the analysis of silence. A further important stage in the reformulation of a psychoanalytical linguistic theory is the work of Edelheit (1969), who used concepts of the structural paradigm of linguistics for an in-depth analysis of psychological concepts. The dialectic relationship between egostructure and linguistic structure is recognized, and the way to a new conception of colloquial speech is thus opened, which finally runs into the metatheoretical considerations of Habermas (1977). Although Jappe (1971:124) realizes the significance of socialization (she falls back on cognitive psychology, on the work of Spitz [1967] and M. Mahler [1969] as well as on Bernstein's sociolinguistics) and of context in determining the unambiguity of the spoken word, she cannot transcend the confines of the structural paradigm of linguistics. This is the very paradigm that regards segmentation and classification as indispensable and largely excludes the analysis of meaning, allowing it at best only at the level of the word and phrase. Note her concluding remark: "It makes a difference whether one conceives of verbalization as 'formulation in words' or as 'expression in speech.' The word can only represent a station on the way to explication; the process as a whole cannot be described other than as linguistic expression, as the development of an 'intermediate' space" (Jappe 1971:142). Her remark again gives final emphasis to the nature of language as a process. To this extent, certain transformational and generative concepts of more recent origin are probably more suitable for an integrated method of observation, but only in a nonnaive application. Because of its theoretical conception, purely generative transformational grammar makes it impossible to incorporate both context and colloquial and everyday linguistic meanings (conceptions of text planning, 3.9). Jappe's view of sociolinguistics and also of communication research represents a quite decisive step forward, as these linguistic approaches transcend transformational grammar in this respect, but she fails to include in her theory the dynamics of interaction and social reality (2.4).

1.2.3. The conception of A. Lorenzer

Lorenzer is of importance in this connection. He attempts to use "pragmatics" conceptions right from the start, which are derived from "late" Wittgenstein's concept of speech-act theory (Lorenzer 1977; Searle 1971) and which are particularly popular today in the linguistic community. Lorenzer, however, adheres too closely to a very abstract and metatheoretical dimension. "Interaction, communication, and verbalization" as interactive processes are at the heart of his conceptions. Once again, there is a lack of detailed analysis, which would very soon have resulted in the need for a differentiated concept of meaning. The diversity of linguistic communication is not considered, yet it is at the heart of work in psycholinguistics and sociolinguistics (2.3, 2.4).

Lorenzer starts with the central concept of understanding. The therapeutic situation initially provides the condition for the analyst to comprehend formally the patient's phrases: "The phrase is unambiguous because it is structured within the scope of a linguistic community. It is the foundation of communication, the operational basis from which the investigation of meanings can gradually be carried out" (1973:91). The meanings must therefore be elaborated by means of "scenic comprehension," by reconstructing the specific private meanings that every patient has individually linked to colloquial language in the course of his life (2.3.4).

> If the therapy (in its perception and in its thinking) has to reconstruct the private language acquisition of the patient, then understanding cannot take place within the framework of a linguistic community. Processes such as we have dealt with in the framework of the concept of "logical understanding" and of "own experience" are then obviously no longer sufficient. An operation which is founded only on the fulfillment of firm anticipatory formulae always falls short at the decisive point, at the point where psychoanalytical understanding must first prove its value: as an ability to transcend that which has always existed and to reassess private acquisition step by step. In short, psychoanalytical understanding must manifest itself as a hermeneutic process. (Lorenzer 1973:136)

As we shall see, Habermas (1977) went on to expound the concept of psychoanalytical hermeneutics metatheoretically (1.2.6).

There are three constitutive factors of Lorenzer's approach that are worth mentioning in the context of this brief outline, as they contain major impulses for interdisciplinary research; these are the concept of private language, the inclusion of Wittgenstein's concept of language games (1967), and the approaches to a materialistic, interactional theory of socialization (Lorenzer 1972).

Lorenzer differentiates between symbolic language usage and "clichés." Symbolic language usage corresponds to the secondary level of process. Clichés, however, are part of neurotic language usage, the expression of the patient's disturbance. Clichés are determined by situation, are irreversible, are subject to compulsive repetition, and are incomprehensible to the patient and his environment (Lorenzer 1973:110).[3] A desymbolization of colloquial meanings in the course of the repression of the patient's traumatic experiences has taken place. Yet the referential nature of the symbol is maintained, and its validity for the interaction, its dynamic and energetic relevance, is not lost but expresses itself in compulsive behavior (Lorenzer 1973:117 ff.). In the same manner, the emotional content of the original scene is retained in its full intensity. Thus it can happen that the patient uses expressions that are initially incomprehensible in response to certain stimuli that are otherwise not remarkable. Lorenzer illustrates his linguistic concept in the resolution of the "horse phobia of little Hans" (Lorenzer 1973: 127 ff.). The concept of the cliché, of private language, has proved useful in the analysis of schizophrenic language usage (Leodolter 1975c) (1.2.5). The inclusion of Wittgenstein's concept of language games enabled Lorenzer to resolve this initially remarkable contradiction (how can signifying content that is tacitly communicated be understood if no path other than communicated symbols appears to lead to them): "The concept of language games actually does take a surprising turn with regard to this problem. In accordance with this concept, access is open to outsiders . . . to the alienated sense fundamentally via another path: through participation in life practice" (Lorenzer 1973:197).

In the therapeutic situation, the analyst takes part, as it were, in a language game that has also lost its symbolic character (because of the transference). Understanding results from the uneffaced affiliation to the linguistic community (Lorenzer 1973:198). The rules of the language games are similar to those of the repressed scenes due to the compulsive repetition.

Although some terms of linguistic origin are used imprecisely, the significance of this concept of language game for a pragmatic linguistic approach cannot be overlooked. Language is embedded in the context of situation, meanings are comprehensible as a result of situational and personal usage (Leodolter 1975a, b). The concrete text analysis is missing; at this level of abstraction, adequate textual indications cannot be found (although this has been attempted— see Leithäuser et al. 1977). I believe that the approach is above all of metatheoretical interest and opens up new perspectives on actual analysis. Habermas's view (1969, 1977) will also be mentioned, particularly with regard to the hermeneutic method (1.2.6).

Finally, Lorenzer's concept of socialization must also be mentioned (Lorenzer 1972). Although the mother-child dyad was recognized by Spitz (1967) and others as an essential concept for socialization, Lorenzer goes even further in the development of his theory. Every action of the small child with his primary parental figure must be conceived as an interaction; to this extent each individual life history can be depicted as a succession of situational experiences. "Society" is imparted to the child via the primary parental person, via his actions, language, and neuroses. The breaks in the life history are marked by clichés. The typology of the interrupted life practice serves to form specific socialization patterns. Detailed sociolinguistic investigations can be applied at this point (2.4). Moreover, Lorenzer, again at a very abstract level, stimulates interdisciplinary research between psychoanalysis, sociology, and sociolinguistics and psycholinguistics.

All these more recent attempts (only two have been mentioned here by way of example) must be credited with turning away from purely neurological concepts (such as were in many cases represented by Freud) and with opening up more recent linguistic and sociolinguistic approaches and perspectives, though without always examining the scientific and epistemological standpoint of the concepts that they chose.

1.2.4. J. Lacan's neostructuralist approach

The approach of Lacan (1975) is characterized by three constitutive assumptions. This approach represents quite a different research tradition from that seen in Lorenzer and his radicalized essential assumptions of psychoanalysis at one point in particular: a difference is no longer made between drive structure and speech structure; language as such cannot be detached from the human being; every human being is language (Leclaire 1979:6). Psychic symptoms do not, therefore, manifest themselves in language, among other things, but are themselves language ("langage").

Furthermore, the concept of the specific, other "logic of the unconscious" is important ("le discours," "la logique de l'inconscient"). This is not a new idea; even Freud in *The Interpretation of Dreams* noticed the reversal of "normal" logic (1976a, II/III:112). The object of the psychoanalytical cure is the revelation of the structure of the other logic, which, however, is conceived as general and not historically individual. There is thus no reference to private language. The grammar of the unconscious is systematic and decipherable. The discovery procedure (I intentionally use this structural term here) is similar to free association: associations, linked to key words, reveal unconscious contents. The example cited by Leclaire (1979), however, is extremely reminiscent of phonetic symbolism; one gets the impression that the analyst is playing with meaningless words without showing an interest in the context and the suppressed meanings. It is not clear either whether the interpretation alone is at the linguistic level or whether essential concepts of depth psychology are in fact applied.

The linguistic theory that influenced Lacan was Jakobson's structuralism (Jakobson 1971). Psychoanalysis as linguistic analysis (but not in the hermeneutic sense) uses segmentation and classification of expressions to reveal the disturbance. The result is a concentration on "the word," and not on the text or on communication.

Even with intensive reading, it therefore remains questionable whether a new terminology has been imposed only on concepts and a conventional technology, or whether the search for the "grammar of the unconscious" has in fact become the basis of a new psychoanalysis and a new technique (Althusser 1970).

If, therefore, Lacan regards the structure of the unconscious as the structure of language itself (though interrupted by social tradition), this does not solve the problem as to the nature of the ambiguity, the kind of "systematic distortion" to which suppressed contents have fallen prey. In place of *condensation* and *displacement*, Lacan uses *metaphor* and *metonymy*, which determine the autonomy of the "signifiant," the symbolic meaning (1958:296). Nevertheless, how can the transition from the autonomous unconscious to the life history of the individual be dealt with, which, as Lorenzer correctly observes in the reconstruction of the disrupted language game, must also be taken into consideration (1.2.3). At any rate, contextless, autonomous linguistic analysis in the structural sense is not able to perform this task.

Two further conceptions are of relevance in this context, these being Habermas's theory of systematically distorted communication (Habermas 1969) and the theory and empirical studies of schizophrenia research, which for the first time involves the return to family interaction and communication as a matter of priority while investigating psychic processes. It therefore appears expedient to consider schizophrenia research, even if only briefly. It is impossible to deal with this field in detail, and this would interfere with the intention of this book, as it deals rather with neurotic disturbances and corresponding speech behavior. Nevertheless, the observation of psychotic disturbances such as schizophrenia does give us insight into important linguistic processes and problems of interactive communication: It is precisely here that one finds manifest material, disturbed speech, of a type that cannot be observed in the case of less serious illnesses. At the same time, the theories on the cause and origin of schizophrenia are exceptionally manifold, while the factor of family socialization has without exception been recognized as relevant; important fundamentals for interaction, for the functioning of human behavior in society, have been discovered and researched in the light of extreme "other" communication.

1.2.5. Schizophrenia research

Let us start with Watzlawick's first axiom (Watzlawick et al. 1972: 50 ff.), with the impossibility of not communicating—that is, that verbal and nonverbal exchange processes take place in every interaction, in every gathering, which, even if communication is not always successful, always represent signals, always form communicative acts. To this extent, unsuccessful communication should never be interpreted as an inability but as "talking at cross-purposes" or "mutual impact" or "conflict." In principle, however, every communicative act is of significance and attempts to impart something. This also applies to schizophrenic "blathering," which on closer observation turns out to be quite structured and full of meanings; it merely obeys laws different from those governing everyday communication. In fact, this blathering is related to a fairly everyday phenomenon, that of the dream (Leodolter 1975c:90). Very similar logical and temporal-spatial displacements can be observed in both cases, and the categories of displacement and condensation can quite meaningfully be applied to schizophrenic texts. The failure of communication is attributed by Watzlawick and his colleagues to the intermingling of the content level and the relational level, a differentiation that has subsequently left its mark on extensive fields of communication and interaction research; other theories, such as the speech-act theory, have approached quite similar phenomena and adopted them terminologically (Searle 1971; Austin 1971).

Contrary to neurotic speech behavior, in which only partial areas of the ego are affected, in the illness of schizophrenia, there is a splitting of the personality, the ego, which manifestly expresses itself in the use of private language, that is, there are not only latent private connotations present which must be worked through but a completely different language is used for certain subjects closely associated with the individual's life history. It is not the monological competence (in the sense used by Chomsky) that is disturbed (this has been verified in the light of an empirical investigation) but the dialogic competence (Leodolter 1975c:86 ff.). It is a characteristic of psychically disturbed speech behavior, however, that the use of private symbolism does not happen intentionally but unconsciously and compulsively: clichés are inserted (1.2.3) which stand out from everyday language particularly because of the fact that they are dependent on a situational stimulus and occur compulsively. As will be demonstrated later, these characteristics of neurotic and psychotic language necessitate a qualitative text description at several levels (2.3, 5.3, 5.4).

Attempts to discover the cause of schizophrenic disturbances have been made in various scientific disciplines. On the one hand, this is certainly a somatic illness for which there is as yet no clear medical and psychiatric explanation; on the other hand, the roots can be found in family interaction and communication, which have resulted in a split personality because of a person's inability to assimilate these factors. This attempt at explanation is particularly interesting here, as this also applies to neurotic symptoms and at the same time provides a point of departure for psycholinguistic and sociolinguistic research (2.4). We shall subsequently also be interested in the communicative mechanisms that occur within group therapy and in particular with the extent to which earlier modes of behavior can be repeated in the therapeutic situation and whether new object relationships and interactions are experienced as distorted as a result of transferences. This is discussed in detail elsewhere (2.1, 2.2, 2.4).

Family interaction, which must be regarded as schizophrenogenic, is certainly an extreme case, which therefore involves, for example, an excess of double-bind situations (Watzlawick et al. 1972), mystification (in Laing's sense—see Laing 1969) or concealment, as the phenomenon of continuous distortion of reality is-described (Wynne 1969); the fact that such interactions occur in almost every family situation, although not at such frequent intervals, has in the meantime been thoroughly proved (Bateson et al. 1969). The double-bind situation in particular offers a very good example of disturbed communication (Watzlawick et al. 1972: 224 ff.): In this case there is a complete divergence between the relational and the contextual level, with the result that the small child does not even have the possibility of arriving at a compromise solution from a conflict situation. An obvious example of this is the case in which the child is told that it is loved but is given a slap at the same time; at the relational level in the interaction, this clearly means a marked withdrawal of affection. One could give many examples, but it is sufficient to refer to the abundant literature on this subject (Leodolter 1975c:94 ff.). A further important aspect is mentioned by Lorenzer, who attempts to achieve an integration between the interactional and the genetic viewpoint in his theory of socialization (Lorenzer 1972): He maintains that lower-class socialization tends to result in more psychotic illness than a middle-class upbringing. The reason is to be found in the nonverbal family interaction of the lower classes and in the existence of rigid non-verbal negative sanctions. This theory should be checked in the light of a large random sample that excludes the factor of hospitalization and refers to members of the lower class who are dependent on public psychiatric institutions (Hollingshead and Redlich 1975). While it would exceed the scope of the present work to consider in detail this complex of questions, the conflict with opinions and theories on class- and sex-specific socialization follows in the commentary (2.4). At this point, only brief mention should be made of the fact that this form of dichotomization and the characteristic of lower-class language and socialization does not conform with the theoretical approach and empirical experience represented here. The lower class is not speechless but—on the contrary—much more open, emotional, and verbally spontaneous than the middle class, although there may possibly be shortcomings with regard to verbalization of the relational level in the course of linguistic socialization. In particular, the concepts of family interaction and communication from the antipsychiatry (Bateson et al. 1969) and the Wynne group (Wynne 1969) mention a very close family nucleus, which is probably more typical of the middle class than of the lower class. In the lower class, at least as far as male children are concerned, socialization is effected largely by peer groups that certainly exceed the confines of the small family (Labov 1972).

Following these brief remarks on schizophrenia, several important points have been selected by way of summary. We shall encounter these later—although in a different form—when talking about neurotic disturbances and corresponding speech behavior. The functions and method of therapeutic communication are not discussed at this stage, however (Leodolter 1975c:91 ff.):

1. Psychotic disturbances such as schizophrenia exhibit manifest linguistically deviant phenomena.
2. These occur not only latently in the form of private connotations but also explicitly as entire texts.
3. These texts use their own structures, obey their own laws, and can be linguistically comprehended and described.
4. Schizophrenic language can be regarded as private language with typical structures; the content is determined by individual history and cannot be understood or interpreted without a knowledge of the patient's history.
5. Some manifestations of schizophrenic communication can be found in everyday interaction and in dreams.
6. The causes of schizophrenic disturbances include mechanisms of communication and interaction in the family. In other words, both interactive sociological, sociopsychological, and socialization factors play an important role.
7. Schizophrenic language and communicative behavior are usually unconscious, that is, not intentional and occurring compulsively; they can therefore be associated with the term *cliché* (see 1.2.3).
8. In many cases resolution of the clichés (which in this case relate not only to the individual sphere of the ego but also result in a split personality) is admissible in psychotherapy (Brody and Redlich 1957). This involves a translation of private language into colloquial language after the processing of traumatic experiences and the resolution of the disturbed communication mechanisms. There are thus many features in common with neurotic speech behavior, as will be shown later (2.3). Schema 1 serves to illustrate these extreme communication disturbances so that it is subse-

SCHEMA 1
COMMUNICATION BETWEEN DOCTOR AND SCHIZOPHRENIC PATIENT
(Leodolter 1975c:92)

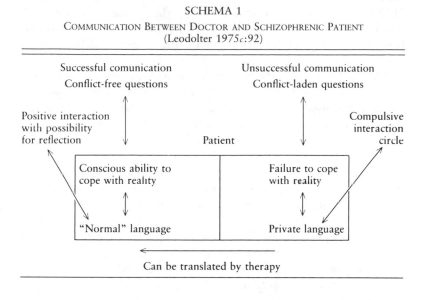

quently possible to differentiate other types of speech behavior on the one hand from this extreme, and on the other, from "normal" colloquial language.

1.2.6. Psychoanalysis as self-reflection

In the following section I would like to refer to a further important interdisciplinary approach to the clarification of disturbed speech: this is Habermas's discussion of "distorted communication" (1969). Habermas (1977:262 ff.) dealt with psychoanalysis, among other things, on a metatheoretical and epistemological level and attempted to describe the characteristic features of psychoanalytical hermeneutics and to point out the "scientistic misconception" of psychoanalysis, which—as can easily be understood—has necessarily arisen from the contradiction between the hermeneutic method and natural scientific pretensions of medicine. In this context it is not so much metatheoretical considerations that are of interest, although they do affect our own methodology, but the extremely differentiated attempt to conceive psychoanalysis as speech analysis. Although Habermas to some extent leans on Lorenzer

(1973), the theoretical framework and the considerations of colloquial language and symbolic organization are a direct exposi-
tion and attempt at integration with the theory and practice of
psychoanalysis.

We shall subsequently be dealing with three aspects of Habermas's considerations: the comprehensive and wide concept of language that is used often in pragmatics (2.3.2), the concept of scenic
comprehension as basic to the psychoanalytical and hermeneutic
method (which acquires particular relevance for the interpretation
of therapeutic communication) (5.2), and at last a broad outline of
the concept of self-reflection as one of the central functions of
psychotherapeutic happenings (this is subsequently of importance
above all in the discussion of therapeutic effect with respect to
linguistic alterations in speech behavior) (2.5).

The concept of private language and "paleosymbolism" has already played a role in the observation of schizophrenic speech
behavior and is also included in the differentiated analysis of therapeutic communication (2.3.4, 2.3.5).

Habermas's approach to colloquial language (1977:206 ff.) stays
in the tradition of analytical philosophy, the concept of the language
game, but its conclusions transcend it with reference to the theory
of the ideal speech situation (Habermas 1971). Colloquial language
comprises three categories of personal expressions: linguistic
expressions, actions, and experiential expressions.

> If linguistic expressions occur in an absolute form which makes their
> content dependent on the situation of the communication, "the diversity
> of times and persons," then comprehension is monological: . . . Only
> expressions in pure language can be completely understood in this sense.
> On the other hand, the more the linguistic expressions adhere to a
> concrete life context, the more important their position in a specific
> dialogic relationship becomes: the "transport" is no longer external to
> the content of the expression. Complete comprehension is obscured
> because there is no longer general agreement on an invariable meaning.
> (Habermas 1977:207)

Verbal language can attempt to give a situation very differentiated treatment, but a gap remains between individual historical
intention and linguistic objectification. This gap can only be closed
with the aid of interpretation. Two categories of the human being's
utterances can be used in the interpretation, however: first are

actions, although here, too, that which is specific to the individual is not clearly apparent; second is the experiential expression, which refers to all mimic, gesticulative, and emotional reactions.

> Hermeneutically the experiential expression is understood as a signal for unexpressed intentions and the inexpressible relationship of an ego to its objectifications. The experiential expression is not therefore on the same level as phrases and actions. On the one hand it is closer to the spontaneous life context than the symbolic expressions of colloquial language and communicative actions: it refers unambiguously to a certain organism in an unrepeatable situation. On the other hand, the experiential expression lacks cognitive content that could completely be interpreted in phrases of actions. (Habermas 1977:210)

The essential thing about this concept is not only the assumption of the different dimensions of colloquial language and the value of hermeneutic interpretation itself in everyday life but also, above all, the consequences of these considerations in the analysis of disturbed and therapeutic communication. This is where we find one of the most important characteristics: the incompatibility (or inconsistency) of the three levels. They no longer supplement one another. The linguistic objective has disintegrated; the particular feature of colloquial language—its reflexivity (it is able to interpret itself)—is inactive with reference to a specific life sphere ("the inner foreign land") (Freud 1973e, XV:62): Conscious verbalization is only possible again after processing of the symptom, which manifests itself linguistically in the manner described. I should like to return to an earlier definition that I made with reference to verbalization as one of the fundamental processes in therapeutic communication.

> By verbalization we mean a process in which there is a transformation of the communicative contents from the normative, activity-related, and physical, expressive level of communication to the level of verbality. The meaning of interaction-related normative action motives in actual social action is understood by the interaction partners in the sense of averbal action communication on the basis of the normativity of action motives that are generally valid in a social context. These action motives are expressed at the normative, activity-related communication level; they are raised to the level of verbal language, or made explicit. (Leodolter and Leodolter 1976a:114)

The individual is not aware of the discrepancy between the various levels and even "deceives himself, as it were." (Freud 1976:247). A "normal" interpretative effort on the basis of everyday knowledge is not sufficient to eliminate such a disturbance; the symptom remains comprehensible to the individual and his environment. The interpretation that is effected in the therapeutic situation is different; it is not "purely" hermeneutic but is based on the concept of scenic comprehension.

Psychoanalysis as linguistic analysis starts from the assumption that the depth-hermeneutic deciphering of specifically incomprehensible objectifications represents an understanding and equation of scenes in the therapeutic situation, in everyday life, and the primal scene. This naturally presupposes the psychoanalytical concept of typical phases of maturity and of their disturbances, of the small child in the family and of the child's conflicts with the primary parental person. It is only against this theoretical, conceptual background that the doctor in the transference situation, in which he is forced by the patient into the role of the conflict-laden primary parental person, is in a position to comprehend the repetition of scenes from early childhood and to compile a lexicon of private linguistic meanings for symptomatic utterances. According to Habermas, "The depth hermeneutics which Freud contrasts with Dilthey's philological hermeneutics refer to texts which indicate the self-deceptions on the part of the author" (1977:267).

The doctor teaches the patient to understand himself, to reflect about himself in the reconstruction of the primal scene; this makes the patient aware of his own process of learning. Scenic comprehension thus possesses explanatory power, in contrast to "pure" hermeneutics (see 2.2, 3.7, and 3.8 on the role of the therapeutic setting and transference between doctor and patient). At the same time, the growing awareness has practical consequences; the individual becomes able to act in a new way: self-reflection becomes a preliminary stage to action. Habermas continues:

> Three further characteristics demonstrate that analytical discovery is self-reflection. Initially two moments are equally included in it: the cognitive and the affective-motivational moment. It is criticism in the sense that insight is inherent in the analytical force of the resolution of dogmatic attitudes. Criticism ends in an alteration of the affective-motivational basis, in the same way as it also begins with the need for

practical change. Criticism would not have the power to destroy false awareness if it were not inspired by a passion for criticism. (Habermas 1977:286)

It is obvious from all these remarks how very much the psychotherapeutic concept is tied to a theory of colloquial language, a theory, which although not developed by Freud in his time, is implicit in his interpretation. Alteration and resolution of resistance and defense are effected by means of language: "The question: How does a thought become conscious? could therefore be more appropriately worded: How does a thought become pre-conscious? And the answer would be: by being brought into connection with the corresponding word images" (Freud 1976c, XIII:247).

In the context of repression, Habermas talks about an excommunication model (the social meaning is repressed, the symbol taken out of the common usage) about an "appropriation of the significant content" (Habermas 1977:295). Thus private language develops. The concept of private language has already been dealt with in the description of Lorenzer's concept and of schizophrenia and schizophrenic communication (1.2.3, 1.2.5).

The approach that Habermas offers is naturally a metatheoretical and epistemological one in accordance with his intention. There is, therefore, no detailed, concrete treatment of therapeutic communication itself. A detailed analysis of what "really" happens in the therapeutic situation must be carried out, and this can only be done with the aid of linguistic means; empirical investigations must also be made to determine whether the therapeutic effect is in fact tied to language or is linguistically expressed and whether the individual is able communicatively to effect self-reflection as a first step toward an alteration in practice (4.3, 5.4, 5.5). In the description of the empirical investigations that have been carried out, it will become evident that Habermas's concept cannot be reconstructed unambiguously—the linguistic analysis is more complex than might be supposed from Habermas's model of colloquial language, and the question of the therapeutic effect of language is considerably more difficult than purely theoretical considerations are prepared to admit. Nevertheless, several aspects of the concept are important. For example, the detailed description of the specific characteristics of therapeutic hermeneutics is relevant for the analysis of therapeutic discourse; it contrasts with the purely subjective interpretation and can be reconstructed on the basis of underlying theoretical concepts and the processes in the therapeutic situation (scenic comprehension). This will receive closer consideration in the discussion of the methods of text analysis (5.2).

The question of self-reflection, of psychoanalysis as a general interpretation of educational processes, also remains relevant in several respects: first, in the investigation of what the therapeutic group has meant for each individual patient (6.4); second, in what extent the intersubjective factor can be elucidated by the exact analysis of speech behavior (5.4, 5.5); and third, methodologically, in the definition of psychotherapy and thus also of interdisciplinary approaches from the natural scientific paradigm (2.3). Finally, a sociological dimension can be established as derived from socio-linguistic theoretical concepts. For example, there is the question as to whether typical class- and sex-specific speech behavior mechanisms have an effect (2.4). Colloquial language is by no means a homogeneous medium. What, therefore, is the effect of sociolinguistic variation? Do language barriers exist? From our experience we know that the model of an ideal speech situation, of mutual understanding, never fully exists in reality—even in normal communication (Krappmann 1972:70 ff.).

Several aspects will be illuminated more closely in the brief description of linguistic studies in the interdisciplinary field of linguistics and psychotherapy; these last subjects played an outstanding role in our own empirical investigation. The following brief outline of existing investigations concentrates particularly on the methodological and methodical framework and on the various attempts at integrating therapeutic and linguistic concepts.

1.3. Linguistics and psychotherapy

The interest of linguistics in therapeutic communication has greatly increased in recent years and has, indeed, only recently begun. The reasons for this lie, on the one hand, in the development of pragmatics and speech-act theory and on the other hand, in the pretension of linguistics actually dealing with empirical material. First, because therapy occurs in a precisely defined setting, amid the familiarity of the institution and its rules, the material from therapeutic situations makes it possible to explain important fundamental conditions of human communication. From a logical research viewpoint, it is always meaningful and useful to use material from extreme communication situations, as it is easier to grasp everyday communication in the definition of such interactions. This interest must be regarded as fundamental research. Second, there is the scientific and historical development that led from rigid structuralism and transformational grammar to pragmatics. (Pragmatics deals with the significance and intention of speech acts.) The tendency has therefore been to follow in the footsteps of Wittgenstein (1967), Schütz (1960), and symbolic interactionism (Goffman 1959). This was of prime importance in taking a speech situation in which explanation, scenic comprehension, and hermeneutic interpretation are actively integrated as immanent action schemata and are not presented merely as methodological concepts. These methodologies can therefore be subjected to realistic examination. Third, language-game therapy is a speech situation in which the action is almost exclusively verbal, with the consequence of intended self-reflection and alteration; it thus involves speaking in direct connection with human practice (2.2.2). There is one further motive that can be mentioned, an interest in the processes of socialization and the acquisition of language and behavior. Psychoanalysis provides us with a concept of socialization, yet it is clear from previous investigations that language is the means of socialization and is acquired through socialization. Psycholinguistic and sociolinguistic fundamental research are the obvious choices here as research orientations (2.4). We know that neurotic symptoms have their roots in childhood and can be traced back to certain communicative mechanisms and that such pathogenic mechanisms are repeated in the transference situation. It is therefore possible to gather experience of disturbed family interactions and develop guidelines and postulates for alternative pedagogics. Labov and Fanshel (1977) summarize the reasons for and interest in linguistic therapy research in two passages in their recent work:

> It is certainly no accident that many of the systematic studies of conversation have focused upon therapeutic sessions. . . . There is an important social need to understand the conversational exchange that takes place in therapy. These conversations are often quite extended, so we have access to a great deal of information about the speakers. The participants become involved in tense and emotional interchanges, which present some of the most difficult problems for the understanding of the mechanism of conversation and its coherence. This emotional climate is also an advantage in diminishing the observer effect. There

is no doubt that speakers never lose their awareness that the conversations are being recorded, but their involvement in the emotional dynamics of the exchanges reduces the amount of attention that can be given to the monitoring of their speech. There is no reason to confine the study of conversation to therapeutic sessions, but for all the reasons just given, it seems likely that therapy will continue to serve as a strategic research site for our understanding of conversation. (Labov and Fanshel 1977:353–354)

This specifies the methodic advantages of a study of the therapeutic situation. In another passage the basic motives are also mentioned:

We can see such analyses developing in two different directions. On the one hand, many students of conversation are more interested in the substance of interpersonal exchange than in the rules and structure of conversation. The rules of discourse may have only incidental interest for them. For many students of psychotherapy, a major concern will be the isolation of the underlying propositions that govern therapy in different settings, and this method will allow them to show how such propositions are embedded in the conversational exchange itself. . . . The other direction of development is a more technical one: the separation and identification of paralinguistic cues, the codification of methods of expansion, and the systematic development of rules of discourse. This is the natural area of interest for linguists who have been involved in formal analysis at lower levels of organisation. . . . An analyst also gains insight through microanalysis. Some of this knowledge will be grounded on objective evidence and some on more subjective evidence. But we cannot escape the strong conviction that we now know more about Rhoda [a patient] and the therapist than we would have gained from a simple reading of their conversation. . . . (Labov and Fanshel 1977:359–360)

Several approaches will subsequently be mentioned by way of example, particularly from the methodical viewpoints of the interpretative techniques used and because of cognitive interests. It is by no means possible to list here all the investigations of therapeutic communication. Although this would provide bibliographical information, it would also serve rather to confuse than to illuminate the points that seem important to us. Similarly, we are less interested in the scientific and historical aspect than in the actual level of research (Flader and Wodak-Leodolter 1979:v–x).

1.3.1. Speech-act-oriented analyses

Initial attempts in the direction of a speech-act-oriented analysis were made by Goeppert and Goeppert (1973, 1975). Transcribed psychotherapeutic discourses were examined according to various criteria, such as person used, temporal and spatial reference, intention, speech acts, and so on, and provided with a psychoanalytical commentary. The linguistic criteria are taken from Habermas's classification of types of speech act (1971:115 ff.) and Posner's theory of annotation (1972:53 ff.). The transition to psychoanalytical interpretation cannot be reconstructed; linguistic and psychoanalytical interpretation stand side by side. Nor has the choice of indicators been accounted for. Indicators had to be derived from a theory on the rules of therapeutic communication and are only meaningful in such a setting. In all other attempts at the analyses of speech acts, it is quite obvious that the categories are typical of each discourse and that there are various typologies and hierarchies of relevant speech acts depending on the speech situation.[4] Therapeutic communication is, once again, diverse, and this should also find expression in the linguistic analysis, in a multilevel analysis against the background of a linguistic model of therapeutic communication (2.3). One cannot, however, criticize initial attempts for not already incorporating an entire development, for much can be learned for further analyses, particularly from such hesitant steps. The two studies of the Goepperts (1973, 1975) were both of great importance scientifically, as they were almost best-sellers and made the German public aware of this important new research field.

Frankenberg's analysis of a married couple's therapeutic discourse (1976) offers a much more differentiated approach. At this stage the problems of a case study with an example and the question of how certain utterances can unambiguously be allocated to a category of speech act will not be examined. This will be done in detail in our own methodological considerations (5.2). Frankenberg's interpretation of a married couple's therapeutic discourse is effected at several levels and sets out principally to explore the gap between intended act, strategy, and interactional goal (Frankenberg 1976:71 ff.)—that is, every communicative act has its own immanent communicative function and may possibly then be used differently as a discourse strategy ("defunctionalized") and has a certain goal with reference to the interaction and the interaction partners. This presupposes at least two things: first, that each utterance is unambiguous in its function and goal, and second, that this typology disregards the specificity of therapeutic communication—the diversity, the position of latent and unconscious functions, desires, needs, and objectives in the communication. These can, however, be registered with the aid of psychotherapeutic concepts and when used would tremendously reduce the subjectivity of the classification. What is more, Frankenberg is unable to recover his own pretensions and intentions and fails to achieve the goal formulated initially to describe communicative mechanisms in the small family (in particular, strategies of reproach and justification) and to incorporate them in a theory of socialization (1976:38 ff.) It proved possible in the light of empirical material, however, to differentiate the mechanism of reproach and justification by way of illustration and to explicate forms of expression of this strategy. To do this it was not absolutely necessary to use therapeutic discourse; a "normal" marital conflict might possibly also have been sufficient. Such material is now, however, easily accessible, and although the decision to investigate the therapeutic situation is understandable, this speech situation and its peculiarities were not explicitly integrated in the analysis, a methodic procedure that is not quite correct. It is to Frankenberg's credit that he was possibly the first person to deal with a therapeutic discourse completely and quite differentially, though the methodological weaknesses cannot be overlooked.

Since the research noted above, this kind of multilevel analysis of speech acts with different categories and different levels has been continued. Yet people became more and more convinced that the allocation of individual expressions to individual categories and the substantiation of these categories remained fairly problematical. Similarly, the psychotherapeutic interpretation, if carried out at all, seems fairly ad hoc, and in most of these investigations there are no theories of therapeutic communication on the ambiguity of language and knowledge about psychoanalytical interpretative categories. Without pretension to generalizable statements, the studies often present interesting material, differentiated descriptions, approaches for further reflection, and impulses for larger empirical investigations and development of hypotheses and theories.

Klann (1979) made an important step forward in her attempt to interpret a fictitious everyday text (*Scenes from a Marriage*) with regard to the value of affective processes against the background of psychotherapeutic knowledge. Her theory, that similar processes direct communication in everyday life and in therapy, is quite plausible, but the processes are usually obscure and irresolvable: the therapeutic setting and the therapist are missing, and the unconscious motives are not discussed, even if they show their effectiveness directly. Everything that is too intimate is glossed over by the speaker with a view to maintaining his own image. In spite of the tremendous structural differences between everyday communication and therapeutic communication, differentiated analysis of the affective level reveals that a number of unconscious contents do indeed become apparent. The problem of allocation and construction is just as much present in this book as it is in the above-mentioned works. Yet the attempt to examine everyday communication for the psychic knowledge and ignorance (Klann 1979:129 ff.) of the speakers represents an important application of the knowledge of the therapeutic process and of the dialogic rules that occur there. We are able to acquire greater comprehension and understanding of everyday life. The result is an insight into the important and essential form in which affective processes control everyday communication and how these can also be experienced through active verbal linguistic processes, particularly in conflict situations in which dialogue fails in spite of attempts at communication. The three levels of colloquial language exhibit contradictions, not only in neurotically disturbed speech behavior but also in everyday life (1.2.6). It should be noted that the dialogue Klann investigated leads us to expect strongly neurotic mechanisms in both interaction partners. These must stay speculative considerations, however, which are impossible to substantiate because of the fictitious nature of the text. This is, therefore, an example of how knowledge gained from therapeutic communication can be useful in everyday practice, and an example in which the analysis, particularly of the affective-motivational level, is new and innovative.

On the other hand, in the scientific investigation of everyday dialogue it is not only permissible, but also desirable that the communicative techniques of therapeutic interaction should be applied and that a difference should be made between the therapeutic effect of the latter in their cognitive content and communicative procedures in everyday communication processes. However, this must be done with strict consideration for the differences between therapeutic and everyday communication and interaction processes. (Klann 1979:153)

1.3.2. The expansion model

In their detailed analysis of a psychotherapeutic discourse, Labov and Fanshel (1977) demonstrated how one can interpret extremely small sections of text using a multitude of different methods and gain an understanding of the therapeutic process and also of the patient, her illness, and life history. The individual steps of the analysis are presented before dealing critically with this study (Wodak-Leodolter 1978a:100 ff.):

1. The case study consists of a microanalysis of five small sections of discourse that are considered as typical of various phases of therapy.
2. The family and life history of the patient are described, and this knowledge is used explicitly in the interpretation.
3. The researchers examine the therapy sessions along with the therapist, using the playback method in order to hear her opinion about the interpretation that has been made and to receive explanations of her course of action. As a result, the authors acquire a great deal of knowledge about the psychotherapeutic technique and about important phases in the psychotherapy of the patient.
4. In an initial theoretical section, the authors develop their method of conversational analysis: general rules of therapeutic discourse (typical speech acts) are extrapolated and subsequently detailed for the particular case. Four levels are included in the therapeutic discourse: therapy, interview, narrative, and family.

> The outermost frame is the institution of psychotherapy. In the preceding section we have outlined the ways in which it affects speech behaviour. Within that frame we find the therapeutic interview marked by a type of metalanguage. . . . Embedded within the therapeutic interview are the narratives and discussions of everyday life, we find brief excerpts from family style, with its characteristic linguistic features. Shifts from one frame to another are characteristic of ordinary conversation, as Goffman (1974) has shown. For us, the recognition of distinct frames is particularly valuable because they determine so directly the linguistic forms that we will be examining. In our formal analysis of the therapeutic session to follow, we will identify each utterance with brackets that locate it within one of the stylistic frames outlined above. (Labov and Fanshel 1977:36–37)

The differentiation of these "frames" seems appropriate; it is also evident that they manifest themselves in different linguistic forms. Suprasegmental units are also considered in the characterization of speech styles.

5. "Expansion" is an essential part of the text analysis of both authors: Using the background knowledge of the authors, each sequence is expanded to a complete text, that is, incompleted sentences and sequences are enlarged; indirect and implicit content is made explicit for concrete analysis (Labov and Fanshel 1977:49 ff.).

6. Typical rules and utterance patterns are listed in the form of propositions. Some refer to the therapeutic situation, others to the particular case. These predicates are inserted into the text in order to identify typical and recurrent themes and relationships.

7. Finally, the interaction is expressed in the categories of speech-act analysis. In this manner, a multidimensional analysis (cross-sectional analysis) is obtained: the therapeutic situation, the specific case, individual texts, the psychotherapeutic process, the analytical technique, verbal and nonverbal content are included in the description (Labov and Fanshel 1977:37 ff.).

In spite of the differentiation and complexity of the analysis, several critical remarks must still be made. The entire investigation fails to progress further than the level described; this is a case study from which we get to see only five small text passages. It is not clear whether on the basis of this case study, important assertions should be made about the therapeutic process, about speech behavior in therapy, about the illness of the patient (anorexia nervosa), a psychosomatic illness, or about the very specific background of the girl (she comes from a "typical" lower-middle-class family). Although all these components are included in the analysis, particularly by means of the frames, their value even as an explanation for speech behavior fails to be considered (how, for example, does the therapy of a psychosomatic illness differ from that of another neurotic disturbance?). The investigation is certainly good as a case study, and the devices developed are manageable; but the question remains as to whether these devices can be transferred to other therapeutic processes. What is more, the method of expansion also entails certain problems. It is essential for text analysis and interpretation, but the criteria for the enlargement of direct speech are missing; yet if the expansion is only of an interpretative nature (even in this case, psychotherapeutic categories would have been appropriate), then it cannot be taken as an object of text analysis; it then has a metafunction. In my opinion, the diversity of language in the therapeutic situation is not therefore adequately grasped: on the contrary, from a methodological point of view, the levels have become mixed up. While there is a differentiated description of a very special case, there is no theory about therapeutic communication in which the specific case could be arranged (even the title of the book, *Therapeutic Discourse,* leads us to suppose that the authors are not interested only in the development of linguistic devices).

In spite of these critical considerations, the work has made an important contribution to the interest in linguistic therapy research and certainly provides the most detailed analysis of psychotherapeutic discourse to date. Although our investigation to some extent contains the methods of both approaches described so far, it also offers a theoretical frame (an interdisciplinary one—see 2.3), and therapeutic discourse is combined with elements of the theory of cognitive planning procedures (storytelling) (3.9). The advantages of this procedure will be described later.

1.3.3. The procedure in conversational analysis

Conversational analysis as the scientific description of extremely small speech units ("turns") represents an approach that sets out to explicate the processes controlling dialogue in everyday life— and in some cases even to record them formally. It is not, therefore, surprising that an attempt should be made to research psychotherapy more closely as a certain institutionally organized form of discourse with the aid of these devices. Flader formulates the intention of such a procedure as follows: "I want to . . . represent the investigation of an excerpt from a psychoanalytical discourse which is regarded as an attempt to classify mutual comprehensive control in psychoanalytical discourse as an interactive phenomenon. This attempt is part of a larger project on which I am working and which pursues the question of how psychoanalytical discourse functions" (Flader 1979:25).

The interesting thing about this approach—which is allied to the tradition of ethnomethodology[5]—is the attempt to reconstruct the therapeutic dialogue without explicit categorical knowledge of psychotherapy. What, then, from the viewpoint of textual immanence, is the nature of the interpretative routines and active habits of the patient, which reflect his everyday knowledge, and how is the gradual reorganization of this everyday knowledge and the elimination of systematic distortion effected by the analyst? The advantage of such an analysis is its text orientation; every individual utterance, every sequence, is minutely examined for implicit ambiguities. The doctor's procedure (often intuitive), his choice of a meaning, are made explicit as a communicative strategy. Communication conflicts are therefore due to nonreciprocity of utterance patterns, which is often the case, particularly in the case of constructions on the part of the doctor and when the patient's resistance is encountered.

In spite of the precision of such a method, it deceives itself: the text is central; all communicative interactions that occur are supposed to be explained from the text; typical features of the therapeutic discourse are elaborated. Yet, the knowledge of therapy and technique that the investigator possesses is naturally included in the interpretation; he knows, of course, that this is a therapeutic discourse. This is a "hermeneutic circle" valid for every social scientific text interpretation.

A similar approach is represented by Trömel-Plötz (1979:56 ff.); in contrast to the attempt described above, however, she observes even smaller, minimal sequences. Using very differentiated semantic analyses, she attempts to characterize the nature of the intervening utterance of the analyst. In these analyses, the effect of therapeutic intervention is examined in connection with the various types of operations that a therapist carries out by using an intervening utterance on the explicit and latent meanings of the previous utterance by the patient. These operations include the redefinition of certain signifying elements, the displacement of the focus of attention from central to marginal elements, the rejection of certain signifying elements, and the confirmation of others.

Yet the corpus remains small, and the interaction and therapy levels are ignored. Such an investigation would be particularly interesting in confrontation with the psychotherapeutic theory of technique, which is also neglected in their examples. What remains unclear is the extent to which therapeutic discourse is different from everyday conversation; there is no attempt to explain why the therapist chose precisely one intervention and not another. Nevertheless, on the basis of their detailed explanation of the empirical corpus, such studies do represent a preliminary move toward theoretically oriented investigations and approaches to interdisciplinary research.

1.3.4. Two further approaches to therapy research: transformational grammar and the Uzdnaze school
1.3.4.1. Generative-transformational syntax and therapeutic discourse

Introductions or guidelines to many scientific fields are often published in the United States, particularly for laymen, thus also to the field of psychotherapy. In a two-volume work, Grindler and Bandler (1976) attempt to explicate the psychotherapeutic technique against the background of generative-transformational syntax. According to them, the ambiguity of patients' utterances is based on several syntactic deep structures, and the therapist can therefore guess the meaning of the utterances on the basis of his knowledge of transformational syntactic operations (for example, a deletion transformation.) It is not by chance that I have chosen the word *guessed* in this context. The therapeutic process is regarded as something magical, and the therapist is a practitioner of "witchcraft," which can now be qualified by transformational grammar as something scientifically objectifiable. It is a thoroughly commendable enterprise, recommending exploratory techniques on the basis of linguistic analysis, but one that cannot succeed in this manner. The approach fails to consider several things:

1. Therapeutic discourse moves at the text level. Therefore, it is inappropriate to apply a sentential grammar.
2. Without exception, the approaches described so far reflect the complexity of therapeutic communication and the diversity of meaning. Yet this is exactly what cannot be investigated with a syntax- or grammatically-based theory that does not include local context and colloquial meaning.
3. Psychoanalytical theory and technique are not included in the analysis; the entire institutional frame seems to have been ignored.

In our case, sentential grammar can at best serve as an instrument in the frame of text-oriented analysis for the recording of individual syntactical phenomena. Yet the unreflected application of a theory that immanently excludes any consideration of everyday language meanings and their vagueness distorts the object of the investigation in an inadmissible manner and does not do justice to it (it is not expedient to buy simplification on the basis of ad hoc reduction).

1.3.4.2. Attitude research

The appearance of linguistic therapy research in the Soviet Union is scientifically and sociologically significant. Three large volumes entitled *The Unconscious* (Prangishvili et al. 1978) were published recently and should be included in our attempt to characterize the current standard of research. Uzdnaze's situation in the twenties is directly comparable with the situation of Freud in the year 1891. Both began on the basis of small studies in order to advance into large new areas of theory. Freud took his orientation from neurology, while Uzdnaze took his bearings from the behavioristic paradigm. By means of his experiments, Uzdnaze arrived at concepts of the unconscious, of feelings, and of verbalization. Lobner discusses the concept of Uzdnaze as follows:

> To illustrate this concept, its application in experimental phonetic symbolism may be mentioned: the Uzdnaze School has shown that unfamiliar "meaningless" words . . . carry a high information value. The experimental choice of new names for objects shows high inter-individual correlation, and the chosen name then begins to exert a reverse influence: it shapes the mode of experience of the denoted content of the object. The conclusion is that a "linguistic set" (which evolves through the interaction between the subject's personality and the objective reality) actually constitutes the psychological basis of what has been called the feeling of a language (Sprachgefühl). The evolution and the features and variations of the "linguistic set" can be examined experimentally. (Lobner 1979:21–22)

This represents quite a large step away from the simple stimulus-response schema, as does the fact that *set* is regarded both consciously and unconsciously. We shall now have to wait and see to what extent Soviet psychology and linguistic research will adopt these conceptual approaches, what results will be produced by the continuous experiments and investigations that in many cases are already being carried out on a large scale within institutions. I want to conclude this overview with a quotation from the foreword to volume three, *Cognition, Communication, Personality* (Prangishvili et al. 1978, III). It would be contrary to the intentions of these approaches to work through the entire literature in detail, and it seems more sensible to outline the most important and salient characteristics of each analysis in order to delimit our own research work, our own theoretical and methodical frame, and to emphasize its attachment, historical roots, and points of intersection with other concepts:

> The theoretical and experimental evidence adduced in the present volume points to the great role of the activity of the unconscious in the dynamics of the higher, ontogenetically most recently formed manifestations of man's mental activity. The history of the development of the concepts of the unconscious indicates that one of the main obstacles in the way of this development has hitherto been the simplified view holding that the most complex manifestations of man's spiritual life are the sphere in which all the components of the mental process are conscious whereas the unconscious is accorded at best only participation at the level of "elementary" mind, or, in other words, all that has the nature of automatisms or fixed dynamic stereotypes. Today there is hardly any need to argue the untenability of such treatment. (Prangishvili et al. 1978, III:23)

1.4. Summary

This brief description of historical developments and current approaches is designed to assist entry into the interdisciplinary field of psychotherapy and linguistics. It has been shown how closely linked the therapeutic procedure is with a theory of colloquial language and meaning: without such a theoretical frame, it would seem difficult to deal adequately with therapeutic communication. It has also been shown how much linguistic, socializing processes shape the individual, even with respect to his neurotic disturbances. A knowledge of these processes is therefore the precondition for understanding the mechanisms in the course of therapy. This book can by no means offer a satisfactory answer to all the open questions that have been raised. It, too, can only represent a step further in the scientific research of communicative processes in therapeutic communication; it may possibly illuminate several points, raise new questions, and in this manner provide an incentive to further research. Nevertheless, the sense of interdisciplinary work in the field of linguistic therapy research seems to us to be justified by the relevance of the object of investigation. The tremendous historical tradition and current scientific interest prove that our efforts are in the right direction.

2

Formation of Hypotheses

2.1. Introduction

This chapter describes the theoretical background to the empirical investigation of therapeutic communication in groups. It is here in particular that the interdisciplinary approach is explicitly evident: linguistic, sociolinguistic, and psycholinguistic concepts, theories, and models are applied. In many cases they run parallel to one another, and in some cases integration is possible.

To begin with, it is necessary to give a brief description of the therapeutic situation in groups with the aim of drafting a model of therapeutic communication. The main idea is to examine therapeutic discourse at three levels of meaning in order to be able to deal with the complexity of events (2.3). At the same time, the linguistically accessible level is explicitly analyzed; communicative functions and appropriate linguistic behavior strategies are taxonomically recorded (2.3.2). The sociological dimension is also relevant to this problem. We are interested not only in the theoretical definition of the therapeutic process but also in class- and sex-specific (speech) behavior in the group situation (2.4). Concepts from sociology and social psychology must therefore be used in our theoretical considerations in order to establish a framework of hypotheses that will not only be immanently relevant to communication processes in therapy but will also integrate the factors of class and sex as independent variables. Many of the motives and reasons for this approach have already been mentioned (1.2, 1.3), while others are described at a suitable point. Finally, empirical investigation will be used to illustrate the extent to which the theoretical background is valid and the claims made can be verified (4.3, 5.4, 5.5).

2.2. Therapeutic communication in the group
2.2.1. The method of group therapy

The researcher in the field of group therapy is faced with a diversity of schools and opinions that are not easy to order systematically

(Buchinger 1979:6 ff.). In this context only a few essential concepts, such as a differentiation between individual therapy and group therapy, seem to be relevant. Apart from three minor attempts (Erb and Knobloch 1979; Lenga and Gutwinski 1979; Meyer-Hermann 1979), this field has not attracted much interest from a linguistic point of view. Yet psychotherapeutic studies, many of which even use tape recordings, lack linguistic methods, theories, and procedures that would make it possible to corroborate or test intuitive perceptions systematically in the light of empirical data (Pagès 1974; Slater 1978.)[1]

Both in group therapy and in group dynamics, the group is artificially composed. In contrast to group dynamics, however, the primary task of group therapy is not to impart group dynamic mechanisms. We are far more interested in the alteration of the individual within the context of the group and in the development of the group process, and this can only be understood using the dialectics of individual psychodynamics and group behavior. This diversity is expressed verbally in the mixing of private language and group language, phenomena that will be examined in this chapter (2.3.3, 2.3.4).

In contrast to individual therapy, there is more free verbal, uncontrolled interaction, more action, more participation by the therapist. A comparison with a play is useful here: the alteration of one participant depends on a corresponding alteration in others. Greater importance is attached to the *here* and *now* than in individual therapy; there is less coming to terms with the past, coupled with future perspectives (*then* and *there*). (These aspects do, however, vary greatly in the various schools and conceptions in the field of group therapy.)

Thus Slavson (1960:6), for example, sees only a gradual difference between individual and group therapy. According to his conception, it is more a matter of individual therapies in the group, the positive transference to the therapist being supplemented by other members of the group. Wolf and Schwarz (1962) also share this view. In my opinion, too little attention is paid to the group process, which does in fact develop quite independently, assuming typical patterns, particularly of a linguistic nature (3.8). Group roles and transference mechanisms are encountered, which Schindler (1957–1958), Kutter (1970, 1971), and others have convincingly described—from a therapeutic viewpoint. Bion (1961), Argelander (1972, 1974), Heigl-Evers (1972), and Schindler (1957–1958) treat the group as an independent entity, but they ignore the individual in the process.

From a scientific and sociological point of view, what we have here is obviously a polarization of two extreme standpoints. If we regard group processes through linguistic "glasses," neither position is conclusive: the level of the individual and the level of the group (both manifest and latent) continually interact with and are dependent upon one another. The most important perceptions that can be made from group therapy can be briefly summed up as follows (Buchinger 1979:7 ff.):

1. Relativization of one's own person: One must accept the fact that one is not always the center of attention, and that others are just as important.
2. Forming of contacts and relationships.
3. Relativization of one's own jealousy: One is reassured by the fact that others also have similar problems.
4. Acquisition of differentiated problem and conflict solutions.
5. Acquisition of insight into reality: The group reflects inter-active processes like a social microcosm.
6. Acquisition of flexibility: The group structure changes continually.
7. Relief from isolation: The feeling of cohesion and solidarity relieves the feeling of loneliness.
8. Establishment of a learning situation: Social learning based on insight is possible within the group.

It is by no means my intention to express preference for one therapeutic method over another. Different therapies with specific points of emphasis are indicated for different syndromes (Strotzka 1975:361 ff.). Many phenomena of therapeutic communication in groups are also encountered in other therapeutic methods.

There are many reasons for our decision to investigate a group linguistically. These are dealt with in the following theoretical section and include a specific sociolinguistic interest. An ethical factor also plays an important role, however, and that is the fact that individual therapy is constitutively based on anonymity and on the dual relationship between analyst and patient. These are deeply compromised by a tape recording or by observation (3.4). The presence of an observer in open group therapy is less disturbing, however. The extent to which it is possible to infer individual analysis on the basis of therapeutic group communication remains un-answered. Nevertheless, objective and differentiated hypotheses on therapeutic processes in general are formulated which promote explicit and systematic therapy research in this manner (4.2, 6.6).

2.2.2. Therapeutic communication versus everyday communication: An attempt at a pragmatic and psycholinguistic comprehension of the therapeutic speech situation
2.2.2.1. The therapeutic setting[2]

Previous works have demonstrated that the external conditions of a speech situation have a decisive effect on the speech behavior of the participants (Dressler et al. 1972:4 ff., Leodolter 1975b: 142 ff.; Wodak-Leodolter 1980). The speech behavior of the persons involved is greatly influenced by the room, time, and place of the communicative action. The therapeutic situation can be regarded as a language game that complies with certain rules, some of which are manifestly and explicitly defined while others are latent. These formal conditions must be described if one wishes to obtain a linguistic description of communicative procedures. What, then, is the difference between therapeutic communication and everyday speech?

The therapeutic situation is a very restrictive, closed speech situation: The room is always the same, the time of the meeting remains unchanged for years, the duration of the interaction is determined beforehand. For example, the group under investigation may meet four times a week at an exactly determined time for one and a half hours in the group room at the Vienna Crisis Intervention Center. The therapeutic session begins when the therapist enters the room, and any communication that takes place before or after is pre- or posttherapy talk (Turner 1972). These precise regulations acquire different functions within the therapy itself. The patients (who are undergoing acute crises in their lives) are given a great deal of security; they do not need to worry each time when and where the next therapeutic session will take place, as this has been established once and for all. In crisis intervention, where the patients' main problems consist of isolation and difficulties in making contact, the certainty of being able to meet people four evenings a week, of being able to come to the group, of belonging somewhere, is of decisive importance (6.4).

However, the determination of time, duration, and place is also relevant to the progress of the therapy, within the therapeutic technique. If part of the therapeutic process consists of acquiring a more conscious attitude to life by occasionally questioning reality, the commitment that the therapeutic setting represents offers an opportunity of resolving obligations that have been subjectively experienced as compulsive, of conscious assimilation of problems and of acquiring insight into reality. The external conditions of the therapeutic setting can therefore be the topic of the therapy itself, as can be seen from analysis of individual sections of dialogue from therapeutic sessions (3.8).

2.2.2.2. The therapist

Although this work does not concentrate on technical questions, it is nevertheless necessary to examine the role of the therapist more closely, as his presence is a constitutive factor of the therapeutic process (Anker and Duffey 1958:314 ff.; Graupe 1975:47 ff.). The presence of the therapist constitutes a fundamental difference from conditions characterizing "normal" groups. The therapist represents competent authority but is not a member of the group and cannot be equated with the "alpha figure" described by Schindler (1957–1958:313). He occupies a unique position: Although he is present in the group, offering a target for transference, he is always in a separate position. The therapeutic technique being used in each case has an effect on the casting of the therapist's role, which can be one of total abstinence, that is, in which the therapist remains neutral, scarcely intervening in the group interaction and giving no information about his person, or he can become an active member of the group, such as is often the case in modern forms of therapy (Jager 1975:343 ff.; Graupe 1975:73 ff.). In the group dealt with here, the classical role of the therapist tends to be preferred, although here, too, depending on the person of the therapist, there is a wide range of therapeutic styles. This question is considered in greater detail in the light of the empirical material collected (3.8.2, 6.4, 6.5).

2.2.2.3. Rules of the speech situation

After outlining the external background of the therapeutic session, it is interesting to note the contextual and qualitative differences between such a group and normal groups. Before this difference can be explicitly defined, it is necessary to describe therapeutic communication in detail and compare it with the experience gained from other nontherapeutic groups. The fundamental hypothesis states that both the content and structure of therapeutic communication differ significantly from those of everyday communication. This results from the formal conditions and from the "basic rule" of any psychoanalytically oriented therapy, which states that one should say everything that occurs to one in the situation (Flader and Grodzicki 1978). In other words, the rules of normal conversation, which serve primarily to maintain an image, no longer apply. Embarrassment, exposure, and shame are excluded (Goffman 1959, 1974:54 ff.); there are no rituals of politeness; both positive and negative sanctions are initially precluded, and the therapy room becomes a sort of "free zone" (Wodak-Leodolter 1979:39). It is also important that nothing reach the outside world: an important rule states that everything said remains secret and anonymous.

Below is a list of these explicit rules (the list does not pretend to be complete):

1. One can, and should, say everything that occurs to one (the basic rule).
2. One can, if one wishes, talk about oneself.
3. Any subject is permissible.
4. There are no rituals of politeness.
5. One can cry, laugh, shout, and so on.
6. There is no need to keep up a certain image.
7. One may reenact conflicts and allow one's aggressions free rein.

The implicit precepts are as follows:

1. One should stay for the entire one and one-half hours.
2. One should arrive punctually.
3. One should listen to the others and try to help them.
4. One should try to speak openly about one's own problems.

These rules do not have to be obeyed, but anyone who fails to observe them is immediately confronted with group pressure. Moreover, a person's motives for not adhering to such rules can themselves become the subject of therapeutic communication.

This list alone makes it obvious that the rules that apply here are different from those governing everyday group conversation. Many studies on social behavior in normal groups (Richter 1972; Bales 1950) clearly prove that something qualitatively new—a group with its own behavior mechanisms, its own typical topics, and its own group jargon—very soon forms from a random collection of people (Brown and Levinson 1979). Once established, these mechanisms are comparatively rigid and can scarcely be altered any more. The individual members of the normal group are assigned typical roles, group roles that determine and govern the individual's opportunities and behavior (Popitz 1967). A group structure forms, with a group leader (alpha figure), with specialists for specific topics or activities (beta figures), and with relatively passive members who follow instructions (gamma figures). There is generally an enemy figure, as well, who is stigmatized by the group, causing the group to stabilize around him (Schindler 1957–1958). The individuals of the group join together in the struggle against an outsider. Such a structure has its own mechanisms for the resolution of conflicts and problems, its own objectives and values (ideologies); once securely established in this manner, it can exist unchanged for a very long time. Accustomed strategies of argumentation and discussion and typical roles remain firmly established, and anyone who rebels must usually leave the group; in extreme cases the group breaks up.

According to the hypothesis postulated above, it is precisely this last factor—the question of the group's breakup—that makes a therapeutic group different. Here, too, there are central topics (3.7.3), typical roles, and strategies of argumentation and discussion (3.8), but these mechanisms can be changed without precipitating the group's breakup. The individuals change, the group structure is flexible, the group as a whole goes through various phases and continues to exist in spite of everything. What is the reason for the continuance of such dynamics, apart from the special setting described, the dialogue rules, and the presence of the therapist?

2.2.2.4. Metacommunication

In this context, it is worth mentioning one special feature of therapeutic communication, and that is the role and the position of metacommunication in the therapeutic process (3.8.3). This aspect has already been discussed in the presentation of Habermas's approach (albeit from a different standpoint). Metacommunication, or communication at the relational level (Watzlawick et al. 1972: 41 ff.), has several functions. Completed actions and experiences are reflected upon and worked through; strategies for the resolution of conflicts and problems are discussed, relationships and relational mechanisms explained. This metacommunicative level is an extremely relevant and characteristic component of therapy. Reflection and working-through are not the only central aspects: Under the guidance and influence of the therapist it is also possible to resolve set mechanisms and transferences. Metacommunication within a therapeutic setting makes it possible to alter existing circumstances without too great a break with the past, to impart insight in the form of explanations and interpretations that leave their mark both intellectually and emotionally. In normal groups, never-ending discussions of relationships often occur, which typically follow a particularly rigid pattern and cover other, deeper problems or repeatedly deal only with one aspect of a problem as a symptom (Richter 1972). In contrast to such discussions, in the therapeutic group it is impossible to cling to any one position in the long run. There are naturally struggles for power, but the therapist (or even members of the group) can uncover such structures by repeated interpretations and explanations without this necessarily resulting immediately in a complete break with or exclusion of individual members of the group (3.8.2, 3.8.6). Alternative behavior patterns are offered, created, considered, and finally put into action: reflection becomes the precondition for change, for "emancipation." The possibility of continuous verbal reflection on past events (working-through) and future events (tentative action) makes therapeutic discourse different from other human communicative relationships.

2.2.3. The concepts of the unconscious and transference

It is impossible to understand therapeutic communication without resorting to important assumptions of psychotherapy. However, by this I do not mean that the entire communication process has to be broken down into psychotherapeutic categories and terminology. This can under no circumstances be the aim of a psycholinguistically and sociolinguistically oriented interdisciplinary study. It is necessary to introduce explicitly only two fundamental concepts in order to carry out further linguistic analysis. In contrast to other behavioristic theories and epistemological (cybernetic) interaction models (Cube 1971:122 ff.), I assume that interaction and communication are "open" processes in which the participants are guided by a variety of motives that can also be of an ambivalent and contradictory nature (Krappmann 1972:32 ff.). The individuals participating are by no means always aware of these motives. The assumption that there are unconscious motives, an "unconscious" element that to a large extent determines the actions of the individual, is of constitutive importance to any understanding of therapeutic communication. In group communication it is not only what is said that is important but also why it is said and what the speaker is consciously and unconsciously trying to achieve by saying it. The unconscious sphere is naturally only partly accessible to linguistic analysis, as the life history, expectations, and traumatic experiences of the participant are not known (2.3.3, 2.3.4).

Though it is not possible here to deal with the theoretical concept of the unconscious, it would be expedient at least to indicate the connection with the hypotheses of Freud (1976*a*, II/III:546) and Lorenzer (1973:195 ff.). The small child is obliged to suppress, or move to the unconscious sphere, certain instinctive needs that he is not allowed to satisfy because they have been verbally or nonverbally forbidden by the primary parental figure. These instinctive needs can now become displaced, sublimated or repressed because of a rupture in the relationship to the parents. Symptoms and clichés are formed as a result, however; these are compulsive actions with corresponding speech behavior that refer to suppressed topics or actions without the individual or his environment being aware of their quality. The individual has no comprehension of his symptoms (a condition called inner alienation) (1.2.6). During the reconstruction of the disturbed language game in the therapeutic process, the individual becomes aware of the suppressed instinctive needs and their contents and is able to work through and resolve the traumatic scenes, and thus also the symptom: *id* then becomes *ego* (Becker 1975:204 ff.).

The second important psychotherapeutic concept that makes it possible to understand group communication is that of transference (LaPlanche and Pontalis 1975, II:550 ff.; Freud 1973*d* XI:447 ff.). In every interaction, not only the predominant relationship, the here and now, determines the structure of the interaction; previous important experiences and relationship patterns also play an essential role in the current interaction. The individual transfers—normally unconsciously—what he has already experienced (often compulsively) into new relationships (Becker 1975:185 ff.). The therapist refuses to enter into a real relationship with the patient (the patient often finds this attitude extremely frustrating, as figuratively speaking he is continually running up against a wall). Yet it is precisely this abstaining and neutral attitude that allows the crystallization of such pathogenic structures (3.8.2) (Menninger and Holzman 1973:77 ff.). Without involving his partner, the patient establishes an interaction structure and communication, which, though they are often distorted, are analogous to his other relationships and can be consciously worked through at the metalevel. This also happens in the group; transfer patterns that are often pathogenic are resolved by the therapeutic free zone and the presence of the neutral, impartial therapist.

The concepts of the unconscious and transference are thus essential to an understanding of the group dynamics and communication mechanisms in any therapeutic situation. Although every individual contributes his own specific life history, expectations, needs, and desires, there are still typical patterns that become established in groups, typical transference figures that thus verify the theoretical concepts mentioned here (2.3.3).

2.2.4. The group as substitute family—family transference

The small child is involved in a group—the family—from early childhood on. Although the primary parental figures are initially of paramount importance to the child, the family, relatives, and even other acquaintances soon gain in significance. In spite of the conflicting relationships in the family (conflicts between brothers and sisters, conflicts with authority, the oedipal conflict, the ban on incest), this primary parental group offers safety, warmth, and security.[3] The need for these factors is a very elementary, childish one that is usually still strongly present in adulthood. It is promoted by a variety of environmental factors, such as isolation in the city, alienation in one's job, and stress and the breakup of the small family unit (Richter 1972). At school the child is confronted with a group structure for a second time; this is the peer group. The results of socialization research have shown that the peer group also has a decisive effect on the child, and class- and sex-specific differences also develop (Whyte 1973) (2.4). At work and during higher education, the developing adult is subsequently placed in new groups, whether these are his colleagues at work, at the university, in sports clubs, or the like. Although different rules and behavior patterns prevail in all these groups, certain constitutive factors of group solidarity remain the same. Particularly in adulthood, the human being appears to seek out groups, or substitute families, whether of the same sex or of both sexes: the small family by itself does not offer a replacement for the large family of previous times. Humans seek out those with similar interests, finding safety and security again in groups (2.3.3, 3.8.4).

An easily perceptible consequence of such socialization mechanisms is the fact that even adults—on the search for substitute families—regard the groups that they encounter during their lives and to which they belong, as families. In many instances they also behave in the manner that they learned as children, and have expectations similar to those that they can rightly place in families, but which are not appropriate for colleagues at work or other associates.

Family transference thus takes place in groups (Kutter 1971); therefore, communication mechanisms and behavioral strategies from childhood are repeated and can be worked through and resolved in the therapeutic group.

The individual necessarily always reacts in the same manner, transferring earlier childhood experiences, to a situational stimulus when interactive mechanisms similar to those encountered in the family situation occur in the group. Such neurotic reactions (clichés) can be considered metacommunicatively by separating the present from past experiences (1.2.3, 1.2.6).

The therapeutic group is therefore a collection of people who contribute a number of neurotic (private) transferences as a result of their individual life histories: at the same time, interactive processes take place that develop in a typical manner. These two levels (the past and the here and now) continuously merge with one another, influence one another, and manifest themselves at the verbal level (2.3.3).

Following this excursion into socialization theory, let us now return to our attempt to explain communication in a therapeutic group explicitly at a theoretical linguistic level. The dimensions that play a role in psychotherapy have already been outlined (the transference level in the group and the psychopathology of the individual). It has also been argued that there are qualitative differences between therapeutic and everyday communication, and the relevance of sociological factors has been indicated. These basic insights and hypotheses determine the three-level model of therapeutic communication.

2.3. The three-level model of therapeutic communication
2.3.1 A new concept of meaning

Therapeutic discourse in the group represents a complex phenomenon. Its diversity is determined by three factors: by the actual communication that takes place and the group dynamics (the here and now); by the family transference; and by the expectations and life history of the individual. As a result, it follows that verbal interaction and communication reflect these three factors.

The verbal expressions and texts encountered in a therapeutic situation are therefore constituted by three significative components: colloquial meaning, which is based on mutual dependence within a speech community; group meaning, which relates the value of the spoken word to the latent transference level in the group; and finally, private semantics,[4] the expression of individual life history, psychogenesis, and pathogenesis and the position of the patient in the social structure of society.

A threefold frame of interpretation is thus able to register and interpret adequately the full meaning of therapeutic discourse. The concept of meaning such as has been used recently in linguistics (Searle 1971:68 ff.; Wittgenstein 1967) must be extended by two dimensions that certainly also have an effect on everyday communication (Klann 1979) but that are tangible only in a clearly defined therapeutic setting. At least since the revolutionary work of Ogden and Richards (1972), Morris (1938), and Bühler (1934), it has been a generally accepted fact that linguistics and linguistic schools have not managed to produce a working definition of the term *meaning*.

Brekle (1972:60) is of the opinion that the usage theory (Wittgenstein 1967; Searle 1971) offers considerable advantages compared to a narrower concept of "meaning" (principally the degree of reality). This theory contrasts with generative-transformational concepts (Katz 1970:142),[5] structural hypotheses (Schifko 1975;

Brekle 1972), and Mel´čuk's integrative approach (1974, 1976), which combines transformational and structural elements (meaning ↔ text model).[6] Brekle puts forward the following definition:

> By the meaning of a linguistic symbol we do not mean a concrete object like this table, but a quantity of conceptual features the structure of which imparts the meaning of a symbol. Now it can be maintained that a concept or complex of concepts can be regarded as the meaning of a linguistic symbol if this concept is uniquely linked with a certain sign in the standard speech usage of a certain speech community. (Brekle 1972:55)

This definition does not, of course, cover private meaning, or connotation (2.3.5). Schifko (1975:112) does differentiate between subjective and social connotations; the former cannot be integrated in the linguistic system. Yet there are no limits, such as criteria, for differentiation (Kerbrat-Orecchioni 1977:106 ff.).

Lyons (1977:1 ff.) tackles the problem of meaning more cautiously by discussing the different ways in which the term is used, proving the impossibility of working out a definition on the basis of this example.

Palmer (1976:4) expresses some scepticism when he quotes a dialogue from L. Carroll's *Alice in Wonderland* (1965): "'Then you should say what you mean,' the March Hare went on. 'I do,' Alice hastily replied; 'at least—at least I mean what I say—that's the same thing, you know.' 'Not the same thing a bit,' said the Hatter."

Even followers of the usage theory, however, do not reach the emotional and unconscious level of spoken texts, although Cavell (Cavell ed. 1976:72) draws a comparison between Freud and Wittgenstein and summarizes the basic assumptions as follows:

> We learn and teach words in certain contexts, and then we are expected, and expect others to be able to project them into further contexts. Nothing insures that this projection will take place . . . , just as nothing insures that we will make, and understand, the same projections. That on the whole we do is a matter of our sharing routes of interest and feeling, modes of response, senses of humor . . . —all the whirl of organism Wittgenstein calls "forms of life." (Cavell ed. 1976:52)

Only through microanalysis of therapeutic discourse (in a group) we may be able to find more precise interpretations of the spoken word, as the verification of the interpretation is often explicitly contained in the text. In my opinion, however, the concept of the usage theory (which I have always supported) must be extended by the dimensions of affect and unconscious content.

It remains to be said that even in individual therapy—analogously to the model presented here—communication is determined by three perspectives. The working relationship between analyst and patient (i.e., the healthy ego) represents the first, the colloquial level. Regression to earlier communicative strategies (revival of scenes in the relationship with the therapist) represents the second, the transference level; finally, there are the real personal and social characteristics of both doctor and patient, composing the individual level (Schröter 1979:180 ff.).

2.3.2. The colloquial level

This level comprises the utterances made in a group therapy situation that can be comprehended in their everyday colloquial meaning. Patients describe their problems, talk about group activities, discuss relationships, and carry out conflicts (3.8). Although everything that takes place in the therapeutic situation has a particular meaning for the group process and the individual (latent meaning), attention is initially focused on the text as such, without further interrogation or interpretation. In view of the fact that the open group for potential suicide candidates is designed in the first place to deal with patients' real problems, the use of colloquial meaning in any linguistic analysis is both necessary and legitimate (5.4, 5.5).

2.3.2.1. Taxonomic framework for the description of the colloquial level

Therapeutic communication within a group session involves several types of speech acts, various classes of texts such as dialogue, conflict discussion, and problem presentation. In descriptions of the course of the session and the individual variables, the communicative procedures that take place (3.8) are illustrated with excerpts from the text. Before an explicit linguistic analysis can be carried out, it is both necessary and indispensable to classify the different text types and classes taxonomically (detailed text analyses are contained in 3.9, 3.10, 5.4, and 5.5).

In contrast to Labov and Fanshel (1977), who differentiate between classificatory types of speech act in their analysis of a psychotherapeutic conversation, it seems expedient to assume larger, functionally defined units, or "speech strategies." This method enables us to avoid several theoretical and methodological difficulties that would otherwise be insuperable. First, by definition, speech acts are limited to individual expressions. Particularly in therapeutic conversation, we are frequently confronted with larger units. Second, the definition of the speech act as a constitutive factor also involves the intentionality of the speaker (Searle 1971:76 ff.). This is bound to cause inconsistencies, particularly when unconscious topics play a part. Third, it is extremely difficult to assign individual expressions unambiguously to categories in the taxonomy of speech acts (Wunderlich 1979:282 ff.) (5.2).

If, however, we start from a category of more inclusive, functional speech strategies that can be implemented both by speech acts (in dialogue, for example) and by other text types, it is possible to carry out a conclusive analysis of therapeutic communication at the colloquial level. This approach is related to the concepts of Halliday (1976:3 ff.) and Barnes and Todd (1977:24 ff.), which also resort to the function of verbal expression as the most important principle of classification.[7] These linguistic and text-linguistic implements can be adapted to the class or type of text in actual text analysis (e.g. speech-act sequences in conflict dialogues, expansion model in interventions, and storytelling grammar in longer narrative passages) (3.9).

Therapeutic communication is broken down initially into a content level and a metalevel. The criterion for this classification is the topic of the text, in other words, whether the speaker introduces problems that are unrelated to the therapy or whether the therapeutic process itself is under discussion or the conversation is at the metacommunicative level. As Meyer-Hermann (1979) conclusively demonstrates, a number of different expressions fall within this category; I would describe these expressions as reflexive speech strategies. They include the following: (1) Reflection on one's own language, thoughts, tentative acts, working-through: (2) establishment of contexts, production of hierarchies, and classificatory terms; (3) evaluation of one's own actions and those of others; and (4) relationship to the group process—summaries and deliberate introduction of new topics.

The content level involves four types of action. Two relate to the formal textual level, two to the content level:

1. Discourse strategies. This category includes all speech strategies that get the conversation going, initiate a change of speakers, terminate discussions, and so on. To an extent, this category corresponds to the phenomena observed in Sacks's conversational analysis (turn-taking) (Sacks 1972).
2. Logical strategies. These include logical connections, argumentation, temporal and spatial classification, and categorization.
3. Behavioral strategies. Here we find problem presentation, conflict strategies, competitive behavior, question-answer strategies, interventions, and supporting strategies.
4. Cognitive-emotional strategies. This category is composed of suggested solutions, attempts at interpretation, and expression of feelings.

This list is by no means complete. Each text unit naturally contains elements of all these categories. The typical combination in each case results in specific text types (3.9, 3.10). It seems reasonable to separate these for the purpose of analysis, as it would otherwise be impossible to describe deviations at the above-mentioned levels. For example, problem presentation by members of the lower and middle classes differs above all at the discourse level (different strategies for turn taking; different narrative structures to express the same event). Normal and schizophrenic speech differ mainly in the nature of the logical (discourse) processes used (Wodak-Leodolter 1978*b*, Leodolter 1975*c*). Sex-specific differences are found mainly in the cognitive-emotional level in the nature and amount of verbalization of an emotional state (Davitz 1967). It is not, therefore, possible to allocate speech strategies exclusively to one category or the other. On the contrary, they relate primarily to a certain category but contain elements from other categories as well.

The importance of specific types of speech acts is more evident as a result: Certain behavioral strategies are generally realized in the form of speech acts (conflicts, questions, answers) (3.8, 3.10), while other behavioral strategies, such as problem presentation, take the form of narrative units (3.9). The transference level in the group and even the individual level can be temporarily resolved into a content level and a metalevel. In this case, however, it is necessary to resort to psychodynamic categories that enable us to recognize typical unconscious conflicts, feelings, and relationships.

Schema 2 sums up this classification, though it also includes factors discussed in the following sections (2.3.3, 2.3.4, 2.4).

2.3.3. The level of group language

In order to avoid possible misunderstanding, it should be emphasized from the start that we are dealing here not with a completely different language or with another dialogue that has taken place simultaneously, but with a second dimension of meaning that allows us to interpret the meaning of each expression by reference to group dynamics. A second set of categories is applied to the text (5.4, 5.5). Because of the peculiarities of the therapeutic setting, many of the transference factors of individual patients are manifest in the group situation in their relationships to one another and to the therapist. Typical group structures and processes, hierarchies, and conflicts, normally unnoticed and at first unconscious, take their course (2.2). Every utterance made by the individual participant must therefore be analyzed not only with respect to its colloquial meaning but also with regard to its value and its function in a group context. What did the speaker intend to achieve by his utterance? Why did he address a particular member of the group? Why does a conflict occur between two particular people?

There are naturally many possible explanations at this level: probable interpretations can be put forward and theoretically substantiated on the basis of our knowledge of typical group processes and the mechanisms that occur (5.2).

Despite the diversity of existing taxonomies and hypotheses about group processes, major phenomena become apparent, regardless of whether the psychoanalytical concept of individual therapy (the structural model) is transferred to the group or whether fundamentally different circumstances are involved (Grumiller 1975; Bion 1961; Schindler 1957–1958; Pohlen 1972; Kutter 1971; Heigl-Evers 1972; Finger 1976; Slater 1978). Common to all interpretations is the fact that the group passes through different distinguishable phases. Thus Bion (1961:165 ff.), for example, differentiates between three fundamental attitudes ("basic assumptions"), those of dependence, formation of pairs, and struggle/flight.

SCHEMA 2

The Structure of Therapeutic Communication in the Group—
the Three-Level Model of Therapeutic Communication

Level 1	Level 2	Level 3
Real interaction (GROUP DYNAMICS, manifest material)	Transference level in the group (PSYCHODYNAMICS, latent, unconscious material)	Individual level (PSYCHOGENESIS, life history)
COLLOQUIAL meaning	GROUP-SPECIFIC meaning	PRIVATE meaning
Content level → Metalevel	Content level → Metalevel	Content level → Metalevel

Level 1:

Content level → Formal text level, Content text level

Formal text level → Discourse strategies, Logical strategies

Content text level → Behavior strategies, Cognitive-emotional strategies

Metalevel → Reflexive speech strategies

Discourse strategies → Types of formal-discourse actions

Logical strategies → Text-logical actions

Behavior strategies → Speech-act patterns

Cognitive-emotional strategies → Cognitive-emotional actions

Reflexive speech strategies → Types of meta-communication

Level 2:

Content level → Psychodynamic categories (process, feelings)

Metalevel → Comprehension patterns

Level 3:

Content level → Connotations, symbols

Metalevel → Meaning of group process for individual patients

Duration, type of therapy, expectations of therapy
Status and position (social roles) of patient and therapist

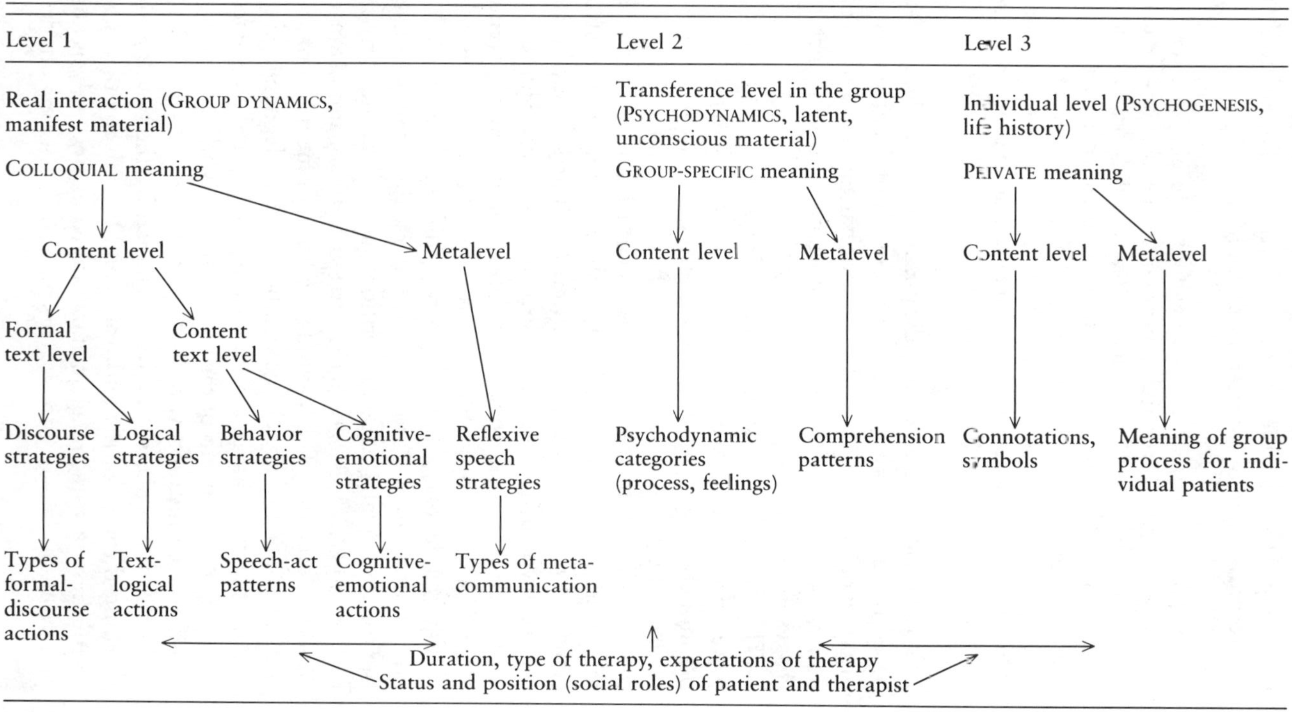

According to Bion, these fundamental attitudes serve to maintain the group. They hide the fear that the group will break up if dreaded (repressed) forms of interaction prevail.[8]

> The group is thus subject to a twofold disturbing of interaction and understanding: this is the result of primal sensations or interaction forms, such as greed, envy, aggression, sexual desire. Once instinctive, these needs are subject to social censure: either in direct or indirect confrontation, i.e., with a previously formed instance of the super-ego. They are not allowed to prevail, but are averted or forced into a compromise with the aid of specific fantasies: dependence, struggle-flight, formation of pairs. (Finger 1976:78–79)

It is a logical step to assume the occurrence of collective fantasies, based on family transference: "The course of events in groups and organizations is determined by emotional fantasies of a collective nature, which, however, for the most part remain unconscious" (Pagès 1974:9).

The real colloquial level (Finger 1976:84) acts as a counterweight to regressive, collective fantasies and rituals (Slater 1978:2 ff.). In her model of linguistic interaction in groups, however, Finger (1976) neglects the private language level of the individual. She also makes the mistake of differentiating between a level of "verbal topics" and a second, "conscious level of the symbolic group structure" (Finger 1976:89). This division into two parts is not justifiable if one believes in a concept of speech strategies. The verbal level cannot be separated from actions and human behavior (Habermas 1977:206 ff.). Finger (1976:73 ff.) conclusively shows what important conflicts typically play a role in family transference. These are relationships to brothers and sisters, the oedipal situation (in the form of rivalry and competition), as well as the early mother-child dyad (2.2.3, 2.2.4). Slater attributes major importance to the concept of revolt: "The 'banding together' of members of the group in a kind of hostile attack against the group leader assigned to them, and on the other hand, a process: the growing independence of the members of the group of the leader, and notwithstanding this their growing identification with him" (1978:3).

The group process is therefore shaped by the development and working-through of the authority conflict with the therapist.

All these factors are again encountered in any analysis and interpretation of transference factors in group therapy. It does not, therefore, seem necessary to prescribe one taxonomy or another on principle (2.2). The major assumptions that determine the interpretation have already been mentioned: the concepts of defense mechanisms (Bion 1961), collective fantasies, and family transference (Slater 1978; Finger 1976; Kutter 1971). Finger (1976:91) makes an attempt at integrating the various group concepts.

All the phenomena listed here are typically manifest in verbal communication (either as symbols or as clichés):

> To the extent that the process of integration in the group is also a process of eliminating language destruction, it is more than a formal repetition of the infantile process of socialization. With the reconstruction of language a process begins which allows the private language of the individual to filter gradually into the speech community. To an increasing extent this becomes equivalent to a new socialization process which makes it possible to transform old interaction patterns into new ones and to modify and improve old ways of solving conflicts. (Finger 1976:91)

2.3.4. The level of private language

Communication in a group conceals yet another aspect besides that of manifestly apprehensible verbal language and group meanings. Each individual always unconsciously associates specific meanings with his verbal utterances; these are his own connotations and can only be understood in the context of his life history and expectations.

As we have already seen (1.2.3, 2.2.4), the small child learns language behavior through specific interaction with his primary parental figures. The experience gained in these first interactions has a cognitive and emotional effect on the child. Although over the course of time the child learns to abstract the interactions experienced with the primary parental figure, the emotional component of these first experiences remains and is passed on. Colloquial language games, therefore, contain a private component. If the language games are "disturbed," in other words, if they are suppressed into the subconscious, the private components form part of a concealing cliché. Private meanings can be resolved into their cognitive and emotional components only by the therapeutic process. The primal scenes are reconstructed; residual private meanings return to the conscious and are assimilated (1.2.3, 1.2.6).

Private meanings and private language are quite clearly apparent in psychotic patients, particularly schizophrenics (Navratil 1974: 43 ff.). In my own investigation of schizophrenic speech behavior, I found that the so-called disturbed speech of these patients had quite different structures that bore many similarities to the mechanisms of dream texts, or, in other words, unconscious material (Leodolter 1975c:90). This private language can be translated back into colloquial language using psychotherapeutic methods (Green 1974; Parker 1974). As a result, neurotic, and even normal, people always add their private symbols and connotations to everyday speech, though they are not as apparent as those of schizophrenics (1.2.5).

Group dynamics play a decisive role in group behavior, as do the psychogenesis and pathogenesis of the individual, the expectations of the individual, and his experiences and knowledge. When comprehended in a broader sense, private linguistic elements are only apparent against the background of each life history and the history of individual object relationships, which are not accessible from observation of the group situation alone. The most one can do, therefore, is establish hypotheses that can then be verified with the aid of individual therapy.

2.3.5. Linguistic description of private meaning

In this context, it should be noted that there can be no discussion of symbols (Lorenzer 1970), as the analysis concentrates on the linguistically accessible level, resorting less to psychotherapeutic interpretations.

One point is always of considerable interest, however, and that is the question of how private meaning can be integrated in any linguistic description (5.2, 5.4, 5.5). The terminological debate over the concept of symbols apparently misses the heart of the problem, and in order to forstall this discussion, I suggest using the term *private meaning* in the sense of "connotation."

In my opinion, Schifko (1975:11–12) extends the definition of connotation too far: "Connotation is the catchment area for everything that is not denotation in the narrower sense of the word, for K. Bühler's function of appeal and presentation, for chronological, topological, sociological, and stylistic variants, unless the latter have already been partly excluded as not belonging to functional language."

Kerbrat-Orecchioni (1977:86 ff.) places still further restrictions on the meaning of connotation. She follows Bally (1930) and differentiates principally between two types of connotation: emotional, and that attributable to environment. (Kerbrat-Orecchioni 1977:89). In her opinion, though, there are absolutely no explicitly descriptive methods for defining connotation.

We are interested here not only in typical symbols, such as dream symbols or the neologisms of schizophrenics, but in individual features that should be integrated into any semantic description of words or sentences and that would take into consideration private communicative and emotional components.

Although the behavioristic approach of apprehending connotation in the framework of the semantic profile (Osgood et al. 1957) can be criticized for its conception of stimulus-response behavior, one essential point holds true: The decision between pairs of opposites, such as good/evil and beautiful/ugly, attributed to individual terms indicates the emotional value of language. Group and individual values are always integrated in colloquial meaning, although individual values result from the very early experiences and interactions in which such terms are first practiced (2.2.4). It is, therefore, conceivable that such individual values could be grouped together in a description of the features of individual terms.

Yet when we analyze texts from therapeutic discourse, we are dealing not with individual terms but with the meanings of sentences and texts, speech acts that evoke a transference of emotions and values from previously experienced scenes. In any adequate analysis, it would therefore be necessary to trace speech interactions back to very central scenes that occur in the socialization process. Such scenes are highly charged emotionally. An example might be the attitude toward the therapist's authority, which in real interaction certainly contains many elements of previously experienced scenes with the parental figures. Therefore, from the speech behavior of the individual toward the therapist in each case, it is possible to extrapolate private language elements and evaluations that can be traced back to scenes experienced in childhood. The first step in an attempt to record private language and connotation would therefore involve the categorization of speech acts into classes of interactions associated with typical scenes experienced in childhood. The understanding of such interactions could then be listed against this background (what are the possible modes of behavior toward authority, for example?). The typical features of these types of expression could then be described.

An initial attempt in this direction is to be made in the qualitative analysis of the text class that will be denoted problem presentation in group therapy. Private variations are also encountered here, in addition to class- and sex-specific differences (3.9, 3.10). However, the speech situation "I am going to talk about a problem" has a parallel to childhood as children often relate stories and experiences, both real and imaginary.

Finally, schema 3 presents the model of therapeutic communication and the many components. Schema 3 breaks down the various dimensions that play a role in group interaction. As a result, every utterance, every text can and should be analyzed at three levels of meaning. This implies the three-level model of therapeutic communication, with a new, precisely defined concept of meaning in a therapeutic setting (2.3). The effect of the sociological dimension is considered in the context of class- and sex-specific socialization (2.4).

2.4. Remarks on class- and sex-specific socialization
2.4.1. The effect of sociological factors on therapeutic communication and the therapeutic process: social class and psychotherapy
2.4.1.1. Class-specific language behavior: results, objectives, methods

A great deal of sociolinguistic literature has emphasized and even empirically demonstrated that there are class-specific differences in speech behavior in both open and closed situations.[9] These differences are attributed to socialization factors and are neither hereditary nor dependent on intelligence.

Investigations of children and adults in school and in court settings have also shown that various types of language behavior (styles) depend on situations or phases within situations (Leodolter 1975a,b). This does not involve two distinct styles that are constantly applicable to the working class on the one hand and to the middle class on the other. Rather, they are variable from one situation to another and realized in the form of situational perfor-

SCHEMA 3

INTERACTION LEVELS IN GROUP THERAPY*

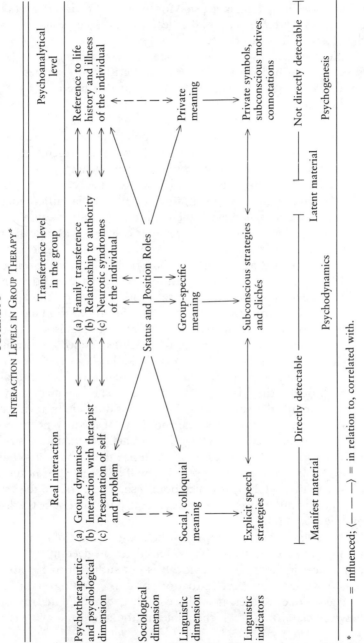

* —— = influenced; ⟨— — —⟩ = in relation to, correlated with.

mance strategies. In the process of socialization, children learn certain rules of social and language behavior because of their different types of families, different parental roles, and different situations that they have to learn to master.

Thus, several aspects of Bernstein's classical theory (1970*a*), which has been discussed in detail and criticized elsewhere (Leodolter 1975*a*:52 ff.), need to be specified and altered. His sharp division into working class and middle class is not commensurate with social reality. This differentiation is based on Marx's theory of class and is therefore certainly applicable to macrostructural conditions—but not to microstructural analysis, which frequently starts from the family as the central social phenomenon. Thus, if one deals with microstructural analyses, it is necessary to resort to stratification models in which more complex social differentiation occurs. This is not, however, intended to be a confrontation of two extreme and incompatible theories that compete with one another in the explanation and description of the same social phenomena. On the contrary, I agree with the assertions of Strasser (Strasser et al. 1979) that we are dealing with different phenomena that relate on the one hand to macrostructural processes and on the other, to microstructural processes. The fact that the stratification model has its own reality is evident from empirical sociolinguistic investigations in which certain styles and variations cannot be attributed either to the working class or to the middle class. The speech behavior of the lower middle class in particular varies significantly from those of other classes (2.4.2.3). This is also confirmed by the present empirical investigation (4.3.1). This different behavior must be seen in the context of social mobility, of identity problems in leaving the social class to which the parents belong, and of striving for prestige, which appears to characterize the higher class (Labov 1966). This interesting phenomenon will be referred to in the empirical analysis (4.3.1), at which point I shall also go into the strong sex-specific differences that are evident, particularly in the lower middle class (2.4.2)

Although Bernstein's approach helped guide sociolinguistics for a long time, it must also be criticized for neglecting sex-specific differences in language behavior. It is not sufficient to explain systematic variation in speech situations by concentrating on the factor of class alone. Rather, it is the complex, differentiated interplay between class and sex which enables us to understand many typical

linguistic phenomena. I shall subsequently prove this both theoretically and empirically (2.4.2, 4.3.1). The present investigation is
the first of its kind and attempts to use the sociological factors of
both class and sex to explain language behavior. It does not, however, follow the direction of Bernstein and his successors or more
recent trends that in their turn emphasize mainly the factor of sex.

Bernstein (1962*a,b*, 1970*a*) attempts to make a sharp division
into middle class and working class, into elaborated code and restricted code, basing his ideas on an epistemological socialization
theory. Yet such a division is not meaningful without reference to
speech situations. On the contrary, microstructural analysis has
demonstrated that, depending on the speech situation, both the
middle and working classes use both codes and many other styles
(Leodolter 1975*a*:279 ff.). This differentiation becomes superfluous
as a result, as it is impossible to validate its power. It therefore
seems important to determine and classify the different strategies
of situational performance, not failing to take social evaluation into
account. In this respect I go along with Bernstein's theory to the
extent that it has shown that the language behavior of the middle
class is ranked higher socially and is more readily accepted in many
speech situations, particularly institutionalized ones. It is evident,
however, especially in the therapeutic situation, where social evaluation is in many cases absent or questioned, that the speech strategies of the working class are quite adequate (4.3.1, 4.4).

2.4.1.2. Do language barriers exist in psychotherapy?

As already mentioned, Bernstein's theory suggests that the working
class expresses itself inadequately in language. I have serious doubts
about this statement in particular. Socialization within the working
class is strongly group oriented (Labov 1972; Whyte 1973); this
would indicate that members of the working class find it easier to
establish relationships. Furthermore, there is no taboo on expressing emotions, as is often found in the middle class. Such expression
is frequently linked to the use of emotional speech styles and thus
also to dialect. The importance of this aspect of class-specific speech
behavior will become evident in the empirical investigation of therapeutic communication, where the ability not only to formulate
emotions abstractly but also to verbalize them—in other words,
to realize them both cognitively and emotionally—determines the

effect of the therapy (3.10, 6.4). In his essay on "Social Class, Language, and Psychotherapy," Bernstein (1970*b*) is the only sociolinguist who has so far dealt with therapeutic communication from sociolinguistic perspectives. He makes assertions that—after the theses outlined above—are no longer surprising but that should be subjected to detailed criticism. In his opinion, members of the working class are precluded from psychotherapy from the start for two reasons: (1) Because of its very structure, the therapeutic situation immanently requires a high ability to verbalize, which members of the working class do not have, as a result of their socialization and the resulting restricted code, and (2) the therapist is normally a member of the middle class and is neither willing nor able to comprehend the language and world of members of the working class, thus making it impossible for the therapy to succeed.

> I begin with the assertion that members of the lower working class do not have the necessary degree of sensitivity and conformity for a psychotherapeutic relationship. This is not due to an innate lack of intelligence, but due to a culturally induced system of speech with a range of meaning and significance too limited to allow a member of the lower working class to orient himself in the therapeutic relationship. On the other hand, the therapist's system of speech gives the therapist expectations which are not shared by patients of the lower working class. By "lower working class" I mean individuals who carry out menial manual work. They represent about 30 percent of the labour force. (Bernstein 1970*b*:84)

Bernstein subsequently lists characteristics of working-class language that deviate from the differentiated mode of expression required in therapy:

> Under these social conditions, which induce a restricted code, the manner of speaking is normally rapid and fluent, articulation aids are limited, the significative content can easily be compressed and dislocated, and is limited to relationships. The standard of choice of words and syntactic selections is low. The way in which something is said is more important than the content of what is said. Finally, it is of decisive importance that the person's assertions regarding individual meanings are more implicit than linguistically elaborated. (Bernstein 1970*b*:89)

Finally, after a description of person- and status-oriented modes of socialization and the commendable habits and appropriate emotional features inherent in them, Bernstein (1970*a*,*b*) comes to the conclusion that successful therapy must involve a change of code. In other words, at the end of the therapy, the working-class patient must have mastered the elaborated code and thus have become adjusted to middle-class language: "The therapy relationship thus results in a change of code for the patient limited to the restricted code, and thus to a tremendous change in the means which he is able to use in order to orient himself in his accustomed environment. We believe that the patient's code changes in successful therapy" (1970*b*:96).

In my view, the opinions that Bernstein puts forward on the psychotherapy of members of the working class are too simple and too condensed. The range of problems encountered contains many more complex and subtle questions, some of which result from the critical remarks made above, others from the institutional conditions of psychotherapy, from the immanent theory itself and from existing empirical studies:

1. Do working-class patients in fact lack an ability to verbalize? (It is only possible to decide this against the background of a theory of communication in the light of a model of ideal therapeutic communication.)
2. How does the socialization of the working class differ from that of the middle class? What are the typical communication mechanisms and communication disturbances encountered in each case? What form of therapy is suitable in each case? (Strotzka 1972:55 ff., 141 ff.).
3. What does a cure mean to the working-class patient? Is he really obliged to acquire the middle-class code? To what extent is it more difficult for him to come to terms with the classical psychoanalytical dyad for structural reasons?
4. Finally, do social factors such as the high cost of long-term therapy, the shortage of versatile therapists, and the internal dispute in psychiatry between medical treatment and psychotherapeutic methods, between treatment of symptoms and a more fundamental approach, play a role in preventing members of the working class from undergoing therapy? In the following section I shall concentrate on the first two questions; it would exceed the limits of this study to deal with the last two questions in detail here.[10]

The remarks on the structure of the therapeutic situation and communication indicate that there is a wide range of very different communicative acts, for example, reflexive speech strategies (that is, those relating principally to the relationship level and requiring an ability to summarize incidents and formulate strategies for problem solving). At the same time, the importance of verbalizing feelings and emotions has been stressed. The basic rule stipulates spontaneity, the admission of ideas, fantasies, desires, needs, and feelings both positive and negative which would otherwise be embarrassing, shameful, and taboo. As yet there is unfortunately little empirical material on the socialization of the working class, particularly as far as the mechanisms of the socialization of female children are concerned. Studies of peer groups have clearly demonstrated that the socialization of the working class takes place primarily in groups of children of the same age. This socialization is more prone to admit the expression of feelings and allow conflicts to be verbally and nonverbally realized while the child develops than do the authoritarian relationships more typically encountered in the middle class (Miller and Swanson 1960). The middle class child therefore acquires more compatible behavior strategies toward authority than the working-class child (Leodolter and Leodolter 1976b).

As a result, it may possibly be better to recommend classical psychotherapy for those who have undergone middle-class socialization, as the scenes, conflicts, and transferences encountered in psychotherapy are strongly reminiscent of childhood patterns. Members of the working class might possibly be better advised to take group therapy, where transferences from previously experienced group scenes will probably be encountered. This position reflects the opinion of several theoretical psychotherapeutic works (Reiter 1973; Junker 1972; Cremerius 1975). The conflicts produced in classical psychoanalysis as a result of class and language barriers are not at all due to a lack of ability to verbalize or to an untrained therapist but to other conditions of socialization (and thus to other childhood experiences and conflicts). Schröter (1979) carries out an empirical investigation of the therapeutic relationship in classical psychoanalysis between working-class patients and middle-class therapists and also comes to the conclusion that this therapeutic method is probably unsuitable for social and structural reasons. The conflict with authority which occurs is intensified and made virtually insoluble by real differences in status and opinion.

Yet I do not wish to imply that psychotherapy as such is therefore unsuitable for members of the working class.

Against the background outlined above, I maintain that although the speech of members of the working class is qualitatively different from that of members of the middle class, it fulfills essential requirements for successful group therapy. At the same time, though, these patients will have to learn many new things in exactly the same way as will members of the middle class. The content and formal structure of their problems will often be different, but it will always be possible to ascertain them. I regard the linguistic indicators that Bernstein uses to characterize working-class speech as inadequate. They are not derived from any linguistic theory and are of a purely quantitative (and intuitive) nature. The different linguistic strategies of situational performance can only be described with the aid of text-linguistic (i.e., suprasyntactic and text-semantic) and sociophonological indicators (3.10).

Finally, I should also like to examine Bernstein's assertion that a "cure" involves acquiring the elaborated code, or in other words, an adaptation to the speech-behavior strategies of the middle class. As mentioned above, this does not involve unilateral adaptation; members of both middle class and working class display neurotic (speech) disorders that must be remedied. In the course of group therapy, both acquire new modes of speech behavior, alternative forms of human practice which each individual must finally select for himself. Unreflected adaptation does not occur because of the constant necessity of reflection. On the contrary, there is a striving for realistic behavior, meaning an objective insight into social necessities coupled with the emancipation of the individual from self-imposed restrictions. This aspect has been given particular mention in the description of Habermas's concept. The question remains as to what extent different opportunities are open to members of the middle and working classes—in other words, whether it is easier for members of the middle class to implement changes in their everyday lives as they become aware of new alternatives. In conclusion, the assumptions on class-specific speech behavior in a therapeutic situation are summarized below (4.2).

1. Members of the working and middle classes use qualitatively different language from one another in a group therapy situation.
2. Members of the working class give free rein to their feelings,

are more spontaneous, and more outgoing; many of their problems are different from those of members of the middle class. Members of the middle class give more consistent presentations, but they lack spontaneity and expression of feeling; the metacommunicative level is more accessible to them.

3. During the course of therapy, members of both working and middle classes acquire new speech-behavior strategies, new identities, and new opportunities for alternative ways of life.

The first empirical phase of the investigation was guided initially by these general hypotheses. In the light of the new findings made, it was then possible to differentiate these assertions contextually and carry out a linguistically qualitative classification of the different rules of situational performance. I concentrated especially on the text type of problem presentation in group therapy: Are there class-specific differences in the manner in which someone relates, presents, and describes his problem in a therapy situation? These synonyms were not chosen at random but represent the possible text-linguistic strategies by means of which a problem presentation can be realized (3.9). At the appropriate time I shall therefore continue the theoretical argumentation of class-specific speech behavior in a therapeutic discourse. The far-reaching and grave consequences for psychiatric practice are immediately apparent. It is obvious that we must break down prejudices against psychic illnesses, institutions, therapeutic methods, and the speech behavior of the working class, so often passed over as an inability to verbalize. The present study may be a first step in this direction (6.4, 6.5, 6.6).

2.4.1.3. The language behavior of the lower middle class

Sociolinguistic investigations (Trudgill 1974; Leodolter 1975a; Wodak-Leodolter and Dressler 1978) have shown both theoretically and empirically that members of the lower middle class must form a separate social strata. Social mobility, which entails immense identity problems, provokes very unstable speech behavior. On the one hand, these people are still rooted in their parent class, while on the other, they consciously attempt to adapt as far as possible to the desirable new class. In other words, the old speech behavior and the old speech identity are still effective, while at the same time, an overadapted, hypercorrect speech behavior is revealed, arising from the need to suppress an origin that the individual himself does not value. Similar phenomena are also encountered with minorities (Dressler and Wodak-Leodolter 1977). This is also apparent in the group therapy investigated. In a state of great excitement and emotion, the individual loses his conscious control, and working-class behavior occurs. Speech behavior is otherwise adapted to the middle class but is much closer to the norm than that of young members of the middle class (Wodak-Leodolter and Dressler 1978:48 ff.).

It is also worth mentioning the tremendous sex-specific differences, which deviate significantly from those of other classes. The role of the woman is negatively evaluated by society, and this, coupled with a negative attitude toward a working-class origin, gives rise to a need to overadapt and avoid any form of dialect. In such cases, women are more aware of their language and more controlled than men, in sharp contrast to the usual cliché. This also conforms to the theoretical and empirical results of investigations into minority situations and of my own study of language in the courtroom (Leodolter 1975a:284 ff.).

2.4.2. Sex-specific language behavior and the therapeutic group
2.4.2.1. Psychotherapy and feminism

My decision to deal with sex-specific language behavior in therapeutic discourse is really not at all surprising. In recent years the opinion has been expressed (particularly in the United States) that psychotherapy should be condemned because of its "antifemale" theory and practice. According to these ideas, it would be expedient to have only monosexual group and therapist relationships, as the socially manifest oppression of women would otherwise merely be repeated (Chesler 1974). At the same time, in many branches of science (and this also applies to linguistics and sociolinguistics), the factor of sex first received attention as a result of the feminist movement. The investigations, most of which are still at the descriptive stage, have clearly demonstrated the significance of the sex of the speaker with respect to speech behavior, particularly in sociolinguistic areas such as minority situations, language variation, and microstructural studies of conversation.[11]

There are therefore several reasons for this interest in the language behavior of men and women in therapeutic groups. It seems essential to define the different rules of situational performance in a linguistically explicit manner, without neglecting to pay particular attention to the interplay of class and sex. This is not principally a matter of deciding which factor is of greater relevance or of establishing a hierarchy. On the contrary, the empirical results prove that the weighting of these two factors changes depending on topic, situation, and therapeutic phase (4.3.1). On the other hand, we are also interested in the extent to which group therapy can deal with the growing social problems of our age, which are closely connected with the changed roles and expectations of the sexes, with the disintegration of the nuclear family, and with the dual strain on women. Is group therapy able to help men and women in acute crises to find an alternative way of life, or emancipation?

Let us start by considering criticism of psychotherapeutic concepts by the feminist movement (Mitchell 1976). Freud cannot be reproached for not presenting the female image of our age. Any scientific paradigm is extremely subject to the influence of the age in which it is conceived. Around the turn of the century in Vienna, the upper middle class from which Freud's patients initially came had different roles and expectations of the sexes from those of the present day. It is not, therefore, surprising that the social conditions of the time should have been incorporated into classical psychoanalytical theory. What is more, every scientific school is subject to social influences and changes, which is why psychotherapeutic theory has often changed so dramatically in the course of the last fifty years, particularly with regard to conceptions of the roles of the sexes.[12] One should not overlook the fact that women very soon began to play an important role in this science in particular long before this was the case in other spheres. I therefore regard the quarrels between feminism and psychotherapy as futile, unless more recent developments are included in the discussion.

2.4.2.2. "Female" and "male" behavior in groups: The balancing identity

The groups of early epochs were largely male dominated. They served the purposes of public life (battle, hunting, politics) (Tiger

1972). The only group in which women took an important part was the family, or the domestic domain. Although the role of mother was highly valued, that of woman as such was not.

Even today, one often finds groups such as sports clubs, dart clubs, political associations, and the like dominated by men: women by themselves are left to hold coffeehouse meetings! At the same time, women are at a strong social disadvantage: Obstacles and prejudices at work and lower rates of pay are the expression of this manifest inequality. Sociolinguistic investigations of conversation have shown that men contribute more to conversation, speak less formally, interrupt women more frequently than the other way around, are more likely to introduce new topics and speak louder than women: they set the tone (Wodak-Leodolter 1977; Smith 1979). Even their favorite topics are different (3.7, 3.8). Men discuss and deal with "important" abstract spheres, while women are "emotional," "irrational," and interested principally in relationships and emotional topics. They "chatter" and "prattle" (Aebischer 1979). Although the clichés and stereotypes listed here appear ridiculous when regarded objectively, they nevertheless strongly affect the evaluation of the sexes by both individual and outsider (6.4).

Many social norms and sanctions are suspended in the therapeutic situation; the group offers a free zone, a testing ground for tentative action (2.2). The here and now is all-important, and an explicit difference is made between inside in the group and outside in real life. To this extent it is possible to differentiate between three levels in an analysis of sex-specific behavior in groups: 1) social conditions—life outside (which must be largely excluded from the present observation) (6.4, 6.6); 2) the group itself (to what extent are certain mechanisms, stereotype modes of behavior, reproduced, and how can they be eliminated?); and 3) the individual (are there typical conflicts within the group shaped by a failure to come to terms with the expectations conditioned by the roles of the sexes?).

If one observes group sessions and if one pays particular attention to the behavior of men and women, one has the impression that although some communication mechanisms are reproduced, other stereotypes are absent or changed in this extreme situation (3.8). It is particularly striking that there are no "typical" men and women, but rather "male" and "female" modes of behavior that can be attributed to either sex. As a result, there are "female" men and "male" women (that is, passive, emotional men and active,

rational women). Differentiating between inborn sex and sociological and social-psychological role attributes and expectations helps
us to describe and explain the variety of forms and modes of behavior observed (Wodak-Leodolter 1979:36 ff.). With the aid of
the metacommunicative level in therapeutic communication, it becomes possible to break stereotypes and acquire new, alternative
modes of behavior, to arrive at a sense of a balancing identity
(Krappmann 1972). Both men and women thus have traditional
male and traditional female modes of behavior, making it possible
to compromise between such existing extremes as passiveness and
activity, emotionality and rationality.

The acquisition of a balancing identity is no guarantee of improved success in handling prejudices and clichés "outside," where
it is normally just inborn sex that counts. However, from interviews
with patients, it is apparent that many of them have been able to
apply this knowledge. Women become more independent, learn to
combine different roles (mother, wife, housewife, worker) more
sensibly; men reject excessive stress and express their feelings more
freely (6.4). Many of the patients' psychic crises result from the
fact that old and new roles are irreconcilable. These patients are
brought up traditionally but strive for intellectually new values and
ideals that cannot be realized before they have been emotionally
and cognitively assimilated. A large number of psychic conflicts and
identity crises crystallize around this discrepancy. The free zone
within the group helps patients initially (particularly in the reproduction of established clichés) to become aware of extreme expectations and values, current ideologies, and traditional upbringing,
finally enabling them to strive for a sensible compromise (initially
in the form of tentative action). Some of the mechanisms reproduced
here do not by any means prevent women from active participation
in the group (3.7.2, 3.7.3). On the contrary, it has been found that
women initially have an easier time than men in therapeutic groups,
as they have always been permitted to suffer and appear weak in
public (Richter 1972). Men have first to acquire this role, which
represents a step toward male emancipation (4.4).

This fact leads us to linguistically interesting speech styles and
strategies: men present their problems differently from women.
Initially, they adopt a strongly defensive attitude, rationalizing and
describing symptoms only, as it is considered quite unmanly to
admit to weaknesses in public. Women, on the other hand, establish

a link with themselves and their life histories, since the weak role is nothing new for them. However, in their search for strategies of problem solving they find it difficult to drop this role, to deal with conflicts more rationally and to give up their passivity (although such typically "female" behavior is also encountered in men).

Against this background, it would now be interesting to examine the interplay among various aspects—sociological role attributes, gender, alterations deriving from the therapeutic process, and finally, the extent to which the insight gained is implemented "outside."

Both a male and a female therapist were deliberately included in the empirical investigation, and in the interviews with patients, the question was posed as to whether the gender of the therapist had any effect. It was quite obvious that the preference expressed for a therapist depended less on gender than on therapeutic style (6.4).

The general hypotheses on which this investigation was based are listed briefly below (they have been extensively elaborated in the course of the empirical study) (4.2):

1. The speech behavior of men and women is significantly different. There are strategies that are used only by men and others used only by women (patterns of problem presentation, certain topics, strategies of image building and competition).
2. There are "male" and "female" modes of behavior that are encountered in both sexes.
3. During the course of the therapy, traditional modes of behavior are clarified, reflected upon, and changed in the direction of a balancing identity.
4. There are class-specific differences in the speech behavior of each sex (2.4.1.2).

Although in the qualitative and quantitative text analysis I shall devote my attention to problem presentation in group therapy, by way of illustration I shall also present other types of text, such as conflict strategies and problem solving strategies (3.8). One question remains, which can only be empirically answered on the basis of self-appraisal by several patients in interviews (6.4): How are the newly acquired speech and social behavior patterns (successfully) implemented in social reality? (or does the therapy remain in its self-defined free zone?). I think that therapeutic methods indicate a way of reducing—even if only slightly—the social discrimination against women. Patients become aware of realistic alternatives and are thus able to take steps toward an emancipated, freer, and happier life.

2.5. The therapeutic effect

In reviewing the standard of research in psychotherapy (Strotzka 1975), one is struck by the fact that a comparatively small number of studies (compared to the number of other publications in this field) have been published on the efficiency of therapeutic methods (Strupp et al. 1977; Frank 1961; Strupp 1973; Graupe 1975; Till 1977; Remplein 1977). Most of the investigations mentioned are based on obtaining the subjective evaluations of patients (based simply on whether they feel better and happier after the conclusion of therapy, and not on any "objective" data).

In the present case (4.3.1, 4.4, 6.4), the attempt to measure therapeutic effect in light of speech behavior is one of the first of its kind. At least some of the changes in the language behavior of the same patient at the beginning and the end of the longitudinal study can be attributed to the effect of the therapy. The changes relate principally to qualitative parameters (3.10).

The quantifying method (4.1, 4.3) is a valid means of evaluating the efficiency of psychotherapy by analyzing therapeutic communication. This method is new, both in the field of linguistics and in that of psychotherapy. Graupe (1975:34) mentions several reasons for the lack of empirical investigations in the field of psychotherapeutic research (research into efficiency in particular):

1. The preconceived rejection of direct intervention in the environment and in the behavior patterns of the patient gives rise to the controversial assumption that there are nonmanipulative psychotherapeutic processes.
2. Traditional psychotherapy assumes that external disturbed behavior is symptomatic of an underlying disturbed process. As a result, the focal point of therapeutic intervention is therefore regarded as being not behavior but, for example, the conflict-laden constellation of motives.

3. It is generally assumed that cognitive and emotional changes always precede and cause behavioral changes. (In social psychology, conversely, it has been shown that external behavior plays an important role with regard to the subsequent alteration of cognitive and emotional processes).

4. The forms of traditional psychotherapy are highly complex; the relationship of theoretical constructions to empirical data not sufficiently stringent; the traditional therapist is not interested in finding adequate empirical evidence for his terms.

Despite these arguments, there are practical reasons for requiring empirical investigations that take the complexity of psychotherapy into account (see also 6.5, 6.6):

> Practical objectives are the elaboration of time- and cost-saving processes. The former could be achieved by reducing therapy to its effective components, leaving out all ineffective aspects, the latter by introducing procedures that could be applied by laymen and assistants using technical aids or in groups. Further practical objectives involve the preparation and modification of processes for patients and target groups that have not previously been reached by therapy or that have been regarded as "untreatable." (Graupe 1975:34)

Remplein (1977) and Bergin and Strupp (1972)—to mention only two studies—emphasize the complexity of the therapeutic process and the resulting difficulties of carrying out an empirical investigation into the effect of therapy. Thus Bergin and Strupp (1972:23, 463 ff.) consider that psychotherapeutic research has brought about a change of attitude. The analyst takes a more critical attitude toward case studies described anecdotally. The resulting difficulties should not be underestimated, however (3.3, 3.5, 4.1). First, any psychotherapy, and even every session, is unique and unrepeatable. The variables of patient, therapist, and environment make it impossible to work with control groups (to resolve such questions as, for example, Is there a difference between therapeutically treated patients and untreated patients?). Moreover, it is impossible to evaluate the effect of the environment. The diversity of communication (2.3)—which has so often been emphasized—initially prevents any generalization. After a critical review of existing empirical, linguistic, and sociopsychological tests, Labov and

Fanshel (1977) are of the opinion that only qualitative analysis is suitable. The authors also argue that the linguistic means at our disposal are not yet sufficiently developed to enable us to effect quantification (Labov and Fanshel 1977:19). I do not agree with this opinion (3.9, 3.10).

Even fundamental metatheoretical objections have been made against any attempt to quantify research into the efficiency of therapy. These have been the result of extreme attitudes toward the methods proposed (3.5). Efficiency studies have therefore mainly used interviews with patients (6.4) (Strupp, Hadley, and Comes-Schwartz 1977; Strupp, Fox, and Lessler 1969; Frank 1961), in which measurement of success is based only on the patients' self-appraisal. (Nobody has as yet been able to define criteria for the category of success; see Graupe 1975:32.)

My opinion is based on the idea that considerable importance must be attached to an objective, significant use of quantifying methods to supplement qualitative and other techniques of investigation in psychotherapeutic research. The limits of quantification (5.4, 5.5) lie in the object under investigation and in the conditions chosen, both of which must be explicitly specified. Other facets of the same object can be examined using other methods, as is the case here (interviews with patients and therapists are qualitatively evaluated and compared with the results of quantitative analysis; see 6.4, 6.5). The decision to use speech behavior as an indicator is justified by the central value of verbal communication in the therapeutic situation (2.3).

The third hypothesis on which this investigation is based could be cautiously formulated as follows: in the course of three years there were changes in the speech behavior of patients that must be attributed at least in part to the therapy. The direction of the change is described as positive and results from an appraisal of psychotherapy as presenting the opportunities of learning to act realistically, of finding happiness, of learning to work and love, and of satisfying one's own needs as far as possible under existing circumstances.

I have often heard the same objection from my patients when I promised them help in the form of relief through a cathartic cure: You yourself say that my suffering is probably linked to my circumstances and fate, which you are unable to alter. How, then, do you intend to help me? I have always replied: I do not doubt that it would be easier for fate than me to relieve your suffering. But you will find that much has been gained if we are successful in transforming your hysterical misery into common bad luck. You will be better able to ward off the latter with a regenerated spirit. (Freud 1977*b*, I:311–312)

3

Empirical Investigation of an Open Therapeutic Group of Potential Suicide Candidates at the Vienna Crisis Intervention Center

3.1. The intention of the empirical investigation

The theoretical concept of therapeutic communication presented here and the hypotheses on class- and sex-specific language behavior were tested on the basis of a three-year empirical longitudinal study. It is impossible to apply the criteria of the exact natural sciences to the present study. Social and sociopsychological processes are too complex, besides being completely unique and unrepeatable in each case. The study therefore sets out to illustrate the hypotheses and theoretical concepts in a differentiated qualitative and quantitative analysis (3.8). It also makes various predictions (4.3, 4.4) and goes on to scrutinize questions of method and the reasons for choosing a case study (3.3).

3.2. The course of the project

Data for the study were collected over a period of three years (1976–1978). There were eight characteristic phases:

1. Familiarization with the institution: I started by spending three months as a trainee at the Vienna Crisis Intervention Center, where I was given a wide range of tasks. I filled out filing cards, accompanied the therapist in open groups, manned the telephone, and sometimes spoke with waiting patients. I soon got to know the habits, values, and everyday life of the institution by asking questions, observing, and reading the doctors' reports.

2. Preliminary study: After I had observed the open group several times and had become used to the communication structures, I recorded four sessions on tape.
3. Preliminary study: These four tapes were subjected to preliminary analysis, and the general hypotheses were elaborated and altered. Individual phases of the sessions were important for further analysis and were dealt with separately (Wodak-Leodolter 1977).
4. Main investigation: After I had carried out the pilot study, elaborated my hypotheses, and studied further literature, I embarked on the main phase of the investigation. In the course of two months, starting exactly a year after the first recording, I recorded sixteen sessions of the same group on tape. My aim was to obtain a broader data base and make it possible to investigate the effect of the therapy (4.5).
5. Notes: At the same time, I made notes of nonverbal reactions. I was also able to look at the doctors' notes at regular intervals and was always given the opportunity to confer with the team.
6. Interviews with patients: In focused interviews, ten patients were asked about their subjective evaluation of the therapy. To this end, I visited the individual patients in their homes, providing they consented. I thus had an opportunity of getting to know their language behavior outside the therapeutic situation and of finding out more about their lives and social surroundings (6.4).
7. Interviews with therapists: I also interviewed a psychiatrist, two psychologists, and a woman social worker about their attitudes toward the therapeutic method and the chances of success and about their opinions on the institution as a whole (6.5).
8. Analysis and interpretation: Finally, I carried out a qualitative and quantitative analysis using all the sources of data at my disposal (recorded sessions, notes, and interviews). Even during this phase, I never lost contact with the institution: I repeatedly conferred, received new information, and reported on provisional results.

Schema 4 clearly illustrates the course of the investigation.

SCHEMA 4

THE COURSE OF THE INVESTIGATION

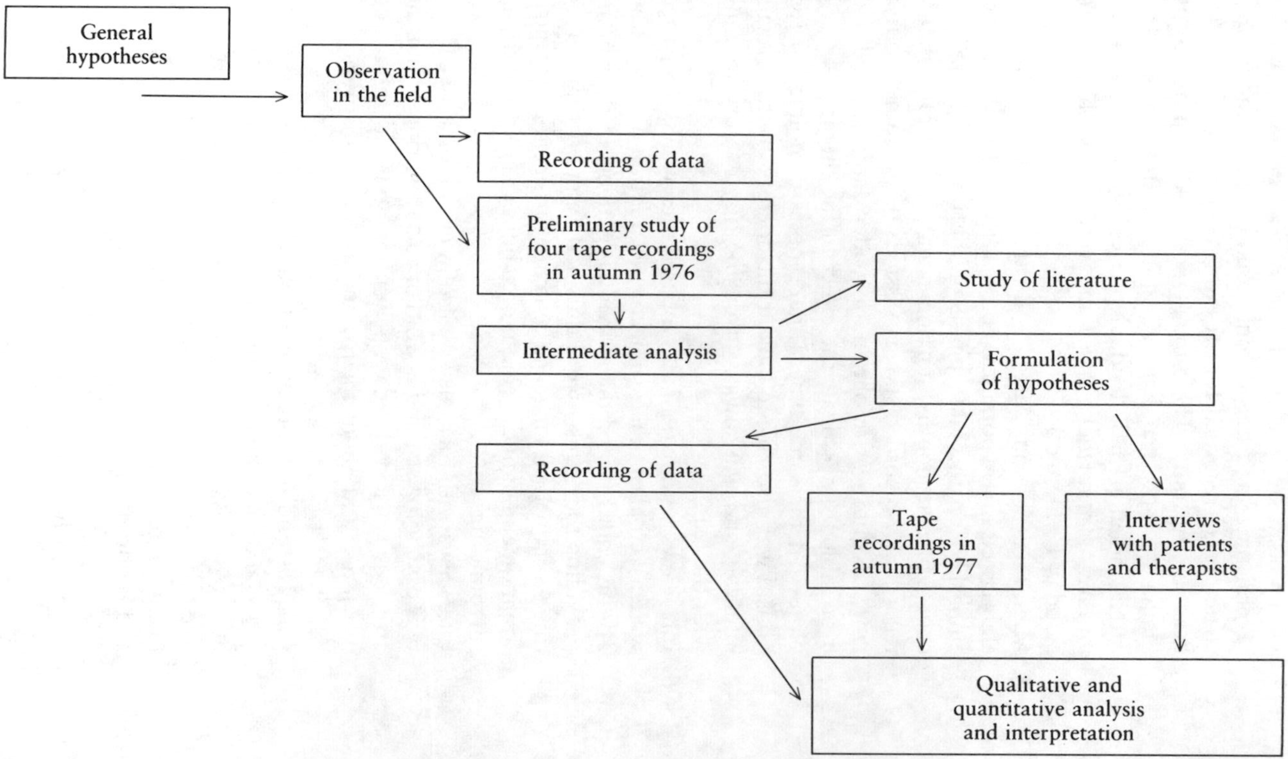

```
General                    Recording of data        Study of          Interviews
hypotheses                                           literature        with patients
                                                                       and therapists
    │              ┌─────────────────────┐               ▲                  │
    ▼              │  Preliminary study   │               │                  ▼
Observation    ──▶ │  of four tape        │               │          Qualitative and
in the field       │  recordings          │         Formulation  ──▶ quantitative analysis
                   │  in autumn 1976      │         of hypotheses     and interpretation
                   └─────────────────────┘               ▲                  ▲
                            │                             │                  │
                            ▼                             │            Tape recordings
                   Intermediate analysis  ───────────────┘            in autumn 1977
                                                          │
                                          Recording of data ────────────────┘
```

3.3. Why a case study?

Regarding the methodology and epistemology of sociological research, there are basically several ways of studying human behavior, or in our case, language behavior:

1. One could study several group therapy sessions in parallel and compare them. In other words, the sessions would be recorded at similar times and generalizable statements would be made on the strength of this data base. The fact that there are too many intervening variables speaks against this method. Patients and therapists are different, and the methods of each therapist are also quite individual, despite typical communication patterns and a similar theoretical background. It would be impossible to cope with the factors of space and time and the different case histories of the patients. In other words, although one would have a larger sample at one's disposal, it would still be impossible to make objective comparisons.

2. One could conceive a laboratory situation in order to eliminate intervening variables and make it possible to measure the therapeutic effect. In this case it would not be necessary to consider the effect of time and other circumstances. Although this sounds interesting and objective from a "scientific" point of view, it stands in complete contradiction to the sense and aim of therapy and the possibilities and ethos of field research. It is impossible to lock people up, and artificial situations have no bearing on everyday life and the everyday behavior of those involved. They relate only to behavior in a laboratory situation. Also, the therapeutic effect is measured in terms of a patient's ability to cope realistically with everyday life, information that could not be integrated in an investigation of this kind. The question remains as to what one could actually measure.

3. Parallel to the therapy group and the patients involved, one could observe an equivalent group of people not undergoing therapy so as to be able to make assertions about the effect of the therapy. But where can one actually find an equivalent group of people? Moreover, it would be unethical if one were actually to deny potential suicide candidates treatment solely in the interests of scientific objectivity.

Because of these considerations, I decided to carry out a case study in the field. A case study allows generalizations to be made over a long period of time, and interviews with patients and therapists, notes, observations, a knowledge of the daily routine of the institution, and theoretical considerations make it possible to obtain a more complete picture.

If one wishes to draw conclusions relating to "real" social behavior (and not merely to self-evaluation, as in a statistical study with questionnaires, for example) when studying the language behavior of human beings, it seems pointless to use an experimental situation. The researcher must go out into the field in order to obtain an insight into the world, and into the way of thinking and the language of the test subjects involved. He should not use an unreal situation that would naturally also entail different language behavior (investigations have shown that every situation has a corresponding range of different styles; see Leodolter 1975*a*; Wodak 1981*a*).

I drew up my research program along these lines with a view to using as many different data sources as possible. Nevertheless, I wanted to keep important factors constant (the group, the times of the meetings, and the therapists remained the same). As has been noted (1.3, 2.2.2), comparatively closed and institutionalized speech situations are best suited for precise empirical investigation, inasmuch as many communication rules are explicit. Furthermore, the constancy of important variables makes it possible to compare recordings made chronologically, enabling the researcher to control intervening variables.

3.4. The ethical dilemma in the research of therapeutic communication

Although the method described above obliges the researcher to take to the field in order to obtain the most genuine and real data possible, the paradox of observation is inevitable, although it is considerably less apparent than in artificially contrived situations. The mere presence of the researcher and the tape recorder distorts the situation from the start and certainly influences the behavior of the persons under observation, albeit to a limited extent. Investigations, however, have convincingly shown that the tape recorder is no longer a disturbing factor after a period of from five to ten minutes; the patients will then actually forget its existence and give free rein to their emotions (Labov 1966; Wodak-Leodolter and Dressler 1978; Dressler and Wodak 1982).

I spoke to the patients, told them about the aims of the therapy and the investigation, and assured them of anonymity. I was very soon accepted and integrated, particularly after the interviews that I carried out in the homes of individual patients. There I had an opportunity of studying their way of life more closely. Awareness of people's personal circumstances facilitates a great deal of insight into their personalities, making it easier to understand their individual suffering and past history. Patients displayed remarkably few inhibitions during the interviews (6.4). On the contrary, they had a great urge to describe their problems to me, even though many of them were of an intimate nature. I was partially forced into the role of therapist, since I had usually appeared together with the therapist.

I was particularly pleased when the patients invited me to eat with them after the therapy sessions (thus integrating me in the group). The patients opened up in the congenial atmosphere of these informal gatherings; they cracked jokes, talked about their daily lives, and asked me about my work and my views on everyday problems. They also asked about the investigation, since, with the permission of the team of the crisis intervention center, I regularly gave them articles and short interim reports to read. In this way I managed to reduce the distance between investigator and subjects. The patients expressed markedly contradictory feelings toward the investigation. Some of them displayed tremendous faith in science ("Go ahead and make the recordings—they will help our children"), while others were very proud to participate in a scientific study. In fact, those patients were almost offended at being represented only by numbers or social class instead of being identified by name. Others, again, were very distrustful and inquisitive. They insisted on having the tapes played to them in order to check what they had said, and discover whether this had been correctly understood. Two women in particular felt self-conscious at times; sometimes they would explicitly refer to the tape recorder (they were "unable" to say things because someone was listening); at other times they would become very excited and aggressive, swearing and afterward apologizing to the tape recorder. Before every session I asked the patients for permission to turn on the tape recorder. Often it took a full five minutes of discussion (though the therapist never intervened) before they were able to reach agreement. I was frequently asked to talk about my scientific interest, a request that I was naturally happy to fulfill.

Only once was I refused permission to make recordings, on the day before Christmas, when patients referred to the forthcoming festivities. Naturally, I obeyed and did not switch the recorder on. I remained for the session to demonstrate my interest not only in the recordings but also—and above all—in the patients themselves. Incidentally, while this session was not structurally different from the others, the patients' request brought to light the latent stress produced by the recordings.

I found it comparatively difficult to establish contact with the patients during the preliminary study. During the main study I tried to enter the therapy room before the others, without the therapist (on the pretext of setting up the tape recorder). This enabled me to gain familiarity with pretherapy talk, and as a result, I was drawn into the discussion. All these minor events made it easier for me to overcome the ethical problems: treating people as human guinea pigs in such extreme situations is difficult to justify. Added to this is the fact that an essential part of the therapy is the maintenance of anonymity and—particularly in individual therapy—the consideration that no uninvolved person should be admitted. In fact, I consider it inadmissible to break this constitutive rule of individual therapy. A different ethical problem is encountered in group therapy, where the presence of observers can be of theoretical and practical value.

It is never possible to avoid this ethical dilemma. One can, however, reduce one's misgivings, mainly by attempting to establish personal contact with the subjects. It helps to tell them about the aims and results of the investigation, allowing them to take part in the research process.[1]

3.5. Methodological considerations—proposal for a compromise

There can be no question here of mentioning and expounding on the large amount of literature on the methodological argument in the social sciences. This has already been done elsewhere (Leodolter 1975*a*:198 ff.; Wodak 1983, 1984). I should merely like to describe the method I used, as it represents a compromise between the extreme standpoints of purely quantifying (natural scientific) methodology and qualitative, cognitive sociology. Two aspects of the methodology used in the present investigation should be particularly emphasized:

1. Many different data sources were used, making it possible to obtain a colorful and complete picture of the object of the investigation. There is a confrontation between self-evaluation and outside assessment, between written and oral material, between unique occurrences and statistical data, and between sessions and the case studies of individual patients. Any method produces distortions when applied exclusively, a fact that considerably influenced my decision to carry out both qualitative and quantitative analysis of the data (4.3, 5.4, 5.5).

2. It is essential to carry out qualitative and quantitative analyses simultaneously. The danger that lies in a purely qualitative analysis of large quantities of data is that one may be biased (subconsciously) in one's selection of typical texts. The entire corpus does not lend itself to meaningful qualitative analysis. Simultaneous quantitative analysis therefore covers the entire corpus and eliminates the bias mentioned above. Even the case studies were also subjected to quantitative analysis, making it possible to draw objective conclusions with the aid of significance tests (4.4). The establishment of coding categories and the selection of individual indicators are dealt with in detail below (3.10). Here, too, greater objectivity was obtained using rating procedures and playback.

To sum up, I do not think it expedient to enter into a discussion of principles. It seems more important to be aware of the limits of every method, applying each accordingly and supplementing it with others as necessary.

3.6. The concept of class[2]

I should like to deal briefly with a point that is either ignored or only briefly touched upon in most sociological studies: the division of a sample into social strata, or classes (2.4.1.1). The term *stratum* was selected in this study for several reasons:

1. As a study of Strasser (Strasser et al. 1979) clearly illustrates, the two terminologies correspond to two different paradigms of sociology, the Marxist approach and a rather more conservative one. They deal with different aspects of reality, however; the term *class* tends to be used in the context of the economic situation, when considering the control and ownership of means of production, whereas the term *stratum* covers the family, socialization, and life history of individuals. As these last points are of particular interest to us, the term *stratum* seems appropriate.
2. The theory of social classes has not so far satisfactorily solved the problem of social mobility and the factor of lower middle class. Yet patients from this social stratum, which represents an important element of our society, are frequently encountered at therapy sessions. The study mentioned above has been moderately successful in establishing a connection between the theories of stratum and class on this point in particular.
3. Not only are the members of the lower middle class a socially relevant factor, they also display behavior that is extremely interesting from a linguistic point of view. As we shall see, the behavior of men and women of this stratum is significantly different from that of members of the working and middle-class strata (4.3, 5.4). These differences have already been mentioned elsewhere. It would therefore be methodologically incorrect to neglect this stratum (2.4.1.3).

These arguments affected my decision to divide the present sample into three strata: lower stratum, lower middle stratum, and middle stratum. Nevertheless, these strata are called "working class," "lower middle class," and "middle class," so I myself have adopted the sociolinguistic terminology used in other Anglo-American literature. This was done according to the criteria of profession, education, and income, and the parents' data were also taken into consideration if available. The upper stratum (upper class) was not represented in the group. The scale used was that of Oevermann (1972—see Leodolter 1975a:208). Furthermore, women were naturally not classified according to their partners but according to their own backgrounds.

3.7. Description of the data
3.7.1. The institution: Vienna Crisis Intervention Center

The problem of suicide and the various theories on this subject cannot be adequately described here, nor is any priority attached to the institutional aspect of the treatment of mentally ill patients and potential suicide candidates.[3] We are interested here solely in one aspect of therapeutic treatment, the open group. Patients may join the "open group" even when therapy has already started whereas "closed groups" do not let new members in. Full details of the therapeutic method will also be given. Till (1977) has already referred to institutional questions in his study of the efficiency of the entire institution; Sonneck—on the other hand—writes about the intentions and goals of crisis intervention:

> Crisis intervention, or the psychosocial treatment of symptoms, illnesses and abnormal attitudes closely connected with crises can either be carried out outside the professional system by relatives, friends or acquaintances, priests, teachers, social welfare workers and family doctors, or within the professional system. The latter covers a wide range of institutions, from consulting and welfare offices to the declared crisis intervention center. (Sonneck 1976:421)

Thus, the aim of such an institution is as follows:

> To enable people involved in crises to mobilize their strength so that they can solve their problems given suitable assistance. . . . It must be possible to achieve the aim of intervention within a short space of time, a change of personality not being the primary objective. Neither should the objective be a return to the status quo ante, but the achievement of a more stable condition by helping the individual to help himself. (Sonneck 1976:421)

These statements are particularly important, as they clearly define the goal of the therapeutic group. This does not involve a fundamental psychoanalytical therapy, but a symptom-oriented method suitable for the treatment of serious crises. Over and above this, the group also discusses conflicts and transference problems, but these are of secondary importance (3.8).

Farberow describes in detail various attempts at instituting group therapy in crisis intervention:

In the interaction during the hour, the therapists are directing, questioning, guiding. If time permits, everyone is encouraged to talk and to interact to each other, i.e., both seek help and give it. The role reversals are impressive. Some of the most intractable problems simply disappear as the same person directs his attention to someone else and becomes his counselor. The focus is on the here and now, or what is occurring in the patient's life which is stimulating the suicidal impulses. (Farberow 1973:13)

Farberow goes on to say that "despite the conceptualization of the 'drop-in' session as non-group, it has been interesting to note the strong tendencies toward group formation" (p. 14) and reminds us that "the goal with the patients in the 'drop-in' sessions is to identify with the center" (p. 16). This means less responsibility for patients than in a truly closed group, although, as described above, the typical patterns and mechanisms of a therapeutic group are immediately established. Identification with the institution rather than with a group or a therapist is a temporary solution. The success rate of the open group is very high (Farberow 1973; Strauss and Sonneck 1978).

In the case of the Vienna Crisis Intervention Center, the group meets four times a week in the evening, Fridays excepted (when there are afternoon sessions). Specific therapists take the group on certain days. Patients are either able to choose the therapist whose therapeutic style they like best or, in acute crises, they can obtain daily support. I limited my recordings to two therapists (one female, one male) so as to keep the variable of therapist constant. Despite the fluctuation of patients, there was a hard core of about twelve patients during the years of the investigation. Eleven patients were rather sporadic visitors, but they also constantly reappeared during the three years of the study.

There are several reasons for my decision to observe and record the open group rather than the "closed group," which is also available at the center. First, the ethical problem would have been much greater. Second—and this is very important—we are interested primarily in analysis at the colloquial level (3.9, 3.10), and this seems most legitimate in an open group, where prime importance is attached not to transference phenomena but to the real problems as such. The two latent levels always play a role and will also be included (as we shall see in 5.4 and 5.5) but are initially of secondary importance in the therapy. As a result, this group does provide all necessary information about therapeutic discourse as there is no major difference between it and a "purely" psychotherapeutic group with regard to the institutional background and the interaction patterns within the group, particularly in view of the characteristic metacommunication (3.8).

The team consists of a manager, four doctors, three psychologists, five social workers, a music therapist, and—for all eventualities—a lawyer. The psychologists, one doctor, and the social workers are employed there full-time. The center works on the team principle, which means that all team members carry out the same work and accept the same responsibility, but to varying extents, depending only on their training. This is so far the only center of its kind in Vienna. About fifteen hundred new patients are contacted every year (almost the same number of men and women). The number of direct individual contacts is about one hundred per month, of which about one-third remain in the care of the center. The social workers make about eighteen hundred home and hospital visits in the course of a year and register six thousand calls; the psychologists, about one thousand calls and about the same number of individual therapeutic sessions; the psychiatrist, six hundred first interviews and twenty-five hundred individual therapy sessions.

There is a fairly wide range of therapeutic forms offered: open and closed groups, medical and psychotherapeutic therapy, short-term and focal therapy, and autogenous training. All treatment is available on the national health service, and as a result, the sample contained patients from every social class.

Most of the patients were in the age group from thirty to thirty-nine, and about two-thirds of the patients are women. Patients either come on their own initiative (the center is open daily from ten in the morning until ten at night; during the night there is an answering service) or after an attempted suicide are referred to the center by the psychiatric clinic, which does not offer crisis intervention.

The average number of visits made by patients is more than four; in the open group, about nine. Every week the professional team itself meets for a joint session, which I was always able to take part in, at which time the problems of difficult patients were discussed. The supervisory staff of the center themselves form a therapeutic group, meeting every two weeks to discuss the problems that inevitably occur in such strenuous jobs. The institution is undergoing expansion as part of the restructuring and reorganization of psychiatric services in Vienna.

3.7.2. The random sample

The random sample was made up of twenty-three patients whom
I observed and recorded in twenty sessions over the course of three
years. Classified by class, five women and three men were middle
class; three women and four men were lower middle class; and four
women and four men were working class. As mentioned above, the
criterion for determination of class was an index based on profession, education, and income. Women who did not work were classified by their training and background. Table 1 shows an overview
of the patients by profession, education, income, and absolute and
relative frequency of contributions to discussion (turns). Each patient was given a number that was retained for all analysis and
description. I differentiated among three age groups and types of
education (under twenty-five, twenty-six to forty, over forty; primary school, secondary school, and higher education). Classification by class had to be carried out on the basis of the status that
existed before the illness, as many patients were unemployed during
their crises, and it would therefore have been impossible to make
a realistic classification.[4]

Although I do not wish to make any statistical assertions (4.3),
one point is clear from tables 2, 3, and 4: most of the contributions
(turns) came from middle-class women of the second age group.

The contributions recorded in tables 2, 3, and 4 do not refer to
every remark made. Only problem presentation in group therapy
was included in both quantitative and qualitative analysis. These
are turns dealing with a topic that involves most emotions of the
patient concerned and that is complete in itself. The length of the
contributions was also taken into account in the quantitative evaluation. A more detailed description of the text type selected is given
in the appropriate passage dealing with the qualitative analysis of
the text corpus in the light of our hypotheses (3.9, 3.10). The
problems dealt with in a total of 1,134 turns relate to nine topics:
(1) contact, (2) work, (3) medications, (4) group metalevel, that is,
discussion of relationships within the group, (5) group activities,
(6) illness, (7) children, (8) parents, and (9) relationships. Table 5
shows the distribution of contributions by individual topics.

Tables 6 and 7 are obtained by analyzing the contributions by
class and sex with reference to the distribution of individual topics
(again descriptive).

Some very interesting questions emerge from this distribution pattern, leading to a differentiation of the general hypotheses with regard to class- and sex-specific differences:

1. Women talk more than men.
2. The problems mainly dealt with by women are different from those of men: Regardless of social class, problems relating to children, parents, and relationships are more "women's" problems, while men tend to talk about problems in the group and at work.
3. The various classes deal with different problems (tables 8 and 9), and there are sex-specific differences within each class as well.

These hypotheses are tested in the overall quantitative analysis. In this case they are purely quantitative differences that nevertheless raise interesting problems, such as the explicit description of the interplay of class and sex based on the indicator of topic selection (4.3.1.12). Yet another explorative hypothesis on class- and sex-specific socialization emerges on the basis of our theoretical considerations: does the selection of topics in the course of twenty sessions change with regard to distribution by class and sex (that is, is it true that the more influence the therapeutic process exerts, the more personal problems are discussed) (4.4)?

Tables 8 and 9 show the distribution of topics by working class, middle class, and sex. The quality of each type of text is illustrated by a problem presentation.

Examples of text topics

The symbols *T* (therapist), *M* (man), and *W* (woman) are used throughout to indicate participants. Section 3.7.3 contains a detailed discussion of the transcription.

Text 1. Topic 1: contact. Session 4, patient 20 (male).

Contact with other people somehow makes me nervous. I also find that when I go to the group, I am sort of jittery all day about going. On the other hand, I want and look for contact with people.

TABLE 1
RANDOM SAMPLE

Patient	Age	Profession	Education	Income (in Austrian shillings)	Class	Absolute frequency*	Relative frequency* (%)
1	40	Unemployed	Higher education	——	Middle class	144	12.7
2	50	Employee	Higher education	5,000	Middle class	52	4.6
3	33	Employee	Master craftsman	10,000	Middle class	133	11.7
4	32	Employee	Higher education	10,000	Middle class	39	3.4
5	50	Housewife	Higher education	——	Middle class	77	6.8
6	30	Hairdresser (unemployed)	Primary school (apprenticeship)	——	Working class	25	2.2
7	35	Worker	Primary school	4,000	Working class	44	3.9
8	45	Cleaning woman	Primary school	4,000	Working class	12	1.1
9	35	Cleaning woman	Primary school	4,000	Working class	24	2.1
10	34	Employee	Primary and secondary school	10,000	Lower middle class	79	7.0
11	20	Nurse	Primary and secondary school	5,000	Lower middle class	36	3.2
12	20	Student	Higher education	——	Lower middle class	30	2.6

13	35	Civil servant	Higher education	10,000	Middle class	51	4.5
14	50	Employee	Higher education	9,000	Middle class	24	2.1
15	35	Civil servant	Higher education	11,000	Middle class	85	7.5
16	23	Unemployed	Primary and secondary school	—	Working class	51	4.5
17	29	Unemployed	Primary and secondary school		Working class	40	3.5
18	35	Worker	Primary and secondary school	3,000	Working class	46	4.1
19	29	Unemployed	Primary and secondary school		Working class	29	2.6
20	35	Employee (unemployed)	Primary school apprenticeship	—	Lower middle class	65	5.7
21	34	Employee (unemployed)	Primary school apprenticeship		Lower middle class	65	5.7
22	45	Employee	Primary school apprenticeship	8,000	Lower middle class	7	0.6
23	38	Tailor	Primary school apprenticeship	9,000	Lower middle class	12	1.1

* Absolute and relative frequency refer to the number of turns analyzed (see 3.7.2).

TABLE 2[5]

AGE/TURNS

Age group	Absolute frequency	Relative frequency (%)
Under 25	117	10.3
Under 40	845	74.5
Over 40	172	15.2

Text 2. Topic 2: work. Session 4, patient 15 (male).

With whom I work. So that is really what the present problem is about, with whom I manage, you see. That is important, but things are already better than before. The only thing that upsets me is number one, with the harassment, which I have already mentioned; number two is, let's say, I react in such a negative way to people who violently—no, not violently— who start shouting that—well I can put up with everything, both in my job and in my private life, just not people shouting at me. If someone shouts at me, I can lose my composure. I can completely lose my composure. My entire self-confidence disappears, do you understand? I can put up with it up to a certain limit, but when somebody shouts at me, for me he becomes a sort of, say, not God, but a big shot compared to me, you see, just because he has shouted at me. He always seems so immensely large compared to me, a tiny little nothing.

Text 3. Topic 3: medications. Session 6, patient 1 (female).

And you were in the Monday group and told us about your suicide attempt, and when I got home I just couldn't handle it. That's how it actually happened. It was a Sunday, or a Tuesday—at any rate, a day on

TABLE 3

CLASS/TURNS

Class	Absolute frequency	Relative frequency (%)
Working class	242	21.3
Lower middle class	287	25.3
Middle class	605	53.4

TABLE 4
Sex/Turns

Sex	Absolute frequency	Relative frequency (%)
Men	439	38.7
Women	695	61.3

which I made a trip to Bisamberg with my last reserves of strength; I could only walk on Bisamberg, and so I took a suppository to help me make it and noticed how I was using up my reserves, and it became clear to me that this suicide is a question of time, you see? It's just a question of time—"how long you can still hold out, how long you can still go on"—then I collapsed yet again. Here, too, you saw me—then I had also taken such a strong dose—and I thought to myself, "now you must stop at once," and so I rang the doctor and told him. Now it's Tuesday, Wednesday, Thursday, Friday, Saturday, Sunday, Monday, the seventh day since the great crisis, but it's still pretty bad.

Text 4. Topic 4: group metalevel. Session 4, patient 16 (male).

May I say something? Well, I have noticed that at the start of the group that the man began with his problem; in her reply the woman immediately mentioned her problem and gave of her best. You in turn gave an answer

TABLE 5
Topic/Turns

Topic	Absolute frequency	Relative frequency (%)
1. Contact	53	4.7
2. Work	166	14.6
3. Medications	59	5.2
4. Group metalevel	53	4.7
5. Group activities	116	10.2
6. Illness	185	16.3
7. Children	77	6.8
8. Parents	144	12.7
9. Relationships	281	24.8

TABLE 6
CLASS/TOPIC

	Topic								
Class	1	2	3	4	5	6	7	8	9
Working class	23	26	14	23	17	59	13	23	44
Lower middle class	10	53	19	10	39	38	15	19	84
Middle class	20	87	26	20	60	88	49	102	153

with your problem, and—everyone just talks about his problem. Only I think that—I think we should—I imagine that we should talk about it a bit, go into it more, if we—we can't solve it anyway.

Text 5. Topic 5: group activities. Session 4, patient 11 (female).

Me? Yes, I have also got something to say, but this is something quite different now [cough], and that is that some time ago I had an idea that I would like to put into practice; I have often been in the psychiatric hospital at Steinhof to visit somebody, and I have always been moved by the people, by the situation there. I don't know whether you know, but there was an article in *Profil* [a weekly magazine], and my idea is that we could introduce some culture into the hospital, and I want to animate the people from the old Arena [a cultural group of the late seventies] to give a performance there, for younger people and for the sick. . . .

Text 6. Topic 6: illness. Session 1, patient 16 (male).

M: I dream a lot anyway, about things, about psychiatrists and mental hospitals, and I think that—that has not yet—Gugging [a psychiatric hospital]—I've not yet really got over it, in my psyche, where I was

TABLE 7
SEX/TOPIC

	Topic								
Sex	1	2	3	4	5	6	7	8	9
Men	33	86	19	32	67	87	28	12	75
Women	20	80	40	21	49	98	49	132	206

TABLE 8

WOMEN/TOPIC/CLASS

Class	Topic									Total
	1	2	3	4	5	6	7	8	9	
Working class	4	11	1	0	6	11	10	20	42	105
Middle class	12	37	25	17	42	81	26	96	109	445
Total	16	48	26	17	48	92	36	116	151	550

ill. I don't know—straitjackets, then this guy collapsed, and bleeding and—

W: Perhaps it's because you think about it all the time, that you're maybe depressive, that it's always there, that—

M: That was not easy, being in the loony bin twice, but—and I, I am aware that I'll certainly never go back there, but still, I didn't know whether or not I would get out, things are so terrible there. I dream about that, too, and I think that the background to my dreams, that I think—all that has its origin. I often dream about drugs, you know, which was also a terrible experience. I often dream about the loony bin; that was also a terrible experience, you know.

Text 7. Topic 7: children. Session 19, patient 5 (female).

The youngest, he was thirteen, and there was a particularly good relationship, which was terribly complicated for me, because I had to run all over the place with him, and at that time he went to the planetarium almost two or three times a week and also assumed that everybody knew anyway what's up above, you know, and he said "people explain that all so prim-

TABLE 9

MEN/TOPIC/CLASS

Class	Topic									Total
	1	2	3	4	5	6	7	8	9	
Working class	19	15	13	23	11	48	3	3	2	137
Middle class	8	50	1	3	18	7	23	6	44	160
Total	27	65	14	26	29	55	26	9	46	297

itively; I know all that anyway," and then he asked me questions, and I sat up at night and learned it so that I would not disappoint him and have to tell him "dear, that's . . ."

Text 8. Topic 8: parents. Session 19, patient 5 (female).

Well, she talks with him anyway. I can't even stand him any more. I mean, we met last Sunday, I couldn't even [stand] his presence—four meters away I could stand and breathe—well, I mean—and I—you can't even describe it, I, I mean, everybody in the group has his own cross to bear, perhaps a worse one, but at the moment that is always the reproach, I can—it's just impossible to talk to the father at all, because if I say "look"— at the moment he is also being treated by Dr. _____ I already told you— by Dr. _____ , I said, "why didn't you go there this week?" Well, I shouldn't have said that, for example, but, well, I'm just about alright, and I take the pills, and I can't talk at the moment, and and Dr. _____ doesn't say either—I mean, I really would like to help, too—You get such a lot of words when you have six patients and talk an hour with each—I mean, he wouldn't do that. You know yourself that psychiatrists just [speak] a few words, and so—they speak, but don't—he can't say, put that in a glass of water . . .

Text 9. Topic 9: relationships. Session 3, patient 8 (female).

Yes, alright: I have a friend, my fiancé, and we broke up because he went back to his wife and child, but he wanted to phone me once a week or more, to ask how I was. Somehow I'm still very fond of the man. He calls up and asks how I am. He upsets my life. Now I've forbidden him to do that, and I hope that I'll be able to get over it now with Mr. _____ , that he'll help me, that he'll take care of me, and that he'll also go out with me, so that I'm in society and so that I can't think about it so much. I wanted to know whether that's a good thing, or whether I'd better leave things as they are.

3.7.3. The Viennese dialect: Peculiarities that were taken into consideration in the transcription of the texts

The transcription of the texts was carried out according to the scheme of Gumperz and Herasimchuk (1972) and partly according to Ehlich and Switalla (1976:89 ff.). Nonverbal actions are placed in parentheses; interruptions are identified by brackets (interruptions hardly ever occur in therapeutic discussion) (2.2.2.3). As remarked above, the names of the patients and therapists are replaced by the symbols *T* for therapist, *M* for man, and *W* for woman. The numbers assigned to patients, sessions, and topics correspond to information in tables 5 and 10. These numbers were consistently retained during the entire empirical investigation (chapters 3–6). This makes it possible to follow individual patients, sessions, and topics through the whole therapy beyond the case studies (4.4). The illustrative texts are also consecutively numbered, and references relate to the number of the text passage (e.g., text 13). Two texts are particularly emphasized and set apart (5.4: text A, 5.5: text B); these two problem presentations are subjected to detailed qualitative analysis. This method of presentation is intended to ensure a continuity between quantitative and qualitative analyses that are often extremely detailed.

The texts from the group sessions reflect the wide variety of styles in Viennese dialect. Several particularly important peculiarities serving as social markers (for class, sex, or personality; see Scherer and Giles 1979) were taken into consideration in the transcription of the texts. The exact phonological derivation and competence model of Viennese dialect are given elsewhere (Leodolter 1975a:252 ff.; Wodak-Leodolter and Dressler 1978). In line with this theoretical analysis, several of the examples listed here—in a sort of miniature lexicon—can be explained as "input shifts," while others are regular manifestations (see Leodolter 1975a:274 ff. in particular, on the formation of the past participle and on vocalization of *l*; see Wodak 1984).

The list giving the quasi-orthographical transcription of important units can be found in Wodak (1981a:108–109). The English translation is standardized. Only a few very meaningful dialect expressions are paraphrased in brackets. It would not have made sense to translate the Viennese dialect into an English or American equivalent that would certainly have different connotations.

3.7.4. The sessions

The external background to the sessions and the typical phases are only briefly described in the presentation of the theoretical considerations (2.2). It is impossible to subject all twenty sessions to qualitative analysis. Therefore, after a description of the distribution of contributions and topics by sessions, I have attempted to

TABLE 10

SESSION/TOPICS

Session	Topics								
	1	2	3	4	5	6	7	8	9
1	0	20	0	4	0	4	0	32	6
2	0	2	0	0	0	4	0	0	2
3	2	8	0	2	0	7	0	4	37
4	7	14	0	4	11	8	0	0	7
5	0	7	0	1	0	4	5	3	9
6	0	16	14	1	5	36	0	15	17
7	1	0	19	5	1	38	1	0	6
8	0	0	0	0	17	11	0	0	38
9	3	30	6	0	4	1	0	16	2
10	0	10	16	0	0	24	1	6	1
11	0	2	0	0	0	0	0	0	18
12	1	3	0	34	35	0	0	5	19
13	0	27	0	0	10	11	3	4	10
14	0	1	0	0	8	2	13	27	13
15	1	2	0	1	0	1	0	0	0
16	0	6	0	0	0	0	16	14	24
17	0	0	0	0	1	0	0	4	0
18	31	11	3	2	15	33	0	5	2
19	2	7	0	0	1	4	31	12	32
20	5	0	0	0	1	0	7	1	38

describe the process of the therapy in the light of the group sessions observed. I have done this with a view to giving at least a continuous impression of episodes in the life of the group (3.8).

It is obvious from table 10 that there are various types of sessions. There are those that are dominated by one or more topics (e.g., 1, 3, 8, 12, 14, 19, 20) and sessions in which several topics are apparently discussed sporadically. It is interesting to note that problems involving relationships, parents, and children are frequently discussed, particularly in the last sessions. Although each session is certainly a self-contained unit with its own group dynamics, there is nevertheless a continuous thread running through all the sessions that points to a development. This can be particularly clearly dem-

TABLE 11
SESSIONS 1–10, WOMEN/TOPIC/CLASS

Class	Topic									Total
	1	2	3	4	5	6	7	8	9	
Working class	0	3	1	0	6	10	5	7	31	63
Lower middle class	0	10	14	0	0	0	1	13	0	38
Middle class	1	19	22	6	6	56	1	49	63	223
Total	1	32	37	6	12	66	7	69	94	324

onstrated in the light of the case studies (4.4). Development during the therapy is by no means best understood to be a straight line with a positive gradient. On the contrary, it is characteristic of therapeutic processes that they often stagnate, and regressions can even be observed. This is especially clear in the group observed, as will subsequently be seen when we examine the development of individual categories (4.3). A return to old behavior patterns corresponds to the introduction of new topics and problems, even with regard to language behavior. There is obviously a break between the first seventeen sessions and the last three, as for the first time patients discuss the topic of sexuality (sessions 19, 20) with increased resistance.

Tables 11 through 14 present an overview of the distribution of topics discussed by class and sex in the course of the first and second ten sessions.[6]

TABLE 12
SESSIONS 11–20, WOMEN/TOPIC/CLASS

Class	Topic									Total
	1	2	3	4	5	6	7	8	9	
Working class	4	8	0	0	0	1	5	13	11	42
Lower middle class	4	22	0	4	1	6	12	3	55	107
Middle class	11	18	3	11	36	25	25	47	46	222
Total	19	48	3	15	37	32	42	63	112	371

TABLE 13
SESSIONS 1–10, MEN/TOPIC/CLASS

Class	Topic									Total
	1	2	3	4	5	6	7	8	9	
Working class	5	10	13	7	0	32	0	1	1	69
Lower middle class	0	18	5	0	19	32	0	2	21	97
Middle class	7	47	1	3	14	4	0	0	9	85
Total	12	75	19	10	33	68	0	3	31	251

It is apparent that middle-class women talk significantly more than do those of other classes. In the first sessions the conversation tended to center on topics 2 through 6, while the contributions of all the social classes later concentrate on 2 (work) and 7, 8 (family) and 9. The lower middle class became considerably more involved during the last sessions. The language behavior of lower-middle-class women is dealt with in detail elsewhere (2.4.1.3, 4.3).

The difference between men and women is particularly evident in topics 4, 7, 8, and 9. Topic 4 (group metalevel) was used more by men and, significantly, by members of the working class; the topic of family tended to be left to the women. Nevertheless, the involvement of men in topics 7, 8, and 9 increased during the course of the therapy.

TABLE 14
SESSION 11–20, MEN/TOPIC/CLASS

Class	Topic									Total
	1	2	3	4	5	6	7	8	9	
Working class	14	5	0	16	11	16	3	2	1	68
Lower middle class	6	0	0	6	19	0	2	1	8	45
Middle class	1	3	0	0	4	3	23	6	35	75
Total	21	11	0	22	34	19	28	9	44	188

The hypotheses on class- and sex-specific differences will be dealt with in the quantitative analysis, as will the course of the therapy with reference to individual indicators (4.3, 4.4). The next section contains a contextual description of the therapeutic process. Several of the variables not included in the detailed qualitative and quantitative evaluation are explained and illustrated.

3.8. The group process

A phenomenological and descriptive list of the characteristic features of a typical session is outlined in the theoretical considerations on therapeutic communication. In the same section, reference is also made to the most important explicit and implicit rules of communication and to the function of metacommunication (2.2.2). The language game designated as therapeutic group session is dealt with in detail below.

Every therapeutic session consists of at least three phases, the beginning, the phase of problem presentation, and the end. Although every session is a complete unit in itself, it is nevertheless possible to trace a gradual development, evident mainly in an alteration in the way that individual patients deal with their own particular problems (4.4).

3.8.1. The group session's beginning

The beginning of a group session illustrates particularly clearly the difference between therapeutic communication and everyday communication. On both formal and informal social occasions, there are usually ritualized conversation beginnings, certain topics that are suitable for this purpose (Goffman 1971; Wodak-Leodolter 1977). The situation is different in a therapy session, where such niceties are out of place and where no attempt is generally made to use them. The entrance of the therapist signals the official beginning: everything discussed beforehand is pretherapy talk and everything talked about afterward, after the therapist has left the room, is posttherapy talk (Turner 1972:370 ff.).

The long period of silence is particularly striking: none of the patients dares to begin. Each of them is aware that they are no longer just chatting but rather that everything happening from here on can be a topic of the therapy itself. Fear and shame are therefore predominant; all spontaneity appears to be suppressed. Apart from this characteristic period of silence, abstract discussion and minor skirmishes are also typical of the start of therapy. If a female therapist leads a group session, the group initially feels without a leader, as their expectation of finding a male therapist and male authority is not fulfilled. Sometimes even the presence of the tape recorder was a topic at the start of the group; discussion of the problem as to whether or not the recording disturbed the patients was quite important.

Text 10. Session 1, beginning.

    [noises of people sitting down, embarrassed laughter]
T: Don't let yourself be put off by it. You'll see, you will immediately forget it.
    [whispering]
T: Mr. _____ , you are already thinking—
M1: I beg your pardon?
T: You are already thinking—
M1: Yes, hidden camera!
    [laughter]
W1: Nobody dares to talk, for one and a half hours . . .
    [whispering, pause, laughter, pause]
T: Perhaps I can begin by asking you, are you put off by the microphone, or is this the usual silence that occurs at the start of the session, until you have warmed up and got to know your neighbors?
M2: I must say, it irritates me—
T: Why?
M2: It disturbs me.
T: What annoys you?
M2: What?
T: What annoys you?
M2: Yes, I think the cause, the reason is that nobody wants to say anything because they don't want to be recorded.
M1: No, I don't think so.
W2: I'm not disturbed by it either.

This was the topic at the beginning of the first session that I recorded on tape. The speaker then changed to a young working-class patient who liked talking about himself a lot, who was comparatively uninhibited, and who therefore felt that the group was addressing him, as nobody else dared to talk about their problems.

Text 11. Session 2, beginning.

M1: Yes, thank you, I have concluded today—now I hope that that's the right thing. You can never tell at the beginning, but it looks good. Better, actually, than I had hoped, even. Because I have also had bad luck, I am really glad that I have at last—that was impossible anyway; I had nothing to do the whole day, and that finished me off mentally.

M2: It's very unpleasant, not having any work, when you just stand around the whole day.

M3: I think that would be the greatest life imaginable, not having any work. Mankind has dreamed of this ever since he has existed.

W1: I think things look quite different in reality. You start being depressive when you find that you are useless and superfluous.

M3: Do you think that work is useful?

W1: Of course it is!

M3: There's one thing I find funny: in the beginning 100 percent of mankind worked to get food in order to feed themselves. Today, the Americans have achieved an extreme value of 4 percent: four percent of the American population is able to feed the other 96 percent. The other 96 percent are employed in the so-called toy industry. In other words, they produce devices where you can turn knobs, push switches, etcetera: cars, televisions, radios, washing machines, things that one really does not need for everyday life.

W1: You do need washing machines!

M3: Somebody once said, "in every man there is a child." The child is able to leave the woman through birth. The man is unable to do this, and so he remains a child his life long and likes playing and is always inventing new devices to play with.

M4: Yes, but women also like playing with these devices. Take the washing machine, for example.

This is a good example of the resistance of the group to deal with its own problems in detail. They prefer to talk about the meaning of work in society generally. After this beginning, the session was dominated by the work problems of a few patients.

Text 12. Session 12, beginning.

    [noises]

T: Tell me your name afterward, please. [inaudible] Are you quite new to the group?

M1: Yes.

T: Who sent you?

M1: [inaudible] [pause]

W1: I brought this lady along.

T: That means we know nothing about you as yet. Please come down with me after the session so that I can fill out a card. For those of you who do not yet know me, I am _____ .

M2: That's nice!

T: Yes, and so [laughter] we can start for a change. Now there are so many of us all of a sudden [pause]

W2: May I say something, please? I would like to thank the group, well, the people whom I know. Thanks to the group, I have now decided to drop my boyfriend. I didn't dare do it, because I thought that [inaudible]

M3: That's fine! [laughter]

This is a very unusual beginning. After a five-minute break, a lower-middle-class patient begins by thanking the group, which has been a great help to her. This beginning is particularly interesting because explicit reference is made to the effect of the therapy. In the course of the session the group discusses the patient's decision to part company with her boyfriend, thus compelling the patient to consider the pros and cons again in detail. This is a classical example of the process of problem solving promoted within a therapy.

Finally, typical strategies at the start of a session in the group studied are summarized below:

1. silence;
2. discussion of the unusual situation of being tape recorded;
3. provocation by the therapist;
4. minor humorous skirmishes by dominant figures in the group;
5. abstract discussion;
6. concentration on one person and his problem;
7. discussion of the initial situation and the prevalent feelings of isolation and lack of leadership;
8. direct introduction of a special problem or a solution to a problem or conflict;
9. ritualized question-and-answer game in order to alleviate the discomfort of the situation and to break the silence;
10. discussion of a minor problem, such as information about institutions, certain medications, and so on.

3.8.2. The therapist

The supporting role of the therapist has already been mentioned (2.2.2.2). The presence of the therapist is a constitutive factor in the therapeutic setting. The various functions of the therapist will subsequently be illustrated in the light of several typical texts. The controversial opinions on sex-specific differences with regard to therapeutic style have already been mentioned (2.4.2.1). In a study of the literature, Cadow (1977) in particular emphasized that women have considerably more empathy than men. As far as my own study is concerned, I was unable to determine any significant differences in this respect, either in the qualitative or quantitative analysis or in the self-assessment of patients and therapists (6.4, 6.5). Due to the abstinent role of the therapists, their contributions are too limited to make a significant contribution to the quantitative analysis. I have, however, already referred to one function a therapist performs in the initial phase of a session, and that is the kind of provocative opening in which a patient is personally addressed about his problem or in which reference is made to the particular situation of the presence of a tape recorder.

The therapist normally moves at the level of metacommunicative activities by summing up, composing problems, indicating conflicts, and, finally, by interpreting group occurrences or individual difficulties and developments. These strategies are of decisive importance for the group therapy as well as being the most significant difference in comparison to everyday group discussion (Trömel-Plötz 1979), even when in such everyday situations there is an authority assumed to possess greater abilities and greater power, as is often the case. Yet this authority is a member of the group and always remains part of the process. The therapist, in contrast, is outside the group. All the power, leadership, omnipotence, and so on, that the group attributes to the therapist springs from the group imagination and from individual fantasies and projections (2.3.3). The therapist offers neutral ground on which conflicts can be projected and settled. Permanent frustration is provoked by the fact that the therapist does not behave like a normal authority, does not provide leadership or fulfill expectations. This is an important part of the learning process and of the acquisition of independence and the resolution of internalized authoritarian figures and compulsions. His very role outside the group enables the therapist to question group mechanisms at a metacommunicative level and to interpret behavior without the group suffering irreparable breaches.

Text 13. Session 3, therapist.

T: I think it's rather like somebody suddenly giving you a large new car, and it really gives you a great deal of pleasure, and—there is a small flaw on the front bumper. I don't want the car because of this flaw. And then you are surprised that you can't drive. And as far as mistaken identities are connected, I think this is a very important thing. This happened to me a couple of times at the clinic. When somebody addresses me as director, I admit to feeling slightly flattered, although I tell them I am not one. If somebody comes up to me and says, "fetch a doctor, quickly," mistaking me for a male nurse, I am simply upset, you understand?
[laughter]
T: People can't tell, because I don't wear a white coat. So these mistakes can only happen until we know one another better. Has that never happened to you; have you never been mistaken for somebody else?

Here the therapist interprets with the aid of a metaphor. It is also interesting to note that he relates an anecdote from his own life, something that would scarcely be possible, for example, in classical psychoanalytical doctor-patient therapy, where the complete abstinence of the therapist is required.

Text 14. Session 3, therapist.

T: I think we should really try to talk about what is happening here and now. Of course it is important that we should relate stories and experiences, but they should at least have some reference to what is going on here. Otherwise we could go straight to a coffeehouse. What motivates us at the moment, what is going on inside ourselves—it is getting warm in here and the air is getting sticky, and the time is up, and nothing has happened. It remains to try [and find out] what motivates us, what we are thinking about, here and now, at this moment. [pause] What are you thinking now, at this moment?

This text offers a good example of the assimilation of events in the group. The therapist refers to the importance of here and now. The therapist's reminder immediately hastens success as the group remembers what has occurred and assesses the prevalent feelings and moods.

Text 15. Session 18, therapist.

T: I think that you are slowly realizing that you are now in control of your life, not me—and certainly not your father or your possible stepmother. You yourself are in control.

W: Mmm.

T: No matter whether or not I have a nice voice.

W: Well, that was—[confusion] But ever since my brother asked what he had done to deserve an abnormal sister, ever since then he has used every means.

T: That you are not normal, that's precisely what it is.

In this case the therapist intervenes drastically. The patient has dominated the greater part of the session, largely by talking about her suffering, which, however, she experiences completely passively, unable to defend herself or change anything. Everything just happens. The pretext used is that the patient has failed to complete a poster for the Christmas celebrations. She has a bad conscience as a result, and the group sympathizes with her. However, the therapist destroys this defense of confronting herself with her real problem with sound interpretations. The patient, however, hardly reacts to this interpretation, but comes back to it several sessions later.

Each therapist naturally has his own quite individual style, but the remarks given here by way of illustration are characteristic of each therapeutic session and are a constitutive element of group activities.

3.8.3. Metacommunication

The value of metacommunication has already been emphasized in the theoretical considerations (2.2.2.4). Metacommunicative utterances are a constitutive feature of therapeutic sessions. This is not to say that there is no metacommunication in everyday communication. Yet the special way in which group activities are verbally worked through, the quality of the tentative actions of individuals, and the search for strategies for the solution of conflicts and problems are different from the practical conclusion of everyday, conversational situations. The acquisition of reflective behavior, or self-reflection, is an important part and aim of therapeutic communication and of therapy itself (1.2.6).

In text 4 a member of the working class criticizes the activities of the group. A patient has introduced his problem at work, but

his problem is not discussed. There follows instead a series of analogous problem presentations. The criticism leads the group to reflect on events and leads to a conflict between one of the patients
involved and the speaker. This induces the group to settle difficulties
and conflicts, to argue and to discuss, and to assimilate fears, such
as, for example, that of losing a loved one (see also 3.8.6).

Text 16. Session 12, patient 3 (female).

W: Do you mind if I tell you, I mean, that I am not attacking anybody,
but I find him so bitter, yes, and in his innermost self—and really,
when somebody says something that they don't really mean or says
something stupid; but I think, oh yes, I think you are so bitter and,
as you say, you want to fortify yourself and find your own ego, etcetera,
which you will find in due time, too, but you are still somewhat—I
don't know, I have the feeling that in your innermost self you are very,
I don't know—or perhaps I just imagine it. [noise] I mean in your life,
or I have only—I mean, I have often seen you, but I really don't know
what exactly your problem is, but you, I don't know, I can—you could
perhaps say of such a person that you have been through a lot in your
youth, or childhood, or dancing school when you were young, or that
you somehow have a certain hardness as a man that a woman may,
that a woman may not have, or like a woman has because she has
had to fight for it, but everything is somehow hard in your case, if I
can put it like that. And now you want things easier, so that your
life—as you say, one should change one's life, that one cannot live like
that. That's the only explanation I can find. To consolidate the whole
thing—or is what I have just said all wrong? But it is just that when
I look at you, yes, I have the feeling that you just stand like iron in
your life.

This text, a recapitulative interpretation of another member of
the group given by a female patient, is a good example of metacommunication centering on the problem of an individual patient
and not mainly on group activities. Such basic criticism as this
would probably be unbearable outside the therapeutic situation. In
this case the patient addressed also deals objectively with the remarks made.

A number of other examples could also be given. Even these
selected passages, however, vividly illustrate the typology of therapeutic metacommunication and the specific features of this
situation.

3.8.4. The development of group cohesion

Although I was not able to observe the entire group process, a certain development was clearly apparent during the years of my study (4.4).

To begin with, there was still a considerable distance between individual members of the group; the custom of going to a restaurant or coffeehouse after the therapeutic session had not yet been introduced. Private meetings were also comparatively rare.

This aspect had changed dramatically by the end of a year. The group had become really bonded together. People spent a lot of time privately with one another and organized joint excursions, a Christmas party, and open houses on weekends and public holidays. They also went to movies or to dances together. A lively social life had taken root, tremendous activity that was naturally headed mainly by the dominant figures of the group. At the same time, the group dynamics had also changed considerably. The relationships between individual members of the group had become closer; the group and the activities of the group had become an important topic of the sessions. Even the implicit and explicit rules of the therapy were discussed, particularly in one instance where there had been a betrayal: a member of the group had divulged important events from the life of a female patient. This indiscretion in the form of idle chatter had serious consequences for the patient, who almost lost her job as a kindergarten teacher as a result.

The following text passages are designed to illustrate how the patients talk about the group (metalevel), the nature of the group activities, and the significance of the group and of the group process for the individual:

Text 17. Session 12, patient 10 (W) (female).

W: Yes, I must say, because now I no longer have the feeling that I am all alone. Of course, I have my children, but I don't talk to them, and nobody listens to me; and, I mean, you have the feeling [in the group] that not only do you have problems yourself, but that the others also have them.

M: Yes, that is also the reason why I come here, too. Then I feel—the contact is important, you know. What do you think?

W: Yes, it is very important. Where can you get to know people these days—I mean, I mean, *really* get to know people, if you can only chat a little—know what I mean?

Here, too, a patient describes what the group means to her, a means of finding genuine human relationships.

Text 18. Session 12, patient 12 (W1) (female).

W1: I think I am already quite hooked on the group.
W2: What?
W1: I'm hooked on the group.
W2: Are you?
W1: Yes.
W2: Do you go every day? Do you go to the group every day?
W1: Yes, you could almost say, substitute mother or substitute father—
M1: Yes, but . . .
W2: Well, why is it so bad, having a substitute mother?
W1: Well, I can't imagine how it will be once I go away again.
M1: Then you'll no doubt find something else, won't you?
W2: Yes, of course.

This short exchange illustrates the patient's phase (she is a student) of extreme dependence on the group very well. The student also attempts to rationalize this by using psychological terminology. The patients reassure her in her fear of dependence.

Text 19. Session 12, patient 19 (male).

M: I have a brief question, which I wanted to raise the whole time today. You see, for a long time I have had the feeling, in the group, that in a way you write me off as a work-shy individual. The question is justified today because there are just enough people here to comment on it. What do you think about it? Was my feeling right? Yes, no, and if yes, why?

A patient projects his feelings of guilt and his bad conscience onto the group, having recourse to the group superego.

Text 20. Session 6, patient 21 (male).

M: That depends, of course, that depends only on the members of the group, because at any time we can—do you mind, I'm here—sorry, I got aggressive there, it's not that I wanted to assert myself. You say that anybody can come from Monday to Friday, during the opening hours of the enterprise, and fetch a key from the reception, and that he can open up, and that he must clear up his mess again afterward, and the more come, the more you take advantage of this.

This describes the independent activity of the group. Separate meetings and groups are organized without the presence of the therapist.

Although only a few passages from the bulk of material have been printed here, the various levels of communication are clearly apparent: metacommunication about the group, communication of the group, and finally, the significance of the group to the individual. The last point in particular is dealt with in detail in the presentation of individual case studies (4.4).

3.8.5. Problem treatment

At this juncture I should like to mention only the aspect of problem treatment, as the explicit qualitative and quantitative text analyses of problem presentation in group therapy are made in 3.9, 3.10, 4.3, 5.4, and 5.5. How does the group react to a problem, how is a problem dealt with in a session, and does this differ from everyday communication? We are dealing here with an important characteristic of therapeutic communication: people try to describe their difficulties as honestly as possible, and the group wants to help. In everyday life, in contrast, problems must be concealed, and those with problems are more liable to reap anger and rejection, or at best sympathy—but seldom help—with their complaints. As it is impossible to reproduce an entire session here, I should like merely to outline the course of problem treatment, illustrating it with text passages. These observations center on the emergence of the problem and the objective questions of the patients (see 5.4 and 5.5 for detailed analysis).

Hesitating and timid, the female patient begins to describe the problem with her father that is affecting her work as well as her entire life. The questions put by members of the group after this very emotional and not very objective description of the problem help the patient to appreciate slowly the full significance of the problem.

The patient's dependence on her parents is particularly clear, as are the tremendous ambivalence and feelings of guilt attached to authority (text 8). Problem solutions are put forward and rejected again, as the patient is not yet able to regard her father and mother with sufficient objectivity. The questions put by the patients force her to see for herself the extent to which this problem overshadows her job and her marriage and to see how passively and defenselessly she behaves.

Text 21. Session 1, patient 3 (W1) (female).

W1: I am so fond of him that I often say, "We'll buy that for daddy"— at the fair, or wherever we are, at an exhibition or something, love suddenly makes itself felt impulsively, and then I think, maybe he'll then say, "Why did you buy that, why and what for—wasn't really necessary—could have bought something else with your money." And now I already think, what will he say about it?

W2: Is that so, what he says about it?

W1: Because he always says something instead of just saying "thank you" or "nice of you" or any old trivial answer that one might give, you know? I mean, I don't buy anything silly anyway; I am careful with money anyway.

W3: Another question, what does your husband think about all this, what does he say about it?

W1: Well, he stands between my mother—well me, for me and says, "Look, you must—for your mother," I mean, everything for you, but my father—there, too, well, not that he [is] bad or anything, but he—

W3: He doesn't like him, does he?

W1: I wouldn't say that—doesn't like him, but he—the way it is with fathers-in-law—I don't know how I should put it: He, he treats him with kid gloves. If you talk to him normally it's all right, but you must, when you talk to him and you finish, you must say, "Yes, daddy, you're right; no, what I've just said was unjust, you—whatever you do, you are always right."

W3: No, thank heavens not! Well I never—

M1: That's lucky!

W1: Lucky?!

W3: That's very positive, because—

W1: That is very positive—

W4: Who will inherit the business one day?

W1: To be honest, everything I've said recently: I don't want it any more; I want to work for about another ten years, until we—well, so far we haven't been in debt, but this year we started building, and we— our debts will then be smaller, and most of them will have been repaid after ten years.

W5: I think you could earn more elsewhere, if you went to work for somebody else.

W1: Yes, but in my case—well, I am still ill, and there are days when I can't even get up and drink a glass of water. Just imagine if I were employed somewhere else, and tell my boss that I am on sick leave.

W5: That would no longer be so!

W1: I beg your pardon?

W5: If you were somewhere else, then—if you were appreciated there.

W1: I don't want you to think I let myself go, but I often find that I am emotionally at a low point.

The narration reminds the patient of earlier scenes, enabling her to connect her depression and her deep-rooted fears. Finally, the discussion centers on work problems and the role of the working woman.

Text 22. Session 1, patient 3 (W1).

W1: That is uninteresting now. Anyway, I wouldn't be that yet.

W3: That's not uninteresting.

W1: Well, I, well, you can't do that in a group; there are so many people here who also have their own problems, I mean, I am now so far that I want to get out, and that I have stopped.

W3: Did the talk help you? Did it help you; did the talk help you?

W1: Yes, to that extent, yes. It's just that now I am even more confused, I mean, everything first has to be, it's like sticking a form into it, the talk, you just do it by yourself—

W3: Yes, that's—

W1: I know, of course, that that are other problems. That's always what I tell myself: what you've got is nothing, other people are sitting here; but at the moment I think of them, who also have a problem now, you know, always, because the others—I don't know—lose a child or a husband or [have] an accident, which a person would really find, but that's—

W3: What do you mean, now, what are you trying to say?

W1: Well, that it's perhaps not so bad after all, that I am perhaps—there's the point again, because I always think when I'm talking about something or doing something, that it's—

W2: —not right—

The group now gives up, and another patient begins to speak. The patient in text 22 in particular changes dramatically over the course of two years. In the discussion of the therapeutic effect, we shall be returning to the presentation of the same problem by this patient at another phase of the therapy (4.4, 5.4, 5.5).

3.8.6. Problems of conflict and profiling

Conflicts are of great importance in group communication. It is the therapeutic free zone that makes it possible to settle conflicts openly without this resulting in irreparable breaches in the relationships between members of the group. There is, moreover, a wide range of conflict strategies, many of them sex-specific. Conflicts between men and women are normally carried out at the level of reproach and justification. Conflicts between men are more aggressive or are transferred to the humorous level. This also involves male profiling strategies. Mock conflicts are presented for the general amusement of everybody (Wodak 1981c).

Text 23. Session 4, beginning, patients 15 (M1) and 20 (M2) (both male).

    [subdued chatting at the beginning; very large group]

M1: There are so many of us today that we could actually split the group if we had two doctors. [general laughter]

T: Really, do you want to split the group?

M1: If it's possible, it might be better.

M2: We've only got one microphone.

M1: Well, you see, people, not everybody can talk.

W1: Everybody can talk loudly.

W2: That should be decided by Dr. _____ and not—

M1: You haven't got a chance to speak with so many people.

M3: Who do you want to talk with, with the mineral water bottle? [laughter—the original text is a play on words]

M1: Well, with the wine bottle of course, just like you.

M3: I don't drink; I'm a teetotaler, on the wagon. Otherwise I'm not abstinent.

Text 24. Session 4, patients 14 (M3), 15 (M1), and 16 (M2).

M1: Because they said, because—well, you know, to start with, I talked for a long time, and now I thought Mr. _____ meant that I talked for too long.

M2: No, that's not what I—at the moment I haven't said it yet, but I will soon.

W1: Do you think that we haven't contributed anything at all?

M2: Well, I don't know, perhaps it's right that everybody should say something, but I think that basically, I don't know.

M1: My own opinion is that everyone should have his say, perhaps; there are not just two people here with things on their minds, there are several people.

M2· Yes, that doesn't work because there are so many people here today.

T: Excuse me: the subgroups should talk to the group.

W1: Yes, I've just said something.

T: What you've just said is important.

W1: I am afraid.

M3: I can't quarrel, because I'm just physically—it really hurts me; I've got such weak nerves that I need a couple of hours to recover. [silence]

T: Perhaps you shouldn't turn your back on your neighbor to your right.

Text 25. Session 2, patients 18 (M1) and 21 (M2).

M1: Actually, I no longer have any feelings of happiness or friendship. But above all, I regard the group as—well, I, I have almost completely mastered severe behavioral disturbances and regard the group as a means of increasing my confidence, and for training, and I regard the therapist as somebody who can show us the way. That is the reason why I come to the group.

M2: The funny thing is just that on the basis of the way in which the group reacts to you and how you react to the group, in the course of time, you should to some extent find out for yourself what the rules are.

M1: Yes, I've already said, if you don't mind, I've—you are not my father.

M2: Yes, but I just wanted to—

M1: You're still not my father; you haven't convinced me.

M2: [inaudible]

M1: Well, I'll find my own way, and one means of doing so is actually the group, the fact that I can take this way, because I am still distrustful, still—what is the right way, what is the healthy way, what does it look like? I am quite convinced that there is a naturalness in every human being, and if I can still learn something, then I will learn it, in order to cope with my life, you see; and that is the reason why I come to the group.

These text passages illustrate typical conflict strategies: (1) reproach-justification conflict; (2) mock conflict (jocularity); (3) conflict on a specific topic (status problem); and (4) relationship conflict (problems of jealousy and envy).

3.9. Linguistic analysis of therapeutic communication: The three-level model and problem presentation in group therapy
3.9.1. Introductory remarks

After the illustrative description of the random sample and important elements of the group therapy session (3.7, 3.8), there now follows an explicit quantitative and qualitative analysis of the text class of problem presentation in group therapy.[7] Starting from the theoretical pragmatic approach to the analysis of therapeutic communication presented in 2.2 and 2.3, problem presentation in group therapy is first assigned a place in the repertoire of speech strategies in the three levels of therapeutic communication (2.3.2.1). Following a description of the functions and structure of this text class, categories are then derived that can be used for the statistical analysis (3.10). The hypotheses on class- and sex-specific language behavior and on therapeutic effect will then be tested in the light of problem presentation in group therapy (2.4, 2.5). The text-linguistic methods are introduced by way of example and are discussed. A complete review of the existing models of conversational and narrative analysis would exceed the scope and intention of this study. I shall, therefore, deal only in detail with approaches directly relating to my own procedure.

3.9.2. Problem presentation in group therapy
3.9.2.1. The concept

Problem presentation in group therapy occupies a central position among group therapy techniques for suicide candidates. The term *problem presentation in group therapy* was deliberately selected as a designation for sections of text devoted to a personal problem and declared by the speaker himself to be his problem. Labov and Waletzky (1967) and Labov and Fanshel (1977) deal with narrative texts, that is, stories in the narrative past, with the typical phases of a narrative, while Quasthoff, for instance, presents narratives in the social welfare office (1979). For my part, I avoid the use of the term *narrative* as a designation for the text class examined here. Problem presentation in group therapy proves to have the definite function of describing an oppressive and acute problem and is realized by patients using different text types (one of these text types can also be the classical narrative form) (2.2). I also deliberately avoid the use of the terms *story* and *event* (Cicourel 1975; Norman and Rumelhart 1975), as these terms suggest a story or a lengthy text containing incidents (events) in the past tense ("narrative past") (Weinrich 1971). It is my view that the term *narrative* becomes hackneyed if every lengthy section of text produced by a speaker is classified as a narrative or has to be measured using Labov and Waletzky's schema (1967)[8] or variations of it (Kraft et al. 1977; van Dijk 1972; Quasthoff 1979). Stylistics and narrative research proffer other terms, such as *depiction, report,* and *description* (Sandig 1978:61 ff., 159 ff.), against which spoken narrative must be defined. The shortcomings of structural and generative-transformational narrative research (Greimas 1966; van Dijk 1972; Gülich and Raible 1977) is that it neglects the concrete speech situation. The structural model (Greimas 1966; Bremond 1973; Todorov 1972) involves the description and classification of a corpus (lengthy text). In many instances, several classes are assumed in the derivation (*Aktantenmodell,* "transaction model") (Gülich and Raible 1977: 207 ff.), though speaker and addressee are again not included in the explicit analysis. Starting with Propp (1928), a difference is indeed made between certain central figures and functions in the text that can be realized in different ways (in various fairy tales and specific to civilizations). Social and psychological dimensions are also included (Lévi-Strauss 1958). The texts dealt with, however, are restricted to fairy tales, myths, narratives, and other literary types. Spontaneous oral texts and the context of the spoken word are not taken into consideration.

The generative-transformational text model offers an interesting approach, particularly the introduction of a macrostructure for the derivation of narrative texts (van Dijk 1972:130 ff.). This, too, is based on Labov and Waletzky's classical narrative model (1967), although in a changed form. Other text types are therefore excluded. It is difficult to justify the methodological approach to narrative via paraphrasing, for which van Dijk (1972:288 ff.) is unable to specify objective criteria, nevertheless then taking the paraphrased text as the basis of his analysis. He fails to consider speech situation, speaker and listener, sociological and psychological variables, which, as we shall see, have a significant effect on the realization of text types (see also Wodak and Schulz 1984; Wodak 1984).[9]

Labov and Fanshel's (1977) procedure with "narratives" taken from the therapeutic situation (1.3.2) is also oriented very one-sidedly toward the classical narrative form (although the patients' texts by no means always conform with the model). What is more, the method of expansion, like van Dijk's "paraphrasing," is used completely subjectively and cannot be reconstructed because explicit psychological, textual, and sociological criteria are missing. Expansion, which justifiably relates to unconscious and latent levels of therapeutic communication, ought to be objectified by applying psychotherapeutic categories (which the therapist also uses in his interpretation) (Labov and Fanshell 1977:49 ff.). Psychological and sociological criteria are present in the form of status predicates (these are the patient's central activities and conflicts, evident from his life history and the therapeutic context and formalized as propositions). These are neither strictly psychotherapeutically nor linguistically derived, however (Labov and Fanshel 1977:51 ff.). Latent levels are also referred to in the text analyses presented here (following the explicit theoretical approach). Psychotherapeutic concepts have been taken into consideration as far as possible (2.2.3). At the same time, it seemed necessary to select the term *problem presentation in group therapy* for the text class analyzed, so as not to make the mistake of being one-sided and of starting exclusively from the classical narrative model. A text class is realized in different ways, depending on social class, sex, and phase of therapy. The text types can probably be derived from a common text thematic macro structure (a cognitive planning strategy) (Norman and Rumelhart 1975; Freedle 1977).

Finally, it is also necessary to justify the use of the term *presentation*. The term is neutral with reference to narrative research, as it has not yet been adopted for a text class. It should on no account be mistaken for Bühler's term, where *presentation* means the most neutral relationship in the organum model, and that is the connection (allocation) of linguistic symbols to subjects and objects, devoid of emotional and social components.

One should single out actual phrases from life in which for the first time it becomes apparent that virtually everything can be defined and attached to the presentational function of linguistic symbols alone. This certainly applies most explicitly to scientific language and culminates in the presentational system of modern logistics. What does the pure logician worry about the expressive values of the symbols which he writes on the board in chalk? . . . and if it is an arbitrary lyricist, he will sometimes write above his door that the logician should stay outside. That again is one of the exaggerations which we do not need to take seriously. In command language, for example, everything is attached to the third person, to an exact appellative function, in the case of words of endearment and expletives, to appeal and express at the same time. (Bühler 1934:31, 32)

The decisive scientific verification of our constitutional formulae, of the organum model of language, is provided if it is found that each of the three relationships, each of the three functions of linguistic symbols opens the door to and relates to a separate field of sociological phenomena and facts. And this is indeed the case. For linguistic expression and linguistic appeal are part of linguistic research as a whole, exhibiting their own structures compared with linguistic presentation. (Bühler 1934:32)

Problem presentation in group therapy does not therefore coincide with the concept of presentation mentioned here. On the contrary, it composes a text class specific to the therapeutic situation, or in Bühler's terminology, containing aspects of expression, appeal, and presentation. It differs from everyday life, from everyday description of problems, because of the interpretation possible in a therapeutic situation, both at a conscious and at an unconscious level; because of its symptomatic nature (the form and content of problem presentation in group therapy expresses the specific illness of a patient); and last, because of the explicit and implicit functions in group therapy, which show marked differences from everyday life. Finally, as shown in section 3.8.5, the working-through of problems and the interventions by other patients and the therapist, the encouragement of emotional factors, and the opportunities for problem solution and tentative action are contextual components of problem presentation in group therapy and characteristic only of therapeutic discourse (5.4, 5.5).

3.9.2.2. Functions of problem presentation in group therapy

According to the theoretical approach, problem presentation in group therapy as a typical communicative strategy in a therapeutic context ought to exhibit considerable differences compared to everyday problem presentation. The degree of openness would appear to be of decisive importance. A therapeutic situation no longer involves establishing or presenting an image that must comply with social values such as achievements, strength, prestige, and status (Goffman 1959). On the contrary, it involves destroying the existing image, which is often the cause of envy and depression because it does not meet requirements and values of society or of one's own superego (internalized standards). Self-disclosure and openness are requirements of the therapeutic situation, and although they cause embarrassment and shame, they nevertheless have a liberating effect. It is not necessary to comply with any preconceived examples, and one can honestly admit one's weaknesses and problems, often experiencing for the first time that one is appreciated and liked in spite of this (or even because of this); the patient finds that self-disclosure does not cause the world to collapse around his ears. In this way the patient is able to formulate and adopt for himself demands, expectations, and values that suit him and are realistic. He is able to form his own identity and free himself from preconceived standards that were impossible to meet. Against the background described above, it is quite obvious that problem presentation in group therapy initially causes many difficulties. Fear of disclosure is initially great if one has previously always been exposed to negative social sanctions when one has not been strong, industrious, successful, and efficient.

Many of the traditional sex-specific differences are encountered here: men ought to be strong; women may be weak. This is why women—at first sight—enter into the therapeutic situation more effectively (Richter 1972) (2.4.2).

At the level of the here and now in the group, problem presentation in group therapy also performs additional functions for the group and the individual in the group. The opportunity of relating a problem in detail makes it possible for the individual to become integrated in the group. Moreover, the feeling of cohesion in the group is produced by the realization that all the members of the group are going through difficult times. The individual is also able to adopt a personality and assume a certain role within the group, or alternatively, the role is ascribed to an individual by the group. The nature of the problem presentation also strongly indicates unconscious transferences (in the sense of family transference) by the individual to the group. If a patient desires mainly comfort and sympathy, he sees himself as poor, helpless, and childish. If, however, he seeks advice or an opportunity to openly compare various strategies for problem solving with other group members against the background of his own decisions, this is already a sign of the emancipation of the individual from the group family (a subsequent phase in Bion's taxonomy—see Bion 1961) and of the partial disintegration of family and authority transference (2.3.3). Finally, both the quality and the subject matter of problem presentation in group therapy are shaped by the life history and expectations of the individual, by his combination of status roles and specific symptoms. However, many of the motives that induce the individual patient to discuss this particular problem at a certain moment are not revealed to the observer. Neither are the private symbols and connotations used in each problem presentation in group therapy (2.3.4). Unconscious connections are not revealed sensu stricto in the crisis group as they are in classical psychoanalysis, for example. Schema 5 presents the position of problem presentation in therapeutic discourse.

3.9.3. Text-thematic macrostructure (cognitive planning strategy)
3.9.3.1. Draft of an integrative model

It is necessary at this point to provide a linguistic model for the text analysis of problem presentation in group therapy. This model contains the constitutive factors of problem presentation and also gives a plausible explanation of the effect of sociological variables, such as class and sex, on the text type realized (Freedle and Duran 1979:205; Hall et al. 1977:169) (2.4.1, 2.4.2).

It seems reasonable to assume a text-thematic macrostructure (Kintsch and van Dijk:7 ff., Gülich and Raible 1977:266) that is systematically realized in a different manner depending on the class and sex of the speaker (in the sense of triggering elements). In other words, to use the terminology of text planning (Cicourel 1975; Norman and Rumelhart 1975), to explicitly follow through the

SCHEMA 5

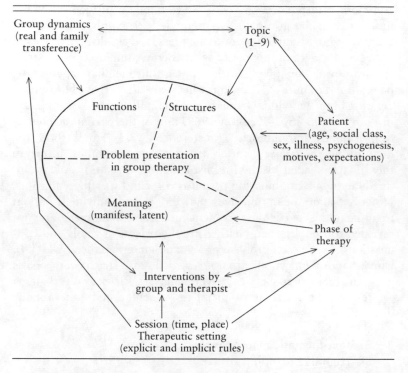

stages from *plans* to *schemata* and *frames* (Schank and Abelson 1977; Goffman 1975:496 ff.).

In the taxonomic classification of therapeutic discourse, it has been argued that each text type (that is, realization pattern of a text class; see Werlich 1975) must be regarded as a combination of different speech strategies (2.3.2.1). Thus, although problem presentation in group therapy falls into the category of behavioral strategies (macrostructurally), at the microstructural level, it also involves discourse strategies and logical and even cognitive-emotional factors. These are constitutive categories contained in a specific combination in every text.

According to our assumptions relating to class- and sex-specific socialization, there are significant differences in the quality of the problem presentation realized (e.g., emotionality and spontaneity in the working class; metacommunicative background in the middle class; introduction of life history in women; rejection of causative explanations in men). In other words, the same topic (e.g., work) is realized in a typical manner depending on the class and sex of the speaker. This fact can be brought into context with various strategies of cognitive planning; the schemata selected for problem presentation in group therapy display various priorities.

3.9.3.2. Cognitive planning and sociolinguistic text analysis

The problem that must be solved is the following: how does one explain the empirical fact that the same topic (in the same speech situation, with the same function) is systematically realized using different text types, and that this is done in a predictable form depending on the class and sex of the speaker?

As we shall see, the qualitative and quantitative analyses of problem presentation in group therapy enable us to make forecasts that specify the probable form in which a problem presentation will be realized (using a certain text type). This has already been claimed by Kintsch and van Dijk (30 ff.), but without their analyzing a suitable corpus or taking sociological variables into consideration (4.3.3).

The text is generated starting from an exactly defined text-thematic macrostructure and following certain planning procedures. The term *schematic structures* is of importance in this context. This refers to conventionalized forms serving the arrangement and verbalization of cognitive experiences.

A number of researchers from a wide range of disciplines have recently dealt with the process of planning and generating texts. They include sociologists (Cicourel 1975; Goffman 1975), linguists (Chafe 1977), psychologists (Rumelhardt and Norman 1975; Freedle 1977, 1979), and computer (artificial intelligence) experts, such as Schank and Abelson (1977). The term *schema* can be traced back to Bartlett (1932), who investigated memory processes (see also Tannen 1979:138 ff., on the history of research). It is not clear in the various different usages of the terms, however, to which level they should be allocated. Are we dealing with psychological concepts or linguistic terms?

Thus Chafe, for example, defines *verbalization* as the conversion of nonverbal knowledge into speech:

> Verbalization is creative in the sense that it requires a speaker to make choices between a multiplicity of available options. The creative choices a speaker must make in the course of verbalization involve precisely this kind of interpretation. They are decisions as to how to assign particulars to types in such a way that the verbal output will serve its purpose with reasonable effectiveness. In the model and terminology I will be using here these types are of three kinds: schemata, frames and categories. (Chafe 1977:41–42)

The experiences are broken down into "chunks" (pieces) (Chafe 1977:45) using the schema (e.g, the structuring of a story). If spatial and temporal sequences and specific persons are then added, Chafe speaks of "frames" (Chafe 1977:46). Classification is eventually effected by adaptation to a certain speech situation. The text-linguistic indicators, however, are missing from this model.

Kintsch and van Dijk go into greater detail, giving rules for the transformation of macrostructures into actual texts. Explicit reference is made to the choice of specific text types: "Schematic structures play an important role in discourse comprehension and production. Without them we would not be able to explain why language users are able to understand a discourse as a story, or why they are able to judge whether a story, or an argument, is correct or not" (Kintsch and van Dijk:9–10).

The schema is the formal representation of the plan: "The schema determines which micro-proposition, or generalization of micro-propositions, is relevant, and thus, which parts of the text will form its gist (Kintsch and van Dijk:26–27). Similarly, the schema, once actualized, will guide the global ordering of the production process, e.g., the order in which the macro-propositions themselves are actualized" (Kintsch and van Dijk:35–36).

Tannen (1979) and Schank and Abelson (1977) take a different approach to the "planning problem." Tannen (1979:179) starts with "structural expectations" (Ross 1975), which organize our knowledge in a culturally specific manner and select certain frames (used in this instance as a psychological concept). Tannen (1979) attempts to illustrate this term using the analysis of a story. She does not, however, devote sufficient attention to the functional aspect of language. It is the function of the text that is of interest in text planning: the choice of a schema or frame will depend on function and speech situation, as we shall see (4.3.3). Only if the concept of function and sociolinguistic variables are included is it possible to understand the phenomenon of different text types for the realization of the same fundamental macrostructure. Different schemata are chosen depending on the class and sex of the speaker.

Ochs (1979:53 ff.), Levy (1979:184 ff.), and Freedle and Duran (1979:206) refer to both functional concepts and sociological variables. Ochs (1979), for example, differentiates between planned and unplanned discourse. Unplanned discourse contains elements of children's language and expresses spontaneity (Ochs 1979:55). Thus, only a consistent text, without strong emotions, can be planned, and this—as illustrated by the example—corresponds more to a very defensive middle-class problem presentation. In my opinion, one cannot differentiate between planned and unplanned (planning is certainly only very seldom a conscious process) but rather between different strategies of planning (every text must be planned). The empirical evidence from the therapeutic situation supports this hypothesis, as in such situations all speakers act "spontaneously," with a greater or lesser degree of resistance. However, none of them has prepared his problem presentation (this would be inconsistent with constitutive features of the therapeutic situation) (2.2.2.1).

Freedle and Duran (1979) discuss the application of this terminology to sociolinguistic phenomena, without, however, making any attempt at integration: "In particular, dialogue rules to us represent higher-order nonlinguistic knowledge scripts about how to organize what to say and how to comprehend verbally instantiated concepts, be they vignettes, scripts, plans, goals, themes" (1979:206).

The authors thus refer to the terminology of Schank and Abelson (1977:17, 41, 69 ff.). This research group is interested in mechanically translatable cognitive planning processes, and there is little reference to linguistic material. The assumption of holes ("slots") that are filled on the basis of the specific situation, speakers, and so on is of importance in the concept of scripts. "A script is a structure that describes appropriate sequences of events in a particular context. A script is made up of slots and requirements about who can fill these slots. . . . Thus, a script is a predetermined stereotyped sequence of actions that defines a well-known situation" (Schank and Abelson 1977:41).

An explanation of private linguistic texts is also offered by Schank and Abelson in the context of their concept (p. 63). They are described as script that is stored in the unconscious (this again excludes the ever-present unconscious aspects of planning!). "Plans" represent chains of scripts aimed at a "goal" (pp. 97, 132) against the background of "themes," which, as background information, serve to make individual actions from the life history of the speaker understandable. The shortcoming of this approach is that a number of sociological and psychological terms are used without reflection. *Theme,* for example, refers to the social roles of the speaker. The authors draft new categories and terms without taking into consideration the differentiated role theory already elaborated by sociologists (an untidy interdisciplinary procedure).

Rehbein (1976*a,b*) lapses into a similar eclecticism when he describes the planning of the action process using an action tree, which—without motivation and without theoretical justification—contains psychological, sociological, and linguistic elements (Rehbein 1976*a*:25 ff.). However, Rehbein is more successful in operationalizing the linguistic corpus than are those of the cognitive school described above.

After this brief digression on several more recent theoretical concepts of text planning, it is possible to risk a tentative answer to the question posed above (see also Wodak 1983): Depending on the class and sex of the speaker, in the precisely defined therapeutic setting, there are typical schemata that are cognitively (unconsciously and consciously) selected in the realization of a problem presentation. The text-thematic macrostructure is systematically verbalized using different text types. The planning processes take place by and large unconsciously; sociological and sociopsychological variables are primarily responsible for the selection of a text type. For the first time it is possible here in the light of the quantity of empirical material to provide "natural" evidence for the assumption of cognitive planning processes and strategies. The knowledge that a frame, like a narrative, is much too narrowly defined is also important. This is more a functional speech strategy of problem presentation that can be realized in similar schemata to those of story, scene, or description of circumstances. At the text level, too, it is therefore possible to speak of systematic variation.

Thus, the sociolinguistic and psycholinguistic results have a direct effect on the elaboration of theories. We therefore propose calling this model the sociopsychological theory of text planning (SPTT) (Wodak and Schulz 1984; Wodak 1984).

3.9.3.3. The macrostructure

Four sample texts (each from a working-class and a middle-class man and woman describing their problems at work) are intended to illustrate the theoretical problem empirically. Typical differences will then be derived after the text-thematic macrostructure is established.

Text 26. Working-class man, patient 16 (M1) (male).

M1: Well, the thing—I am really done for, you could say, but I have to go to work. Often I stand there and think I am being swallowed up by the earth, then I, then I can't see anything any more, I am quite gone [*bin ganz weg*]. . . . Yes, in private industry, I think you are really done for, because I am still free in a way. Not long ago I was up on the, up on the Ringturm, on the eighteenth floor, and I thought the whole, the whole—what do you call it, the thing you hold on to, you know—

M2: Railing?

M1: That's it, the railing would break; I got giddy again [*des Wurlerte 'kriegt*], and thought, should I jump, but then I went to the lift, went down, took a seat in a coffeehouse, and tried like mad to read. I ran round the block, but it didn't work, then it went again.

Text 27. Middle-class man, patient 14 (male).

M: At the moment I really suffer from profuse sweating in the morning when I wake up and until I get up; it's so uncontrollable, and I'm completely washed out. My whole chest and everything is so tense. I'm working as a salesman again, and as I said, my boss seemed very nasty. We've already had a difference of opinion, and when that happens, it happens then, especially in the morning; it's worst then.

T: What's your boss like, then?

M: Well, things may—things will probably settle down, but I still feel the first quarrel—it just came out of the blue. I know that when you're fifty you have to work harder than when you're young and let's say—to fill the job, anyway, everything is so tense that I can't get any rest.

At the weekend I'm afraid, even on Friday, that the whole thing will start up again on Monday. But things are really going quite well, but I know, everything's alright, but the tension, this fear, the whole situation is terrible; it's disastrous for me. In the morning I'm completely whacked and I'm afraid of starting work again. So far I've only taken Deanxit, and not so many of them, at most one, and they don't help in this condition. I don't know—perhaps you can help me—if there's anything—a medication one can take.

Text 28. Working-class woman, patient 9 (female).

W: So he says, "That's got nothing to do with the others"; that's good for me when he says that. Now I can't even look at the paper. Then he says, "You looking again? That's not for you, going out to work. And it's better for you if you stay at home, isn't it?" Then I say, "I know you mean well, but you're trying to get your own way, because you want it." Because, say, I went out to work in the afternoon, and my husband didn't like it, and because I couldn't have his tea waiting on the table for him. It's precooked anyway, and we've got a stove—all he has to do is take it. And then I said, "You don't want me to go because I can't serve your tea for you. You want it all your own way. You can't help me either, because I know that, too, when I get a job again, I'll be better off."

Text 29. Middle-class woman, patient (W1) (female).

W1: I'm afraid in the morning, too, afraid of failing at the office. And sometimes a certain fear of speaking in front of lots of people—that's why I don't find it very easy to talk (embarrassed laughter), but I know that such fear is often unfounded, but unfortunately I'm always afraid. I take Temesta, and that helps me a bit. Sometimes it's stronger and sometimes not so strong. I went through a time when I felt really groggy in the morning; I had to be sick, I had such an aversion, such a fear, a slight nausea until midday, and that happened until I was in a hectic state again—

W2: What are you actually afraid of?

W1: Well, now, let's say I had to type up a very difficult text to begin with, and there are some people there, and I have to type, and now and again I make a spelling mistake in public—that would be very embarrassing for me, you know . . .

W2: Were you afraid before, too?

W1: Yes, but not so much. Actually, it's only since 1954, actually, that I harbor this fear in me, since, let me see, a long time now; that happened when I got married.

The most important categories that will be used for linguistic description are found on the four constitutive levels mentioned, these being logical strategies, discourse strategies, behavioral strategies, and cognitive-emotional strategies (2.3.2.1). Some of the indicators selected for operationalization have been validated in earlier text-linguistic and sociolinguistic investigations (Leodolter 1975*a,c*; Wodak-Leodolter 1977), while others have been tested in the provisional evaluation of the present texts and also used with success by raters (3.10) (see schema 6). The linguistic indicators are listed individually in the discussion of categories prior to quantitative evaluation. Some are given here by way of example:

Discourse strategies: narrative structure (see Quasthoff 1979; Wodak-Leodolter 1980; Gülich and Raible 1977:192 ff.).

Logical strategies: coherence phenomena (Beaugrande and Dressler 1980:40 ff.), deictic conditions (Gülich and Raible 1977: 40 ff.), and relations (Warren et al. 1979).

Behavioral strategies: speaker's perspective (Werlich 1975:46 ff.; Leodolter 1975*c*).

Cognitive-emotional strategies: problem solving (Dörner 1979:49), expression of feelings (Leodolter 1975*a*:260 ff.; Deese 1973; Kolers 1973).

SCHEMA 6

THE MACROSTRUCTURE

Legend:	
T	Text topic
CL	Content level
CT	Content text level
FT	Formal text level
BS	Behavior strategies
CE	Cognitive + emotional strategies
DS	Discourse strategies
DL	Logical strategies
ME	Metalevel
RS	Reflexive strategies

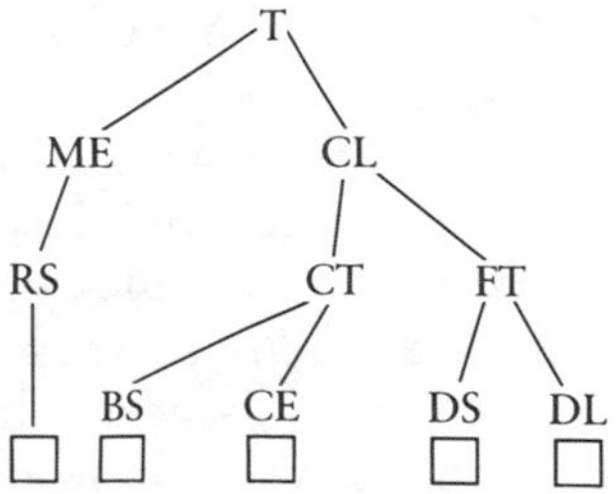

A text model is presented graphically which takes a topic as a basis (e.g., problem at work) and represents the planning strategy (macrostructure) to the superior text class of problem presentation in group therapy (schema 7).

No attempt is made to transform this text-thematic macro-structure step by step into typical text realizations using complex rules (like van Dijk 1972). Individual small grammars ("modulars") execute the steps from frame to schema similar to the representations of artificial intelligence (Schank and Abelson 1977). We are more interested in the determination of constitutive factors (limited to the conscious level of therapeutic communication), as well as in the assumption that the same macrostructure would have to be assumed for the same topic and similar communicative functions within the therapeutic group situation that now produces a specific text type with a certain forecastable probability depending on the specific combination of sociological and psychological parameters (4.3.4).

3.9.3.4. Qualitative-phenomenological analysis of sample texts— preliminaries on quantitative analysis[10]

The four text passages contain marked differences that confirm purely phenomenologically and intuitively the hypotheses on class- and sex-specific behavioral differences. Text 26 and text 28 are fascinating for their vivid and spontaneous descriptions: fear, despair, and ambivalence are reproduced with feeling, in direct speech; the listener has the impression that he experiences the scene. Orientation and coda are missing (if we go by Labov and Waletzky 1967), as are the metacommunicative background and frame and objectivity (distance) with regard to events and problems. A single event is reproduced without reference to the patient's life history and to the relevance of the scene in the everyday life of the speaker. The speaker's perspective is very personal throughout; use of the narrative past as well as the present tense in direct speech, use of short sentences, often cut short, and use of dialect are important characteristics in which complexity and strong emotional involvement are apparent. These texts cannot be classified using Labov and Waletzky's schema (1967). Text 27 and text 29 differ greatly from the problem presentation described above. Both are very coherent and consistent presentations. Text 27 describes a circumstance, a symptom, while text 29 starts with a description of the

SCHEMA 7

Text Planning and Text Generation—Sociopsychological Theory of Text Planning
(Wodak 1983:320)

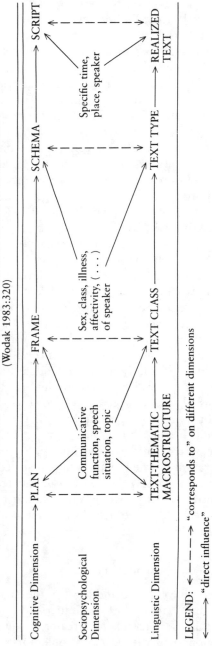

Cognitive Dimension → PLAN → FRAME → SCHEMA → SCRIPT

Sociopsychological Dimension

Communicative function, speech situation, topic

Sex, class, illness, affectivity, (. . . .) of speaker

Specific time, place, speaker

Linguistic Dimension → TEXT-THEMATIC MACROSTRUCTURE → TEXT CLASS → TEXT TYPE → REALIZED TEXT

LEGEND: ← – – – → "corresponds to" on different dimensions

→ "direct influence"

symptom and then goes on to causal questions and references to the patient's life history. Feelings are scarcely expressed, and one can feel tremendous distance. The speaker's perspective in text 27 is mainly impersonal, and there are frequent defense mechanisms in the form of rationalizations. All in all, the four texts can only be fitted into the classical narrative schema with difficulty. The model of the superior text class of problem presentation in group therapy and the categories used must suffice to test the adequacy of these text types and realizations (3.10). Ideal modifications of the macrostructure are drafted in connection with a differentiation of the hypotheses on class- and sex-specific socialization.

However, additional quantitative processing of the texts is indispensable in order to allow us to make generalizations (4.3). The fact that priority is given to qualitative linguistic description does not need to be argued (5.4, 5.5). Driven by an academic interest, the observer's gaze falls on text samples that correspond to the ideal types particularly well, and on the basis of the text passages that he considers typical, the researcher also develops ideal types that must also comply with the theoretical concept. Objective limits and criteria must therefore be established and introduced. It is precisely the therapeutic setting and the uniqueness of every session that initially resist quantifying generalization (2.5). The number of variables that may possibly intervene is correspondingly large and indeterminable, particularly as the individual life history of each patient cannot be generalized. On the other hand, the purely qualitative analysis of such a large quantity of text serves no purpose if one does not try to make generalizations. The goal is to find text types, to establish connections, not to argue taxonomically or, at best, using small case studies (3.3, 3.5).

One is therefore justified in analyzing the discourse for problem presentations using closely defined categories. These presentations are then coded and the assumptions relating to class- and sex-specific language behavior tested. Complexity can be meaningfully reduced only in this manner.

3.9.3.5 Summary: Four ideal types

In contrast to conventional models for the analysis of narrative texts (Labov and Waletzky 1967; Gülich and Raible 1977; Quasthoff 1979), this approach claims greater adequacy of description and explanation. The text class of problem presentation in group therapy comprises several text types that are realized depending on the class and sex of the speaker and on the phase of the therapy; they are also predictable. The text-thematic macrostructure can be regarded as a cognitive planning strategy with reference to constitutive factors correlated with psychological and sociological categories.

On the basis of the category of narrative structure, four ideal types will be derived by way of example which can be used to register the four texts reproduced above. Detailed classification and quantitative analysis to test the hypotheses are carried out in 3.10 and 4.3.

The hypotheses are therefore summarized only briefly here with respect to narrative structure (for working class and middle class). The hypotheses relating to the lower middle class are ignored for the time being, as they present a more complex picture with regard to both theoretical conception and empirical data analyses. This can only be comprehended in the context of all the categories (3.10, 2.4.1.3).

1. Working class and middle class differ significantly with regard to the narrative structure of the same topic (the theory of socialization attributes this to the acquisition of meta-communicative strategies and a taboo on the expression of feelings in the middle class). Members of the middle class use more descriptive reports or narratives; members of the working class use more scenic forms (2.4.2).
2. Men and women differ significantly in the nature of the narrative structure used (the theory of socialization attributes this to the fact that women are accustomed to relating their suffering explicitly and in the context of their life histories). Women, therefore, use scenic or narrative forms; men tend to use descriptive forms (2.4.2).

In the later sections (3.10, 4.3) I shall elaborate on the interplay between class and sex, the expression of feelings, strategies for problem solving, coherence phenomena, and defense mechanisms. (It is obvious from the formulation of the hypotheses that, for example, in the working class, scenic and narrative problem presentation will also be found more among women than among men.)

Scene, circumstance, and narration are three text types used to realize the text-thematic macrostructure (text class) of problem presentation. They can be regarded as equivalent forms, and the first two do not deviate from Labov and Waletzky's schema; all three types have their own relevance to the group therapy situation and their own symptomatic character (despite their common function of describing an acute problem).

It is possible to differentiate linguistically between these three discourse strategies due to the nature of the speaker's perspective, the narrative tense, and the use of metacommunicative speech acts. In narration we are dealing with a classical narrative form (with orientation, complication, evaluation, coda); in scene, we find a typical event without an orienting setting and evaluative position— a picture is suddenly drawn that is usually ended just as abruptly. No metacommunicative generalizations and observations are made.

Circumstance actually involves a topical displacement (in psychotherapeutic terms, we would speak of concealment) or a combination of topics. It is not an example (scene, event, or personal anecdote) that is presented simultaneously with the topic work, but rather the description of a symptom that must be placed in the context of work only as a second priority.

However, these categories by themselves are not sufficient to cover all the text types used for realization. Cognitive-emotional strategies, subconscious processes (defense, expression of feelings), and their assimilation must also be dealt with to facilitate description of all the nuances and changes dependent on therapy in the presentation of the same problem by the same patient (3.10). Finally, we shall also have to ask ourselves what the ideal problem presentation looks like, that would ensure the most effective problem solving (5.4, 5.5).

The four schemata (ignoring all other categories, with the exception of narrative structure) are ideal and are used principally to specify the text model (i.e., text types, schema 8) initially fairly abstract (see again also schema 7 and the sociopsychological theory of text planning [SPTT]).

3.10. Categories, examples, and textual indicators

Before presenting the results of the quantitative analysis and their interpretation with reference to the hypotheses, it is first necessary to explicitly introduce the categories used for the coding of the text class of problem presentation (4.2, 4.3).

SCHEMA 8
SEX AND CLASS SPECIFIC PROBLEM PRESENTATIONS

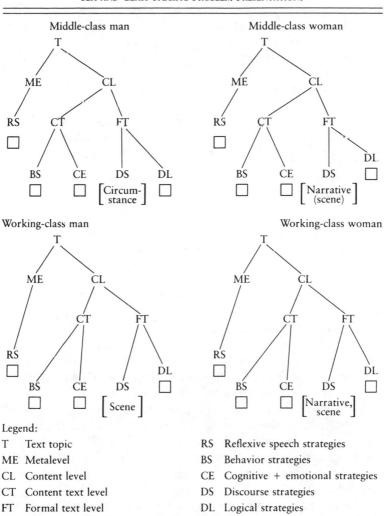

Legend:

T	Text topic	RS	Reflexive speech strategies
ME	Metalevel	BS	Behavior strategies
CL	Content level	CE	Cognitive + emotional strategies
CT	Content text level	DS	Discourse strategies
FT	Formal text level	DL	Logical strategies

The categories are divided into eleven groups. The first three relate to linguistic indicators, the next four to psychotherapeutic aspects, and the last four make up the interactional dimension between patient, group, and therapist.

The problematics of classification have already been mentioned several times (5.2). The question is whether and how it is possible to allocate each expression or each passage unambiguously to a category (Filstead 1971; Cicourel 1970). In the final analysis, the subjective decision always plays a role (albeit a small one). An attempt was made to get around this problem by using raters. The raters, who had no previous close association with the text, were presented with problem presentations. The categories were defined for them, and as outside observers, so to speak, they had to classify the texts. This resulted in an essential degree of objectivity. Problems that could not be solved satisfactorily will be considered and discussed in the qualitative chapter that follows (5.4, 5.5).

3.10.1. Text-linguistic categories
3.10.1.1. Narrative structure

This category is used to describe the text structure of a discourse strategy. Typical forms of problem presentation in group therapy can be placed into three subcategories: scene, narration, and circumstance. The theoretical basis for these categories and for their relationship to class- and sex-specific hypotheses has already been provided (3.9.3.5), and it is therefore only necessary here to specify the criteria for its application.

The indicators selected are: speaker's perspective (Werlich 1975:46 ff.), the presence (or absence) of metacommunicative speaker strategies (2.3.2.1), the narrative tense used (Werlich 1975: 51 ff.), and the coherence of the text (Kallmeyer et al. 1974: 57 ff.): "Every sentence contains a number of constituents that all indicate and limit the root of the viewpoint from which the speaker speaks in a communicative situation and to which all objects, changes and facts described in the text refer. Text constituents that fulfil this function clarify various aspects of the speaker's perspective" (Werlich 1975:46).

The speaker's perspective is determined by person (that is, the choice of the impersonal *one* or *you*, in contrast to the personal *I*), presentation (as a selective speaker's attitude to situational factors), focus, aspect, genus, and modus (Leodolter 1975c:88 ff.).

A difference is made between an opening and a closing focus. *Opening focus* refers to temporal sequences that gradually become more comprehensive, while *closing focus* comprises local and temporal sequential forms that become less and less comprehensive (Werlich 1975:50). "The choice of an aspect . . . indicates how the speaker sees changes and circumstances with reference to segments in the temporal continuum, or how he would like them to be seen. The speaker's perspective of the aspect is thus always closely linked to the choice of tenses" (p. 52).

Although in German the aspect is expressed lexically rather than directly in the form of a verb, the marked and continuous aspect can nevertheless be differentiated. *Genus* refers to the choice of the active or passive aspect and indicates whether the speaker wishes to view changes and circumstances of phenomena as an agent or as happening to him (p. 53). "The choice of modus . . . provides information about the entity attributed by the speaker to persons, objects and facts. There are three main modi from which the speaker can choose: the factual modus, the negative modus and the probable modus" (p. 54).

As will be shown, it is precisely the combinations of these elements that constitute an important criterion in differentiating the three text types.

The choice of the narrative tense is also an important indicator: "The choice of the tense of a verb indicates how the speaker views objects and facts with relation to an axis of orientation formed by his momentary situation, i.e., by the speech act at any moment in time within the temporal continuum" (p. 51).

Finally, the coherence of the text affects the textual structure as a whole (Beaugrande and Dressler 1981:88 ff.). Can the speaker realize his intentions; does the planned strategy reach its goal, the desired reaction from the listener? Is the topic consistently pursued? Are references clear and understandable? Kallmeyer defines *coherence* as "the coherence of dialogue results from connective elements, definition of the topic and the interactive context" (Kallmeyer et al. 1974:58).

This also naturally applies to longer monological sections, such as problem presentation in group therapy, in a wider interactive context. *Scene* is characterized by the absence of metacommunicative speaker strategies. It is a defined, personal speaker's perspective (use of *I*); the presentation is very selective (one event); the focus closes (unique experience); the aspect is marked (description of events); the genus is active, the modus factual; scenes take place in the narrative present with much direct speech. Although there is coherence, the great degree of complication coupled with the absence of metacommunicative signals make understanding difficult for outsiders (text 26).

Narration means the classical narrative form of Labov and Waletzky (1967:23). Orientation, complication, evaluation, resolution, and coda are present and ensure the coherence of the text. The orientation and evaluation provide the metacommunicative frame. The definite, personal speaker's perspective comes to the fore; the focus closes (generalizations are normally only possible in connection with problem solving; see 5.5). The aspect is marked, the genus active or passive ("I have done" or "it happened to me"), the modus factual. There is coherence, and—if the other patients allow— a story will be related from beginning to end, normally without establishing a direct connection to the problem at once (text A, 5.4).

Circumstance means the description of a symptom, of the circumstance in which the speaker suffers. In this case there is no metacommunicative frame at all. The speaker's perspective is impersonal (use of *one* or *you*); the focus opens; problem presentation in group therapy is kept very verbal and formal; the presentation is not selective; the aspect is unmarked (circumstance, continuity); the genus is passive, and the modus, finally, probable ("perhaps it could . . ."). The text is superficially coherent: a circumstance is described coherently, but much remains unclear to the listener because of the use of defense mechanisms (3.9.3.5), and above all, there is no reference to the causes of the patient's case history— these are only implied (text 27). (In some instances it was necessary to use the wider context of the problem presentation in the interpretation of the text samples used. Space considerations preclude explanation in detail here.)

This category is used to check the hypothesis that text types are realized in significantly different ways depending on class and sex (3.9.3.5, 4.3.1.1).

3.10.1.2. Text length

It is best to quantify and register the clauses in problem presentation. Exponentially increasing intervals were used for this purpose, these being, 1, 2–4, 5–16, and 17–256. (Examples appear superfluous in the case of this category, which can be unambiguously registered quantitatively).

This category is important in testing whether (as is so often asserted) there are significant differences between the classes with regard to text length. As we are interested primarily in the qualitative parameters, it is important as a safeguard with respect to a frequently used category such as text length (number of clauses). In the criticism of studies from the Bernstein school (2.4.1.1) it was emphasized that quantifications of this kind are only of limited value, and this is again confirmed here (4.3.1.2).

3.10.1.3. Problem solving

This category registers the degree of involvement with a problem and the stages in the process of solving the problem. Several stages are mentioned in the literature of cognitive psychology on problem solving (Dörner 1979:48): analysis of the situation, choice of a heuristic method, self-reflection, and implementation of the action.

The connection between problem, procedure for problem solving, and language is emphasized (Dörner 1979:53, 54). Three functions in particular are listed: address function (designation), regulation function (connection of trains of thought), and coding function (redesignation). The fact that a number of deep psychological mechanisms play a role at the same time is obvious (an example is given in 3.8.5, where the resistance to recognizing a problem and at the same time naming the causes of it is very clearly apparent).

The essential requirements for the selection of meaningful heuristic methods and operators include the correct appraisal of reality and close scrutiny of the differences between starting point and goal. These are then important indicators of therapeutic effect. All too often, incorrect evaluations of the problem result from resistance, defense, and fear.

Four subcategories were assumed, although it would certainly have been possible to distinguish more stages. A limitation proved necessary, if only for statistical reasons. It would be interesting to know whether certain stages are distributed specific to class and sex. Bernstein's theory might tempt one to assume that members of the working class were incapable of abstract thought and tentative action because of the restricted code (2.4.1.2). Traditional clichés and stereotypes of sex-specific behavior might also encourage one to assume that women are less capable of solving problems than men because of their apparent irrationality (2.4.2.2). It is important to subject such opinions and clichés to systematic investigation in order to be able to remove prejudices with the aid of empirical evidence. At the same time, it would be an indicator of a positive therapeutic effect if problem solutions were mainly encountered toward the end of the therapy. This, too, must be checked (2.5, 4.3.1.3).

Penetration: this is a declaration of intent; the topic is named, the facts established (address function, neutral language behavior).

Text 30. Session 3, patient 23 (male).

M:　I have a problem [coughing]: I had a girlfriend whom I—we split up. Now she's running after me, now she says she's carrying my baby. She says she'll go to the police and report me. [laughter]

Ambivalence is used to refer to hesitation in a problem field. This manifests itself in greater involvement. Several topics are mentioned and heuristic methods considered (definite personal speaker's perspective, excited manner of speaking).

Text 31. Session 6, patient 2 (female).

T:　The problem is now that you have to decide on yes or no.
W:　With money, without money? Flat, yes, okay? See the children, yes, okay? That's always the way.

Objectivity (distance): the procedure for solution appears to be successful; relevant heuristic methods are examined; insight into reality has been obtained (coherent presentation; possible solutions are indicated; definite personal speaker's perspective; neutral manner of speaking).

Text 32. Session 4, patient 16 (male).

M:　With talking, I also had a to and fro for a long time, that is—and even now, and that's why I often still talk nonsense. I tell my wife time and again, "remind me that I don't mince my words." Now I talk; it's getting better and better; when I came I also read something, a

foreign word that one could mention in passing. I was really pleased—
then I didn't notice that I had been talking nonsense. Well, really, that
that—I mean—because—I know I'm not a complete idiot; I do know
a bit, and I mean, I know enough about a lot of things, and now I'd
like to be in a position, at long last, that I can manage; even now, I
still use words when I have no idea what they mean.

Solution: the objective (goal) has been achieved; the procedure
used to solve the problem is discussed; arguments and explanations
are introduced. The problem no longer exists (coherent presentation, neutral manner of speaking, definite personal speaker's
perspective).

Text 33. Session 12, patient 1 (female).

W: Well, I'd really like to contradict that, because I have—an example,
perhaps. I have been coping with myself, or with my difficulties and
problems, for almost two years, you know, and I only saw the light,
so to speak, three weeks ago, like with bookkeeping, where you suddenly realize what it's all about; only three weeks ago, and where I
said to myself, "Alright, and now you must really start working, because now you know what it's all about." And that's why I don't think
I rate the group idea too highly, because I was always against the
group, and I always had the greatest of difficulties, because I just did
not want to go to the group. And the way I see things now, I find it
indispensable and that I have got away from the whole thing, you
know. But I was—until three weeks ago I came here because I had to,
because otherwise I would have been left in the lurch by the doctor.
I didn't want to.

3.10.2. Psychoanalytical categories
3.10.2.1. Defense mechanisms

The following definition of *defense* can be be found in the "Vokabular der Psychoanalyse":

The totality of operations the finality of which lies in limiting or sup-
pressing modification which is liable to endanger the integrity and constancy of the biopsychological individual. Defense is generally directed
against an inner stimulus (instinct) and electively against a stimulus
linked with ideas (memories, fantasies), against a certain situation that
can trigger this stimulus to the extent that it is incompatible with this

balance and therefore averse for the ego. . . . The defense process consists of defense mechanisms integrated to a greater or lesser extent in
the ego. . . . Characterized and permeated by the instinct against which
it is directed in the long run, defense often takes on a compulsive character and takes place, at least in part, unconsciously. (Laplanche and
Pontalis 1975, I:24)

Accordingly, defense processes are unconscious, automatically
controlled processes, mechanisms that contrast strongly with atti-
tudinal actions, such as considered abstention and deliberate denial
(Becker 1979:8). According to the assumptions on class- and sex-
specific socialization, not only can we expect to find significant
differences at the verbal linguistic level but at the emotional level
as well, where the defense processes explicitly manifest themselves
in the texts, or, interpreted as such, appear to be important indicators for the investigation. In accordance with the prevalent assumptions, scenic presentation (working class) should tend to contain
regression, while coherent descriptions by members of the middle
class would tend to contain rationalizations (intellectualizations).
This may also be an important difference between the sexes: men
are not permitted to suffer and therefore rationalize their difficulties, while women are permitted to suffer but are passive and therefore regress more easily than men (Windhoff-Heritier 1976:145 ff.)
(4.3.1.3).

It is precisely here that we find several class-specific differences.
I have already referred to the overadaptation of lower-middle-class
women (2.4.1.3). It is to be expected that here, too, they also behave
differently from working-class and middle-class women. As far as
therapeutic effect is concerned, the number and nature of defense
mechanisms used should decrease when insight is gained into a
problem and it is solved.

Theoretically there should be a further sex-specific difference
with regard to projection and turning against the self. Men are
permitted to give their aggressions free rein and direct their feelings
of guilt against others (identification with the aggressor), while
women produce significantly more feelings of guilt because of their
more substantial superego (Windhoff-Heritier 1976:154). This, too,
should change when the therapy has a positive effect.

The classification is based mainly on the traditional work of
A. Freud (1936). Today there is lively discussion on this subject

(Laplanche and Pontalis 1975, I:32 ff.; Becker 1979:8 ff.), but this cannot be dealt with here. Becker's recent attempt (1979:10 ff.) to divide the defense mechanisms into information-processing mechanisms and attempts to cope with the problem seems sensible (both are naturally unadaptable, distortive, and disorganized). Accordingly, introspection, projection, suppression, and denial would be information-related defense mechanisms, while regression, identification, displacement, and overcompensation would relate to action schemata.

The defense mechanisms investigated are briefly defined and illustrated below:

Rationalization

"Rationalization translates reasons and objectives from one's own experience and behavior unawares into terms which make it possible to interpret connections without aversion. The distorting effects are due to tendencies which the subject is not aware of" (Becker 1979:9). Reinterpretation or intellectualization prevent a deeper insight: one deceives oneself, as it were, with regard to the causes and conditions of one's own actions. Certain strategies of argumentation, reasoning, and justification that the patient uses as a sort of self-defense or consolation for lack of success ("it wouldn't have worked anyway") serve as indicators in the text. At the same time, it is characteristic that psychological or intellectual jargon is also often used. The patient is best able to explain everything himself anyway and needs neither group nor therapist. Priority is given to the cognitive level and not to the emotional life. An example of this can be found in text 27.

Negation

"A process in which the subject, although he/she now gives clear expression to previously suppressed desires, thoughts and feelings, continues to reject them by denying that they are his/her own" (Laplanche and Pontalis 1975, II:598). Allocation to this category is based on the explicit negation of suppressed contents rising to consciousness. This category is thus correspondingly smaller than the category of denial, which tends to be associated with refusal to perceive a fact in the outside world. "There is no firmer proof of the successful exposure of the unconscious than when the subject reacts with the phrase 'I didn't think that' or 'I never thought of that'" (Freud 1976b, XIV:15).

Text 34. Session 1, patient 3 (W2).

W1: Yes, what is the situation, then: are you dependent on your father and your mother, are you dependent on them?
W2: Yes, no, I am not dependent on them. Yes. I am employed in the business that belongs to my father; I mean, I really needn't do it at all, let's say—
W1: So you're not dependent on them?
W2: No, I wouldn't be, but my mother is alone, and she wouldn't be able to cope on her own, you see; she wouldn't be able to manage the business.

Regression

Regression is a return to earlier modi operandi. Previous behavioral patterns are reactivated; in a temporal context this term designates the return of the subject to stages that have already been passed in his development (libidinous stage of object relationships, identifications). Formally regression designates a transition to the behavioral modes of a lower level from the point of view of complexity of structuring and differentiation. This therefore also relates to the verbal and nonverbal linguistic level. Recalled scenes are relived; certain styles of speech associated with such scenes or relationships come to light again, such as childish expressions and group jargon (Laplanche and Pontalis 1975:436; Becker 1979:10).

Text 35. Session 14, patient 1 (female).

W: For a time I didn't get on with my mother particularly well, but in the last year, before she died, I got along with her very well. She once said to a neighbor, "I think I must have done something wrong with my daughter." I only found out about that later; then she was already dead, you know. And then she really tried to establish contact with me, and even when I came home, always. My father and my brother sat watching television and my mother closed the door and talked to me and listened to me, and so on, you know. And my father cannot remember at all when I had my first big success at work, and the flowers that I received, a huge bunch of flowers. I thought to myself, my God, my mommy has helped me to do this, I'll give her the flowers, and I went up full of joy and gave her the flowers.

Denial

This form of defense is particularly evident when the patient refuses to accept the reality of a traumatic experience. In contrast to negation, facts situated principally in the outside world are denied ("process of self-deception with regard to the outside world"—see Becker 1979:9). In the case of negation, linguistic classification is effected if there is explicit denial, mainly with attempts at interpretation or interpretative questions. *Denial* is a broader term and is evident rather from the nature of the presentation of the problem, in other words, initial phases of problem solving and particularly ambivalent conditions.

Text 36. Session 1, patient 3 (W).

M: Some people are taken for a ride, and some people are not taken for a ride. But what do you want anyway in the present situation—money or recognition?

W: Well, I want, let's say, I want to work for six, seven years or five, and to stay at home—

M: So you want to work for six years for 3,500 shillings?

W: No, no, I wouldn't work for that, my good sir; there'd have to be more in it than that. I wouldn't be so foolish again, you know!

M: Because you said—

W: No, I mean because—not that one says it, but—I'd put so much on one side, I mean, there'd have to be something in it!

M: Yes, but you, otherwise, if you didn't get any more, you wouldn't work any more, or would you?

Projection

This term is in common use today and is often applied to many different things, but in this context it is used in a very narrow psychoanalytical (psychotherapeutic) meaning. "Operation by means of which the subject localizes in the other person or thing qualities, feelings, desires, and even 'objects' which he underrates or rejects in himself, from which he excepts himself" (Laplanche and Pontalis 1975, II:400).

Thus the fearful type sees dangers everywhere, the irritated type projects his irritation into his partner so as to recognize it again there. This defense mechanism can be linguistically characterized in several different ways. It is remarkable in problem presentations and descriptions of persons often containing overstated designations and characteristics; in other words, it can be seen in the particularly frequent use of adjectives (matter-of-fact description). Breaks in the argument or dialogue also indicate projective mechanisms, such as aggressive interpretation of utterances that are obviously false or overinterpreted.

Text 37. Session 4, patients 15 (M1) and 16 (M2).

W: He didn't mean it like that.
M1: I don't know.
W: He said so.
M2: What, well, I didn't mean it like that.
M1: That's right, he didn't mean it like that, but that's the way things are at work, too. There may be somebody who immediately starts shouting, like Mr. _____ just did.
W: He didn't shout.
M1: He may not have meant it like that, you know, but I take it wrongly because he shouted like that; you see, I judge the whole thing incorrectly.
W: Because you think in such a complicated way, you really make things worse for others. I found it very unpleasant, because I thought the whole thing was unnecessary.
M1: Well, yes, I thought—
W: That only complicated things.

Turning against the self

"Process by which an independent object is instinctively replaced by one's own person" (Laplanche and Pontalis 1975, II:622).

This defense mechanism is used principally to protect oneself against forbidden aggressive, sadistic, active sentiments ("complete reversal"—see Laplanche and Pontalis 1975, II:593). The subject prefers to direct his aggressions against himself rather than against others. This defense mechanism can be text-linguistically characterized mainly by the metacommunicative background of a problem presentation or by the coda, the summary of a story. Thus the result of the problem presentation is the fact that one is oneself to blame, that everything has been done correctly, that everything is against one, and so on. Depressive people (and women in particular) tend to use this defense mechanism, which is correlated with self-destructive, masochistic tendencies.

Text 38. Session 6, patient 3.

W: Well, but I always protect him, because he was in Stalingrad in the war, with everything that happened there. He is, well, he has had a hard life, but he should leave me to get on with my life. How often I would have taken my life, and time and again grasped at a little piece: no, I mustn't, he was my father. After all, I shouldn't always have thought of him: "you just can't do that to him"; now we'll fetch an ambulance, but I don't know, he must often have had me on his conscience.

3.10.2.2. Affectivity

This category is particularly relevant to the understanding and interpretation of problem presentation in group therapy. Therapeutic work and the assimilation of traumatic experiences and scenes from the patient's life history can only be successful if the affects linked to these historically important situations are relived and assimilated. "However, in language man finds a surrogate for the deed, with the aid of which the affect can be abreacted almost as well" (Freud 1977a, I:87).

It is not by chance that two categories are devoted to the "feelings." We find ourselves confronted with affective conditions that traditionally and culturally accompany a certain idea, a situation, an external stimulus (and that are derived from the two primal instincts, from "Eros" and the death instinct). Yet the therapeutic work can only be regarded as successful if the accompanying affects are actualized and verbalized—in other words, if there is an activity with the feelings.

The various theories on affectivity, on affective conditions, and abreaction to them cannot be dealt with at length in this brief outline. Nevertheless, several aspects should be mentioned. In behavioristically oriented research, a feeling or affective condition is regarded as a reaction to certain external or internal stimuli (Birbaumer 1973:2). This condition can be measured at three levels: at the verbal-subjective level by means of tests and content analysis; at the motorial-nonverbal level, where actions are used as indicators; and finally, at the physiological level, by measuring the corresponding dimensions. Although this approach includes the verbal-linguistic level, in the study of affectivity it is limited to the measurement of physiological dimensions (dermal resistance, electroencephalogram, electrocardiogram). The cognitive components, ideas, and fantasies and the causes of emotions are excluded from the investigation. Furthermore, there must be a situational stimulus, which can then be followed by an affective reaction. "The psychology of learning regards fear as a subjective (emotional, physiological and motorial) reaction to a censorious, aversive stimulus. An aversive stimulus becomes operational defined as a condition which a living being tries to escape, as a condition which it tries to end or to avoid" (Birbaumer 1973:4–5).

This approach cannot explain neurotic emotions that occur pathologically without being triggered by an understandable stimulus. Lang's concept lies closer to the psychoanalytical interpretation and to an expanded linguistic concept (2.3).

> We postulate that emotional behavior represents reactions within several systems: verbal-cognitive, motorial and physiological reactions. Due to inadequate coupling, it is possible, and even usual for emotional cognitions to develop without autonomous activation, for aggressive behavior to develop without an appropriate hostile motive or for autonomous phobic reactions and evasive behavior to develop without insight (Lang 1973:55).

Lazarus and his colleagues (1973) and Epstein (1973) go one stage further. Thus the cognitive school believes that only the cognitive perception of physiological changes gives rise to emotions. The quality of the feeling itself is actually determined by cognitive factors. Epstein (1973:184) discusses the unconscious and conscious perception of feelings, and directed and undirected conditions. This comes closest to my view that neurotic affective conditions and affects—imperceptible to the individual—are initially manifest in situations that do not appear correlated with the strength of the affect (phobias, conversions, hysterias).

To this extent the psychoanalytical concept is important: every instinct is expressed at the two levels of affect and concept, and it is therefore possible for affect and concept to be separated (Laplanche and Pontalis 1975, I:37).

Freud describes this as transposition of the affect. For this reason there are problem presentations by patients that—according to everyday understanding—should be accompanied by strong emotions, but such emotions are not verbalized or transposed (this relates to the category of affective expression). Only by therapeutic work can affect and concept—or cognitive and emotional level—correspond to one another again, or thereafter, the affective condition is successfully transposed to other cognitive or behavioral levels (sublimation). Thus, sublimation is at a different level from the other subcategories of affective expression. "To our great surprise we found that individual hysterial symptoms disappeared immediately and did not return if we were successful in completely illuminating the causative process, thus awakening the associated affect, and if the patient then described the process in the greatest possible detail and put the affect into words" (Freud 1977*a*, I:85).

A more recent classification of affects using psychoanalytical criteria is provided by Engel. "In brief, then I am proposing that affects, as psychic experience, evolve from communicative processes within the organism and between organisms, processes that are intimately concerned with the regulation of those basic life activities which for their success require the presence or participation of an outside organism (object)" (1963:269 ff.).

Engel differentiates between "signal-scanning affects" (affects that test reality), such as fear, shame, guilt, sorrow, joy, and "drive-discharge affects," such as love and aggression. This classification, which I cannot go into any further here without considering the entire psychoanalytical discussion of affects, is based on a differentiated theoretical approach to the origins of affects and allows a clearer explanation and allocation of affective conditions. In dramatic contrast to the behavioristic approach, Engel claims that feelings can only be observed to a limited extent, that we are thus dealing with "derivatives" (p. 294). This underlines the difficulties of an empirical investigation in which one is obliged to resort to interpretation of the two latent levels of meaning in order to allocate individual linguistic expressions to the following categories (2.3, 5.2).

When investigating the therapeutic group, it is necessary to differentiate between neurotic and really appropriate affective conditions. Conditions are neurotic when the reaction is completely inappropriate and incomprehensible; they are real when there is a causative situation (such as a death), and the emotion occurs in association with an appropriate reaction. However, affective expression can be disturbed even in the second case. In other words, sorrow, fear, and the like are rejected and not verbalized.

The combination of both categories therefore serves mainly as an indicator of therapeutic effect. Are affect and concept meaningfully linked to one another or not, and does this change in the course of the therapy? The sociolinguistic problem is also dealt with. From the assumptions on class- and sex-specific socialization, it is apparent that (1) members of the working class probably express their feelings more freely than do members of the lower middle class and middle class; and (2) women (with the exception of lower-middle-class women) express more emotions than do men.

Even with regard to the type of feelings, it is necessary to assume differences resulting from theories on sex-specific development (Windhoff-Heritier 1976: 67 ff., 105 ff.): men are more aggressive than women; women have more feelings of guilt than men! (see also Wodak and Schulz 1984).

The rather childish feelings of shame and spite should occur while regressing to earlier action schemata. Rationalizing patients, however, will tend to dissociate concept and affect (the allocation of individual problem presentations to these categories was checked by raters and the therapist) (4.3.1.5).

Rage

Rage is an aggressive excitement that—in contrast to hate—is not directed at a specific object. Linguistically we allocate this affective condition to the explicit expression of annoyance and aggression, aggressive aversive affects that are directed outward and not against the person himself.

Text 39. Session 6, patient 2 (W).

W: I am so full of rage today and so—if I had a revolver I would shoot all of you today!
M: Me, too?
W: Of course.

Guilt

A great deal of space is devoted to the observation of feelings of guilt in psychoanalytical literature, particularly with reference to the theory of the superego:

> It can designate an affective condition which follows an act regarded by the subject as reprehensible and for which the reason given, inci-dentally, can be more or less adequate (the criminal's qualms of con-science or apparently absurd self-reproaches), or even a diffuse feeling of personal unworthiness with no connection to a certain act which the subject accuses himself of. (Laplanche and Pontalis 1975, II:458)

Engel (1963:281) relates feelings of guilt mainly to the superego and internalized precepts and interdictions. Here, too, linguistic classification is based on semantic criteria: either the patient himself expresses explicit awareness of guilt, feelings of guilt or depressive aversive affects, feelings of inferiority and inadequacy, or—in the second case—a psychotherapeutic interpretation ascribes feelings of guilt to a speaker (second and third levels of meaning in the model of therapeutic communication). There are typical speech acts and speaker strategies that can be classified as revealing feelings of guilt (text 38).

Sorrow

Sorrow is an affective condition that can be defined as a reaction to the loss of a loved object (Freud 1973*b*, X:442–443). The concept of assimilation of sorrow is also important. In other words, the individual concerned relives all the important situations in order to be able to cope with the loss at his leisure, as it were. It is precisely here that we encounter a strong rejection of feelings, a denial of reality, and therefore dissociation. From the content and topic it follows that the problem described should cause a reaction of sor-row, but the patient reports on the event in a factual, neutral manner.

Text 40. Session 2, patient 2 (female).

T: How are you feeling now, Mrs. _____ ?
W: I'm not feeling well at all, actually, I was off work for a week, very depressive, and was full of bad thoughts. And now this is my second day back at work again.

Fear

In contrast to anxiety, fear is described as an undirected affective condition in confrontation with an insurmountable situation (imagined or real) (Freud 1976g, XIV:181 ff.). "Some regard fear as synonymous with anxiety, others equate it to physiological correlatives, while others again insist that it can only be defined in terms of subjective experience. Some discuss the consequences of 'conscious fear,' others regard the expression 'unconscious' fear as a self-contradiction (Epstein 1973:184).

In his theoretical approach, Epstein (1973:211) finally differentiates between anxiety as a motivational concept, activation as a random component of any motivation, and fear as between anxiety and activation. Fear is a primary occurrence—the psychoanalytical concept mentions the birth trauma as the prototype of all subsequent fears (fear of separation). Linguistic classification is based either on explicit expression or on interpretative allocation to the second and third levels of meaning.

Text 41. Session 2, patient 15 (male).

Well, yes, work—when I have the feeling, when there is any way, I've always been interested in that, then I follow it up and I see what—then sometimes I think I would like to switch something on; I don't switch anything on: that is—totally—I don't need anything; eating is almost a nuisance; if I can't get on, I have to drink coffee, then. I'm active the whole time without doing anything; it seems to me that I make the same mistake at work as at—ah—before going to sleep, I find that I have always waited anxiously to see whether I sleep and have noted when I go to sleep. Of course you can't go to sleep like that, and it seems to me that it's about the same with my concentration. I, I'm always afraid I won't be able to concentrate: then I can't concentrate. But I can't stop it; it is difficult, something makes me, then—it's ridiculous; it doesn't get me any further.

Joy

It would exceed the scope of this study to deal with the discussion of libido, the pleasure-unpleasure principle, the pleasure-ego and the real-ego (Engel 1963:286). In the differentiated assumptions that are made regarding the perception of pleasure and joy, we shall therefore be contented with a general definition of the pleasure principle. "According to Freud one of the two principles that dominate psychic activity: all psychic activity has the objective of avoiding unpleasure and seeking pleasure. The pleasure principle is an economic principle to the extent that unpleasure is linked to increasing excitative activities and pleasure to the reduction of the same" (Laplanche and Pontalis 1975, I:297).

Joy is an undirected pleasurable excitement, in contrast to love, which is object related. As in the previous subcategories, here, too, classification is carried out either on the basis of explicit verbalization or interpretation.

Text 42. Session 18, patient 17 (male).

M: It doesn't work with some people, they are so reserved on the street; that makes me a bit sad. But when I am healthy, I really enjoy it a lot. I often talk to people in the street, and what pleasure it gives me!

Love

By *love* we mean any tender and amicable sentiments linked to sexual needs that are directed at an object (see Freud 1976*f*, XIV:63).

Text 43. Session 3, patient 16 (male).

M: Yes, otherwise I forget it. I'm a bit younger than you two, but—I know how I met my wife; she was still really hooked on a foreigner, a Peruvian, and at the time, I, well, I really struggled with myself. I struggled with myself so that I—so that I would get over it, and I was very kind to her. And he doesn't live in Austria. And when she no longer saw him, it all died down with her Michael, and we two started to meet more frequently. And now the time has come. And now Michael doesn't exist any more. And when we talk about him, he's just anybody.

Hate

Hate, like love, is object related, arising from the destructive instinct, as do aggression and rage. The ambivalence between hate and love is often mentioned as a psychological phenomenon and not only as a topic for poetry. "We can take the polarity of love and hate as the opposite of the two types of instinct. We are not at a loss for a representative for Eros, and on the other hand are highly contented with being able to indicate a representative of the elusive death instinct in the destructive instinct, the way for which is paved by hate" (Freud 1976c, XIII:271).

Love and hate are classified either through explicitly expressed feelings or on the basis of latent text meanings (text 8).

Shame

Shame, like disgust, is regarded as a social reaction to the needs of the sexual drive (Freud 1972, V:132). The development of this feeling is strongly linked to certain mechanisms of socialization and cultural taboos. The fact that this feeling is connected with child-hood experiences can often be observed in the everyday treatment of children ("Aren't you ashamed?") and in the reaction of adults, who are "even ashamed of their shame" (Levin 1977:534). In connection with shame, we may encounter sex-specific differences, because the development of sexual inhibitions tends to be promoted in girls (Freud 1972, V:120). Shame may frequently occur in connection with the defense mechanism of regression.

Text 44. Session 20, patient 15 (male).

M1: Yes, I think it is certainly valuable, and it is also necessary. Apart from professional—there are also discussions that go much, much—that go a bit further. That indicates that there are such, such needs, but that there are very high walls—if one can formulate it quite well, but that doesn't always mean that one has the courage to talk about things that really affect you personally. And I know that when one is very involved oneself, it is very difficult to talk about these things, get them off one's chest.

Spite

Spite also has its origins in the very early phases of the socialization process. It is an important reaction of the ego to the requirements of others and must therefore be rated as relation-oriented (Freud 1973b, X:409). We also expect a sex-specific difference: girls are better behaved and more tender; boys are more aggressive and defiant. As in the case of shame, this feeling also contains strong regressive tendencies. Classification to individual problem presentations is effected in the same way as for the other affective conditions.

Text 45. Session 4, patient 20 (M1) (male).

M1: That didn't affect me at all; I laughed because of him.
W1: You still interrupted us!
W2: One doesn't dare talk any more, if—You have the feeling somehow that somebody's making fun of you.
M2: I can only say that I think you must risk having the others laugh at you sometime, too, I mean—
M1: Good, I won't say anything anymore; now we must be quite serious.

3.10.2.3. The expression of affects

This category has already been dealt with theoretically and with regard to the sociolinguistic hypotheses in the previous section (as an activity involving the feelings). The following categories (with the exception of admission and sublimation) fall into the category of defense mechanisms: rejection of affective conditions. The above-mentioned defense mechanisms can also relate to emotions (e.g., feelings are isolated or denied). I have deliberately considered the following three categories (dissociation, hesitation, displacement) separately, however, because these forms of defense are regarded as being specific to emotions and not so much to semantic contents. Problems and feelings can be rationalized, but in our definition, feelings in particular are retarded. Deutsch (1977b:73) and Zilboorg (1977:59) have already referred to this phenomenon, pointing out the absence of expression as a peculiar characteristic in the case of specific emotions. Sperling (1977:174) describes two particular types of affective expression that contrast with the usual forms of defense. These are spacing and crowding, or in other words, separation of emotions or compression of emotions. The former occurs for fear of too strong an affective experience, the second as a result of an almost Dionysian desire for wild excitement. It is precisely such phenomena that should be included in this category. It only remains to define the subcategories in contrast to the expected condition. Once again, the importance of this category as an indicator of therapeutic effect should be emphasized. The ability to link affect and concept together with each other in verbalization can serve as an indicator for the elimination of neurotic patterns.

In previous investigations (Leodolter 1975a:256 ff.; Dressler et al. 1972; Wodak-Leodolter and Dressler 1978), it proved expedient to analyze the sociophonological level as an indicator of psychological phenomena. Thus, for example, in my investigation of interaction in court, five different sociophonological styles were found, ranging from a formal, emphatic style to a stylistic level reflecting great excitement. For technical reasons it was not possible to have all the recordings from the group sessions phonetically transcribed, thus making it impossible to carry out a detailed sociophonological investigation of this speech situation. The parameters already established for Viennese dialect were therefore used.[11] For this reason a difference is made between the presence or absence of affective elements.

In their analysis of therapeutic discourse, Labov and Fanshel (1977:43 ff.) deal only superficially with the various affective levels. Nevertheless, several features are noted, even though they are allocated fairly carelessly to the category of tension. "Hesitation, long pauses, and other forms of disruption are crucial signals in this therapeutic session especially when contrasted with the fluent speech of everyday life" (Labov and Fanshel 1977:43).

The authors also agree that there is no uniform descriptive method and no theory of affective intonation in prosodic research. Both authors argue that it is difficult to effect a classification on the basis of purely phonetic indicators because of the theoretical requirements of communication. "The lack of agreement on the transcription of prosodic cues is not accidental. We feel that this system of communication is utilized by speakers in conversational interaction to communicate signals that are not clear, discrete, or unambiguous" (Labov and Fanshel 1977:46).

Although the purely suprasegmental level is not sufficient for definition (I therefore apply the text-semantic levels for interpretation), there are still more recent approaches to the description of emphasis, suprasegmental phenomena, and intonation with regard to psychological factors. Students of generative phonology agree that further research must be carried out in this field (Dogil 1979a:23 ff.).

Lawendowski (1970:74), Vanderslice and Ladefoged (1972:821), Bolinger (1978:488), and Liberman (1978:61) all give examples in which the use of psychological factors is indispensable for description and explanation. An integrative study along those lines has not yet been carried out, however. Marek (1975:180–255) offers an approach that firmly establishes attitudes and psychological factors.

> It seems that all attitudes can be classified according to some common feature or property which they share, and that intonation is an exponent of that one feature rather than of the highly complex structure of elements which are given a common term "attitude." (Marek 1975:254)

> Instead of modifying the Basic Intonation Contours by such endless lists of specifications of the underlying preformative verbs such as / + doubt/, / + admiration/, / + joy/ etc., we can have a limited number of features common to several attitudes, such as the one we have discussed, that is / + intensity/ realised in the surface syntactic structure as the high or low nuclear tones, which, in different situations, will have different implications. (Marek 1975:255)

Only Ceplitis (1974:188 ff.) and Vitt (1975) attempt to differentiate and classify individual emotions according to physiological and suprasegmental properties, such as tone, timbre, melody, intonation, rhythm, and hesitation (see Goldman-Eisler 1958, 1961, 1968). They differentiate between ten emotions, which are naturally not always clearly defined, forming hybrid terms in many cases. These ten affective conditions correspond to the classification used here.

It will be apparent from this brief outline that there are as yet no clear-cut phonological and phonetic theories and descriptions in this field. Individual indicators can be used, such as timbre, hesitation, falling and rising intonation, tension, pauses. It is inevitable, however, that interpretation should be carried out simultaneously (Maclay and Osgood 1959; Boomer 1965). Both psychotherapeutic criteria, semantic interpretation, and the above-mentioned suprasegmental indicators are therefore used in our classification into affective conditions, affective expression, and strength of affective expression. For the reasons mentioned it is impossible to differentiate unambiguously between individual affective conditions, and I have therefore confined myself to two categories of affective strength: increased presence of these indicators and neutral manner of speaking. A differentiated investigation of this level should

be carried out in the future and may produce an integrative psy-
chophonological and psychophonetical theory; see Vaneček and
Dressler (1975) (4.3.1.6).

Dissociation[12]

The affect has apparently disappeared: problems that should have
a major impact on the patient are described in a neutral, factual
manner. Zilboorg (1977:58 ff.) speaks of the "splitting up of certain
affective reactions." The affect appears to have been suppressed
completely. In this context Deutsch differentiates between "as-if
personalities" and "repressed individuals" whose affective life appears to have been concealed:

> For the "as-if" personality, often endowed with a high unimpaired
> intelligence, distorts the meaning of reality and corrupts affective life
> through intellectualizations and rationalizations, all the while wearing
> the mask of sanity, and without going deeper into the matter, I wish at
> this point to state that this condition is not identical with the coldness
> of repressed individuals in whom there is usually a highly differentiated
> emotional life hidden behind a wall, the loss of affect being either
> manifest or cloaked by overcompensations. (Deutsch 1977a:111)

It is naturally impossible to differentiate between these two types
on the basis of text passages without a closer knowledge of the
patient. Allocation to this category is based on the quality of the
verbalization (text 27).

Hesitation

The affect occurs with hesitation, either because of spacing (that
is, the affect is divided up), or it subsequently emerges entire. The
narrower and wider context of the problem presentation must be
taken into consideration in allocating to this category.

Text 46. Session 5, patient 7 (W).

W: Well, at the moment I can't do anything, you know; yes, I would like
    to go to work again in January. Not now, though; my husband wouldn't
    agree at the moment. Anyway, I'm taking more medications, and at

the moment everything is adjusted to medications, to the—I have troubles with my stomach and intestine. And perhaps that's also where the tiredness comes from.

W: [Ten minutes later] Yes, there's absolutely nobody in my family who still understands me. [weeps]
M: And can you talk about it with your husband . . . ?

Displacement

The affect that one would expect to find in a problem presentation occurs in quite a different place but is easily interpreted as displacement, because of the context.

Text 47. Session 4, patients 15 (M1) and 16 (M2).

M1: But you know, Mr. _____ , what I don't, and you in turn have abilities which I don't know about.
M2: We're pretty much equal.
M1: You don't understand me.
M2: To high society, to the top ten thousand, sort of conversational difficulties—
M1: Well, that depends on you; that doesn't affect me.
M2: That didn't worry me, I'd say—
M1: I think that depends on you. Let's say you feel more inhibited in my presence.
M2: Is that so?
M1: I hope you understand what I'm trying to say. I am talking with you just as I would to anybody else, you know, who might perhaps be intellectually slightly superior; I am talking with you quite normally. I think it's your fault that you are perhaps a bit embarrassed with me.
M2: Embarrassed with you? [laughter] Is that an example?
M1: I really meant that, because you said you were embarrassed with people who were superior to you. By which I don't mean that I am so much better than you, but I mean—
M2: That's all a bit too much for me.
M1: What?
M2: That was a bit too much for me; you are certainly better than I am. [laughter]

M1: That's not the answer I was expecting, Mr. _____ . I am talking to
somebody.

M2: To begin with, when I came to the groups, I had inferiority complexes,
but—that really grew, that was a real . . . There were people, most
of the group—ah—were intellectuals, or at least they talked very
pompously, you know; I didn't know what it was all about, you see.
Then, then—

M1: That happened to me, too; that happened to me, too, you know.
Most of the group, as you say, were intellectuals: I found exactly the
same thing. Now we are all pretty much so high up that there are
no more intellectuals among us. [laughter] Dr. _____ has raised us
all so far that—

M2: I wanted to say something else, actually, that—ah—that one should
be the way one is, and that I am working on myself, and that I am
doing quite well. Now I'm already talking just like a native [*red wie
a Beisser*] and will go to a therapy, a self-therapy.

Admission

The affect is admitted; cognitive and emotional levels correspond
to one another (text 8).

Sublimation

> The process postulated by Freud to explain human actions that appar-
> ently have no relationship with sexuality, although their driving force
> is sexual drive. Freud described principally artistic activity and intel-
> lectual work as sublimations. The drive is called "sublimated" to the
> extent that it is channelled to a new, nonsexual goal and directed at a
> new, nonsexual object. (Laplanche and Pontalis 1975, II:478)

This category is at a different level from the previous ones. The
affect or primal instinct is not displaced, delayed, or suppressed,
but is given a new quality, transferred to another level, with a new
goal and object. The feelings are assimilated cognitively and emotionally; the resulting new action is also completely satisfying, particularly in the light of social and cultural values. (It is impossible
to go into the theory of sublimation here.)

This category refers to problem presentations in group therapy
where the patient is successful in transforming obvious grief, love,

or even aggression into different, meaningful activities. The affect is not rejected; instead, the energy is deliberately used for other objectives. According to our theoretical assumptions, it is precisely here that we should be able to find sex-specific differences and monitor the therapeutic effect (Windhoff-Heritier 1976:154 ff.).

Text 48. Session 13, patient 10 (W) (female).

W: Yes, now I'll be off work for another week, because I'd like them to realize it for once, there. And if they don't realize it, then I must say, I wouldn't like to go, because I don't see why I should. I have been with the company for eight and a half years, and I like working there, you know, but I won't work under such conditions.

M: They won't even throw you out if—

W: Well, but I just don't want to any more, either, because I said that I have my children in the evening and I, I mean, I must be there for them, too. I can't come home like an empty sack, and quite washed out, and I shout at the children because I am so exhausted after working there for eight hours on the trot. I am not going to live like this.

3.10.2.4. The intensity of affective expression

This category covers the intensity (or the presence) of the affect at both a verbal and a nonverbal level. The theoretical assumptions mentioned above are based on this difference. These assumptions relate to the various levels of affective expression and at the same time emphasize that there can be a discrepancy between motor, verbal, and cognitive levels, but that they are not normally completely independent of one another (Scheflen 1973:237 ff.). According to our class- and sex-specific assumptions, there ought to be differences between men and women, as well as between the social classes. Women are permitted to give nonverbal expression to affects, are allowed to cry, laugh, and so on, while men may be loud or verbally violent (e.g, in conflict situations). The mechanisms of socialization would lead us to expect members of the middle class to remain rather neutral, while members of the working class would tend to give free rein to their feelings. Members of the lower middle class would probably try to display particularly rational behavior (4.3.1.7).

Verbal: neutral
Nonverbal: neutral

The problem is presented in a completely neutral manner. This corresponds to sociophonological style 3 in the investigation of the variation of Viennese dialect; (see Leodolter 1975*a*:260). This probably goes hand in hand with a complete rejection of affects (text 27).

Verbal: violent
Nonverbal: neutral

The problem presentation is related very emotionally but with simultaneous motor control (text 26).

Verbal: neutral
Nonverbal: violent

Here there is a marked discrepancy between verbal and nonverbal levels. The patient presents his problem in a verbally factual manner, but his body, gestures, mimicry, and movements reveal a high degree of internal excitement. This category would naturally have to be investigated more closely with the aid of video recordings, although this would qualitatively increase the observer paradox. The allocation of the nonverbal level was made on the basis of my own reports and notes made immediately after the tape recordings (text 12).

Verbal: violent
Nonverbal: violent

Verbal and nonverbal levels are parallel: the affect is expressed through both channels (text 46).

3.10.3. The interactive dimension

The following four types of category relate to the context of the problem presentation: the reaction of patients and therapists to the problem presentation and—if appropriate—the answer of the patient concerned. In accordance with the theoretical considerations of 2.3.2.4, the interactive level in group communication comprises several aspects. Manifest and latent meaning are particularly intricately interwoven here: the analysis concentrates on the real colloquial level (i.e., which speech acts follow the problem presentation, who reacts, and how?). The psychotherapeutic process and the therapeutic technique with reference to the intervention of the therapist (this relates rather to the transference level in the group) are also observed (2.3.2, 2.3.3). Finally, the individual patient reacts in accordance with his personal character structure, his status and position roles, and his place in the relative structure of the group (2.3.4). Linguistic allocation will therefore relate to manifest behavioral patterns and in some instances to indirect speech acts, meanings, and perlocutive aspects. The relevance of the speech-act theory for the analysis of therapeutic communication will be examined again more closely in a digression on qualitative text analysis (5.2).

3.10.3.1. Sex of intervention

According to more recent investigations of sex-specific language behavior, men tend to dominate in mixed dialogues (West and Zimmermann 1975). They interrupt significantly more frequently and initiate topics as well. Nevertheless, in view of the fact that communication in a therapeutic situation differs greatly from that of an everyday situation, it seems at least doubtful whether this pattern is maintained. Women initially find easier access to the therapeutic situation (this has been dealt with in detail in 2.4.2), and this might lead us to expect that they would also talk more. This contrasts with the assumption that men, although they experience difficulties talking about their own problems, probably have hardly any inhibitions about tackling the problems of others, independent of the content of a problem presentation. Investigations of sex-specific language behavior already carried out in the United States are normally concentrated on white members of the middle and upper classes from an intellectual (university) milieu. We should therefore ask whether the mechanisms observed there are repeated in all social classes.

The following hypotheses will therefore be tested in the light of this category (4.2):

1. Men intervene more frequently than women.
2. The intervention depends on the topic: women will probably tend to express their views on children, parents, and relationships.
3. There are class-specific differences (these must remain undifferentiated, as to date there have not been any theoretical or empirical studies of this question. This aspect therefore assumes an exploratory nature in the study) (4.3.1.8).

Men

Allocation to this category was made according to the natural sex of the patients reacting to the problem presentation. If only men reacted, the problem presentation was allocated to this category.

Text 48. Session 15, patients 6 (W) and 15 (M).

W: No, I haven't done anything yet; at the moment I'm on sick leave. [confusion, inaudible] and then perhaps I'll go to work for a few days, and then I go on holiday, yes; I still have four weeks' holiday this year, you know.
M: Of course, and then appeal against being given notice.

Women

Texts were allocated to this category if there were female reactions.

Text 49. Session 20, patients 13 (M), 1 (W1), and 12 (W2).

W1: What country is that?
M: Poland.
W2: And she doesn't come for Christmas, either?
M: No, I will travel to her for Christmas.
W1: That's difficult, anyway; that's how I see it, you know. And you can't, I don't think, talk about yourself.

Mixed

Both men and women take part in the problem presentation.

Text 50. Session 20, patients 13 (M2), 15 (M1), and 1 (W).

M1: But that was a whole series of problems that were self-explanatory. They're still to come—

W: It's probably a problem for him, the sexual problem, where he has actually been parted from his wife for a long time, but by doing so he wanted to show her why things had gone that far, you know; it all began with the sexual problem.

M1: Well, he meant whether or not he should remain faithful to his wife now.

W: Yes. [confusion]

M2: That's a problem for me. I don't expect an answer as to whether I should or not, but—

3.10.3.2. The nature of intervention

This category relates to the quality of the interventions by members of the group to the problem presented by a patient. In the present classification for quantitative analysis, the allocation had to be restricted to the manifest colloquial level of direct speech acts and manifest intentions (2.3.2.1). Only when absolutely necessary were interpretative allocations made. This type of analysis must ignore several important aspects: the tracing of expressions to transference patterns, the analysis of projections, a sociodynamic structure with group roles and the corresponding behavioral strategies, and finally, the differentiation of Bales's character types and their behavioral motives and expressive forms (Bales 1950). This type of differentiated qualitative multilevel analysis would include the entire context of the session, information about the persons involved, and finally, the dynamics of the psychotherapeutic process. A detailed qualitative analysis is demonstrated in sections 5.4 and 5.5 in the light of two selected text passages. The limitation to the manifest text level of the problem presentation is justified not only for technical reasons. The specific therapeutic technique of the crisis intervention center, and in particular the specific position of problem presentation, has already been referred to in section 3.7.1. Problem presentations are not only analyzed in the group with reference to their psychodynamics; priority is given initially to their acute critical nature. As a result, the interventions also deal with the manifest problem presentation, only in some instances with examination of the subconscious mechanisms and the symptomatic nature of the presentation. The taxonomy presented is based on the most common speech acts and types of intervention occurring in all classifications that can be regarded as typical of psychotherapeutic dialogue and that comprise larger text types than individual utterances.[13]

  According to the assumptions regarding class- and sex-specific language behavior, there ought to be significant differences in dialogue (2.4.2). Men react more aggressively than women; women ask more questions and assume comforting and supporting roles; men tend to identify with the role of the therapist and give interpretations and explanations; members of the working class deal with the content of problem presentations, members of the middle class with metacommunicative aspects. Women tend also to introduce their own problems; men prefer to tackle the problems raised by others. As in the previous category (sex of intervention), there will probably be connections with the topic elaborated upon. The significant correlation between the sex of the intervening person and the nature of the intervention is certainly not pure chance. We are especially interested in the question as to whether the nature of the intervention depends on the narrative structure of the problem presentation (which in turn, according to the hypotheses, is class- and sex-specific). In other words, are there typical reactions to a scenic, narrative, or circumstantial description, or does the reaction depend rather on the stage reached in problem solving, on affective expression and content? In this category, too, several hypotheses remain fairly undifferentiated and exploratory because of the limited amount of literature on sex- and class-specific language behavior in groups. The assumption regarding the significantly higher level of aggression and disputatious nature of men is already firmly anchored in the theory of psychoanalysis, as is also the willingness of women to assume mothering roles (Windhoff-Heritier 1976: 42 ff.) (4.3.1.9).

Commentary

This category comprises all comments on a problem presentation, from the smallest segments, such as *hm, ahem,* and *oh,* to statements and factual commentaries. This division is based mainly on Posner's classification of comments (1972) and on Wunderlich's discussion of such speech acts (Wunderlich 1976:337) (text 50).

Question

Open and closed questions fall within this category. During provisional analysis, it was not considered expedient to subdivide this category into open and closed questions (text 49).

Analog problem presentation

This type of intervention seems to be particularly typical of therapeutic communication. Patients tend to introduce similar problems in order to build up an image for themselves, give consolation, and so on. The perlocutive effect of analog problem presentation can either obstruct the patient or serve as a model. People learn from a similar problem for which a solution has already been found. The effect of an analog problem presentation is evident mainly from the subsequent reaction of the patient. Allocation to this category is made using the criteria of the text class of problem presentation in group therapy. These have already been described in detail (text 29).

Interpretation

Interpretation belongs to the class of metacommunicative speech acts, or reflexive speaker strategies (with reference to the taxonomy presented in 2.3.2.1).[14] In contrast to explanation, interpretation is a connective hypothesis intended to give the patient access to the latent meanings of his behavior (Laplanche and Pontalis 1975, I:117). The patient must reflect on the interpretation and can accept or reject it. To this extent the words of the therapist or other patients are of a tentative and hypothetical nature and are by no means a definitive statement. Foulkes (1976:277) establishes that patients often provide interpretations in identification with the therapist. In such instances, patients offering interpretations are often unconsciously involved in competing with the therapist. "These unconscious interpretations are just as important for the person interpreting as for the person who receives them. They are all meaningful in the common pole of opinions in the communication network representing the 'matrix' of the group" (p. 278).

The interpretation may be introduced either with an illocutionary construction, such as "in my opinion," "I believe that," "I would see things this way," or in the form of a question: "is it possible that. . . . " Allocation to this category depends mainly on the metacommunicative content, in other words on the expression of an opinion or a summary of the problem presented.

Text 51. Session 10, patient 9 (male).

I don't know whether I should say this: I have had an idea. We'll see how the group reacts to it. Normally the situation in a family is that the boy is very attached to his mother at a certain phase, and the girl more to the father. Now, in your case, you have always had difficulties, you said; your mother always rings up, and it takes a few seconds, and you can [inaudible] be happy. But at the same time, you said that your, your father could never really get his way with your mother, and as a result (I've just thought about this), the situation is reversed, say—in a way you have linked your personality to your father and cannot break away from your mother as a result, exactly the same as he can't get his way.

Support

This category comprises mainly comforting and encouraging speech acts that are intended to show the patient speaking that he can find protection, support, and assistance in the group. This type of intervention is also necessary for the positive transference and minimization of frustration in the psychotherapeutic situation (Menninger and Holzman 1973:135). Expressions of this nature are generally emotionally colored and include extremely personal offers of help or assurances of affection ("I'll help you," "It's not so bad, really," "We like you").

Text 52. Session 10, patient 1 (female).

W: Yes, because one covers up a lot, but we know you; we are familiar with your difficulties, your whatever, where we can help you, where we can intervene—we know all that already. So with us you can assume a certain amount of confidence, and it ought to be easier for you, shouldn't it.

Advice

This class comprises any expression that contributes to a problem solution. Such expressions normally occur as conjunctives ("in your place I would . . . ") or in the form of questions ("why don't you . . . "). They also follow the illocutionary utterance "I would advise you." All three types listed by Wunderlich occur (Wunderlich 1976:280 ff.): cogent advice, weak advice, and assurances ("if you don't take the ace, you won't win," "if you take the ace, you will win"; "if you don't upset the dog, it won't bite you").

Text 53. Session 10, patient 1 (female).

W: I would like to suggest that you, when you are talking about your problem, that you try, for our sake, too, to talk as though you were talking about somebody else. So—you know how you talk as a teacher; I can imagine that you really have a certain personality in you, don't you. Because the girls wouldn't listen to you in a lesson if you talked like that. I know that from my own experience, because there'd be trouble in ten minutes, right? And try to imagine that we are all impatient now, and not listening to you.

Rejection

Rejection relates to a negation of the problem presentation just heard. The rejection can relate either to the topic (e.g., if it is felt that the topic is being used as a pretext) or to the problem solution suggested. Negative evaluation is expressed, the problem presentation not accepted, a conflict initiated. Rejection can be factual or emotional, and depending on the nature of the utterance, it may initiate a conflict or provoke discussion. It can be expressed very directly ("I think that is wrong, bad") or rather indirectly ("I would have acted differently," "this is the best way," and so on).

Text 54. Session 11, patients 15 (M) and 8 (W).

M: And simply under these conditions, I am not in this condition. I live quite differently: I also have psychic problems; I solve them quite differently.
W: Yes, but you certainly make things easy for yourself!

Obstruction

In contrast to rejection, which relates to the negation of content, though continuing the dialogue, the consequence of obstruction is that the problem presentation is no longer discussed. The obstruction may either consist of an explicit expression of displeasure or uneasiness either with respect to the speaker or the entire subject matter presented ("he's talking yet again"; "the topic is uninteresting") or may involve the abrupt introduction of a quite different topic, with the result that the problem presentation is not elaborated upon. Obstruction can result in the development of a conflict (the patient feels he has been ignored). The therapist or another patient intervenes; the situation is elaborated metacommunicatively; or—finally—it can happen that the obstruction is successful and a new topic is introduced.

Text 55. Session 9, patients 15 (M) and 3 (W).

M: But my wife has made inquiries; apparently I can't give notice. I don't really believe it. [pause]
T: Well, hasn't anybody got anything to say?
W: Yes, I'd just like to say that if the job doesn't suit me, then there can be no notice here. I don't believe that, because if I don't like a job, I can give up my job at any time; there's no such thing as not being able to give notice.

3.10.3.3. Intervention by the therapist

It is not my intention in this section to discuss various techniques of psychotherapy or deal with opportunities for intervention (Menninger and Holzman 1973:124 ff.; Slater 1978). Neither will our interest focus on a detailed qualitative analysis of interventions and their possible classification (Trömel-Plötz 1979). The task at hand is to establish whether there are connections between the topic of the problem presentation, the patients concerned, and therapeutic intervention. In other words, are middle-class patients better understood and given preference? Do the sexes of the therapist and patients actually play a role such that male therapists tend to intervene with women and vice versa, or, as the feminist literature maintains, do women tend to intervene with women (Cadow 1977)? Are there significant differences in the nature of the intervention with reference to the class and sex of the speaker, or do therapeutic interventions depend on the topic under discussion? Are they oriented toward the problem-solving stage or the intensity of the affective expression? Here, too, these questions are of an exploratory nature, as nobody has previously carried out an explicit linguistic analysis of an extensive corpus. Basically, it can be assumed that therapeutic intervention is oriented mainly toward the psychodynamics of the patient and not toward his class or sex (4.3.1.10).

Question: This category comprises all open and closed questions put by the therapist to the patient who has effected a problem presentation (texts 14, 59).

Interpretation: In this instance the connective hypothesis comes from the therapist[15] (text 15).

Rejection: The therapist expresses a negative evaluation of the subject matter presented by the patient (he rejects, for example, a problem solution or even an opinion).

Direct intervention by the therapist occurs comparatively seldom, but is sometimes necessary in order to resolve transference phenomena (e.g., when he is addressed as an adviser or authority). Such utterances are interpreted in a broader context in the qualitative analysis of individual problem presentations (5.4, 5.5).

Text 56. Session 18, therapist.

May I interrupt again? [confusion noises in the group, confused talking] You say you wouldn't have come here at all, but [do so] because I have a pleasant voice; I mean, I'm glad it's my fault that you come; that doesn't worry me at all; but I don't think it's as simple as that.

3.10.3.4. The reaction of patients

The answer of the patient to the interventions made concludes the interaction unit of problem presentation in group therapy. Formal linguistic criteria are decisive for allocation to this category. Starting from the considerations of class- and sex-specific socialization, it can be assumed that women tend to acquire insight more easily than men. Men are more liable to enter into conflicts than women and also ask more counterquestions. Members of the working class will probably behave more aggressively than members of the lower middle class and middle class. This category can naturally only be considered in connection with the two previous ones (4.3.1.11).

Rejection

The patient explicitly rejects a piece of advice, a consolation, or an interpretation without giving further reasons.

Text 57. Session 18, patient 2 (female).

W: I didn't know that, no. I was sent to you at the time and deliberately wrongly—because I was simply afraid where I would be sent to. But you know that exactly.

Counterquestion

The patient does not go into the content of the intervention but withdraws to the metacommunicative level: "Why do you ask that?" or "Why do you, of all people, ask that question?" This is a fairly typical form of resistance in therapeutic work.

Text 58. Session 10, patient 20 (male).

M: Can I just say something briefly: you have known me for some time now. I have been very forgetful, I know; I have already been through situations similar to the one I described today, you know. Has there ever been a situation like the one today?

Repetition

This can also be regarded as a form of resistance; the patient overlooks, as it were, the intervention and repeats his problem, often in an identical formal linguistic manner.

Text 59. Session 2, patient 18 (male).

T: What's the situation with the others?
M: I haven't got a job, for eight days now.
T: What?
M: I haven't got a job.

New aspect

This represents a first step toward further work on the problem presented. The patient provides further material, answers the questions put to him or details the proposed problem solution. This category is normally realized in the form of a further problem presentation (text 21).

Conflict

The patient rejects the intervention and starts a conflict with the intervening person. This, too, can be interpreted as resistance. The conflict can be realized in different ways (3.8.6) (text 24).

Insight

The patient accepts the interpretation and begins to come to terms with it. Explicit acceptance is usually expressed initially ("yes, you are right"), followed either by further material confirming the interpretation or a search for other problem solutions:

> The term In-Sight presupposes an "introspection" which includes both an intellectual and an affective review of experiences which had previously remained in the subconscious. In essence it consists of creating for oneself a fitting and most complete possible picture of the internal world, particularly where there is a discrepancy between it and the external reality. . . . For this reason the ACQUISITION of in-sight is one of the main objectives of the therapeutic process. This insight must extend sufficiently deep to make it possible to alter and finally eliminate the rigid neurotic structure. (Kemper 1971:171)

The acquisition of insight can therefore be regarded as one of the most important indicators of positive therapeutic effect and of successful assimilation and problem solving. According to the hypotheses, there ought to be an increase in insightful reactions in the course of the therapy (2.5).

Text 60. Session 10, patients 11 (W) and 14 (M).

M: Well, you know which question I wanted to ask first, when you spoke about your, well, about your pupil, to what extent do you draw parallels between yourself and your pupil, do you see, that's what I wanted to ask you to begin with. Do you draw any parallels at all between the way you feel and between yourself? One becomes too involved anyway. . . .

W: I do see parallels between the girl and myself, that's right.

3.10.4. Summary: Categories for the description of "problem presentation in group therapy"

The eleven categories and their subcategories thus serve to describe and analyze problem presentations in group therapies (schema 9). These categories are linguistic, psychoanalytic and interactional. I believe that only such an interdisciplinary approach is fruitful in analyzing such a complex phenomenon as therapeutic discourse. Raters coded the 1134 problem presentations for the quantitative analysis. After that, a qualitative analysis proved necessary to illustrate the total complexity and also the limits of quantification in text analysis (5.4, 5.5).

SCHEMA 9

CATEGORIES FOR THE DESCRIPTION OF THE TEXT CLASS PROBLEM PRESENTATION IN GROUP THERAPY

Descriptive categories	Subcategories			
Narrative structure	Scene	Narration	Circumstance	
Text length (clauses)	1	4	16	256
Problem solving	Penetration—ambivalence—distance—solution			
Defense mechanisms	Rationalization—negation—regression—denial—projection—turning against the self			
Affectivity	Rage—guilt—sorrow—fear—joy—love—hate—shame—spite			
Expression of affects	Dissociation—hesitation—displacement—admission—sublimation			
Intensity of affective expression	Verbal: neutral Nonverbal: neutral	Verbal: violent Nonverbal: neutral	Verbal: neutral Nonverbal: violent	Verbal: violent Nonverbal: violent
Sex of intervention	men—women—mixed			
Nature of the intervention	Commentary—question—analog problem presentation—interpretation—support—advice— rejection—obstruction			
Intervention by the therapist	Question—interpretation—rejection			
Reaction of patients	Rejection—counterquestion—repetition—new aspect—conflict—insight			

4
Quantitative Analysis

4.1. Intention and goal

The quantitative analysis is limited to a certain text class in therapeutic communication in groups which is linguistically defined and described exactly (problem presentation in group therapy; see 3.9, 3.10). Selected hypotheses on class- and sex-specific behavior and on the therapeutic effect are tested in the light of a large, statistically representative corpus (4.3). Case studies with individual patients (4.4), focused interviews (6.4), and the qualitative linguistic analysis of disputed passages (5.4, 5.6) locate the quantitative results in the course of the investigation. Without quantitative analysis, these assertions would have remained speculative and illustrative, and the systematic analysis of the mass of texts using linguistically and psychoanalytically founded categories could not have been carried out on a purely qualitative basis. The relevance of the results confirms my efforts and objectives: to enhance sociolinguistic and psycholinguistic theory and psychiatric practice, to shed new light on and explain previously unknown aspects, and to demonstrate the fertility of interdisciplinary research.

4.2. Hypotheses

The hypotheses on which the quantitative analysis is based are listed below (the theoretical background is presented in 2.3, 2.4, 2.5).

I. Hypotheses on class-specific language behavior

  A. General hypotheses

    1. There are significant differences in the language behavior of the working class, the lower middle class, and the middle class.

    2. These differences relate to all levels of therapeutic communication (interaction strategies and linguistic, semantic, syntactic, and phonological levels) (3.9).

3. The differences are of a qualitative and not a purely quantitative nature (turn frequency and other strategies are relevant as indicators, sentence length is of minor importance) (3.10.1).
4. The differences concern the cognitive and the affective spheres of language behavior (3.10.2).
5. This results in differently used strategies of defense and problem solving (3.10.1.3, 3.10.2.1).

B. Differentiation of the hypotheses

  1. Middle class
     a) Members of the middle class give coherent descriptions (3.10.1.1).
     b) Members of the middle class have metacommunicative abilities (2.4.1.2).
     c) Members of the middle class suppress their feelings and dissociate (3.10.2.3).
     d) Members of the middle class describe symptoms and relate stories (3.10.1.1).
     e) In accordance with the differences in the cognitive and affective spheres, members of the middle class tend to rationalize rather than to regress (3.10.2.1).
     f) Members of the middle class are more likely to have problems establishing contact (3.9).

  2. Working class
     a) Members of the working class give sketchy descriptions (3.10.1.1).
     b) Members of the working class do not have metacommunicative abilities (2.4.1.2).
     c) Members of the working class express their feelings (3.10.2.3).
     d) Members of the working class describe individual experiences (3.10.1.1).
     e) Members of the working class tend to regress (3.10.2.1).
     f) Members of the working class are more likely to have problems in their relationships (3.9).

  3. Lower middle class
     a) The language behavior of the lower middle class is

unstable (switching, overadaptation, hypercorrectness) (2.4.1.3).

b) Members of the lower middle class give coherent descriptions (3.10.1.1).

c) Members of the lower middle class tend to suppress their feelings (3.10.2.3).

d) Members of the lower middle class tend to rationalize (3.10.2.1).

e) Members of the lower middle class have problems establishing contact (3.7.2).

II. Hypotheses on sex-specific language behavior

A. General hypotheses

1. There are significant differences in the language behavior of men and women (2.4.2).

2. These differences relate to both the affective and cognitive levels and are manifest at all linguistic levels.

3. In each sex there are also class-specific differences (such as those assumed above).

B. Differentiation of the hypotheses

1. Men

a) Men report symptoms and circumstances that apparently have nothing to do with themselves (3.10.1.1).

b) Their presentations are not set in the context of their life histories.

c) Men reject problems more strongly and therefore use fewer strategies of problem solving (3.10.1.3).

d) Men tend to rationalize and project (3.10.2.1).

e) Men suppress feelings (3.10.2.3).

f) Men are more liable to become involved in conflicts, quarrels, and obstructions than women (3.10.3.2).

g) The main topics are work, group activities and "group metalevel," and contact (3.9).

2. Women

a) Women relate their problems in the context of their life histories (3.10.1.1).

b) They are used to suffering and find it more difficult to take active steps to alter their situations (2.4.2).
c) They have more approaches to problem solving (3.10.1.3).
d) Women regress more and turn feelings more against themselves; they have more feelings of guilt (3.10.2.1).
e) They express their feelings openly (3.10.2.3).
f) Women display more insight and are less ready to enter into conflict (3.10.3.4).
g) Topics are family and—as with men—work (3.9).

3. Class-specific differences and sex
a) There are differences in the language behavior of working-class, lower-middle-class, and middle-class men (2.4.1.2).
b) Working-class men are more emotional and expressive than lower-middle-class and middle-class men (3.10.2.3).
c) Working-class men tend to use scenic presentations (3.10.1.1).
d) There are differences between working-class, lower-middle-class, and middle-class women (2.4.2).
e) Lower-middle-class women overadapt and suppress their feelings (2.4.1.3).
f) Middle-class and working-class women use different narrative structures (3.10.1.1).
g) Middle-class and working-class women use different defense mechanisms (3.10.2.1).

The hypotheses on class-specific differences in each sex cannot be further elaborated. This aspect involves the examination of virgin territory that must be explored (to an extent, descriptively) before the question of how class and sex interact with one another can be fully answered.

III. Hypotheses on therapeutic effect
1. There are significant differences between language behavior during the pilot study and that of subsequent phases (2.5).

2. The narrative structure changes, as does the view of the problem (3.10.1.1).
3. Feelings are expressed more strongly (3.10.2.3).
4. Defenses become weaker and change (3.10.2.1).
5. Reactions are accepted with greater insight (3.10.3.4).
6. Men learn to suffer explicitly (2.4.2.2).
7. Women learn to help themselves, to work actively toward a balancing identity (2.4.2.2).
8. Class-specific behavior changes in all three classes (2.4.1.2).

The therapeutic effect is corroborated by case studies that are analyzed both quantitatively and qualitatively and by focused interviews with the same patients (4.4, 6.4).

4.3. Quantitative testing of the hypotheses

In the following section the individual results of the quantitative analysis are listed, each with respect to a category. It is impossible to give all the detailed results in tables, as this would exceed the limits of this book. Reference to existing detailed analyses will be made at the appropriate places. The results are presented together with their interpretation, and finally, the results are summarized again for the sake of clarity. "Chi-square tests" ($= \chi^2$" tests) and the relationships between (influence of) individual variables were calculated, thus making it possible to predict the occurrence of certain linguistic structures depending on more than one independent variable, with the aid of Goodman's log-linear model (1972). Finally, the therapeutic effect is examined in the light of quantitative and qualitative analysis of individual case studies. The limits of quantification are indicated in chapter 5, which concerns qualitative interpretation. A detailed analysis of two text passages illustrates once again the three-level model (5.4, 5.5). The case studies and interviews with patients and therapists serve to illustrate self-appraisal and to differentiate aspects not quantitatively accessible (6.4, 6.5).

4.3.1. Individual results
4.3.1.1. Narrative structure[1]

As tables 15 through 19 show, there are both significant sex- and class-specific differences (at the 99 percent level). Accordingly,

TABLE 15
NARRATIVE STRUCTURE/CLASS

Narrative structure		Working 1.	Lower middle 2.	Middle 3.	Row total
Narration	1.	50 10.7 20.7 4.4	132 28.2 46.0 11.6	286 61.1 47.3 25.2	468 41.3
Scene	2.	136 44.0 56.2 12.0	39 12.6 13.6 3.4	134 43.4 22.1 11.8	309 27.2
Circumstance	3.	56 15.7 23.1 4.9	116 32.5 40.4 10.2	185 51.8 30.6 16.3	357 31.5
Column Total		242 21.3	287 25.3	605 53.4	1134 100.0

$\chi^2 = 144.38$ $\alpha = .0001$ df = 4

TABLE 16
NARRATIVE STRUCTURE/SEX

Narrative structure		Male 1.	Female 2.	Row total
Narration	1.	157 33.5 35.8 13.8	311 66.5 44.7 27.4	468 41.3
Scene	2.	114 36.9 26.0 10.1	195 63.1 28.1 17.2	309 27.2
Circumstance	3.	168 47.1 38.3 14.8	189 52.9 27.2 16.7	357 31.5
Column Total		439 38.7	695 61.3	1134 100.0

$\chi^2 = 16.17$ $\alpha = .0003$ df = 2

TABLE 17

NARRATIVE STRUCTURE/CLASS/MEN

Narrative structure		Class			Row total
		Working 1.	Lower middle 2.	Middle 3.	
Narration	1.	19 12.1 13.9 4.3	58 36.9 40.8 13.2	80 51.0 50.0 18.2	157 35.8
Scene	2.	84 73.7 61.3 19.1	22 19.3 15.5 5.0	8 7.0 5.0 1.8	114 26.0
Circumstance	3.	34 20.2 24.8 7.7	62 36.9 43.7 14.1	72 42.9 45.0 16.4	168 38.3
Column Total		137 31.2	142 32.3	160 36.4	439 100.0

$\chi^2 = 136.90$ $\alpha = .0001$ $df = 4$

TABLE 18

NARRATIVE STRUCTURE/CLASS/WOMEN

Narrative structure		Class			Row total
		Working 1.	Lower middle 2.	Middle 3.	
Narration	1.	31 10.0 29.5 4.5	74 23.8 51.0 10.6	206 66.2 46.3 29.6	311 44.7
Scene	2.	52 26.7 49.5 7.5	17 8.7 11.7 2.4	126 64.6 28.3 18.1	195 28.1
Circumstance	3.	22 11.6 21.0 3.2	54 28.6 37.2 7.8	113 59.8 25.4 16.3	189 27.2
Column Total		105 15.1	145 20.9	445 64.0	695 100.0

$\chi^2 = 45.41$ $\alpha = .0001$ $df = 4$

TABLE 19

Topic/Sex/Class/Narrative Structure*
Summary of Results of the χ²-Tests of Individual Calculations for Comparison

Sex		Contact	Work	Medications	Group metalevel	Group activities	Illness	Children	Parents	Relationships
						Topic				
Male		$\chi^2 = 11,6309$ $\alpha = 0,02$ df = 4	$\chi^2 = 16,11$ $\alpha = 0,01$ df = 4	$\chi^2 = 7,9$ $\alpha = 0,09$ df = 4	$\chi^2 = 13,27$ $\alpha = 0,01$ df = 4	$\chi^2 = 25,3$ $\alpha = 0,01$ df = 4	$\chi^2 = 15,84$ $\alpha = 0,01$ df = 4	$\chi^2 = 24,5$ $\alpha = 0,01$ df = 4	$\chi^2 = 4,8$ $\alpha = 0,3$ df = 4	$\chi^2 = 13,4$ $\alpha = 0,01$ df = 4
Female		$\chi^2 = 4,2$ $\alpha = 0,3$ df = 4	$\chi^2 = 2,8$ $\alpha = 0,5$ df = 4	$\chi^2 = 13,6$ $\alpha = 0,0$ df = 4	$\chi^2 = 1,1$ $\alpha = 0,5$ df = 4	$\chi^2 = 6,2$ $\alpha = 0,1$ df = 4	$\chi^2 = 7,6$ $\alpha = 0,1$ df = 4	$\chi^2 = 17,8$ $\alpha = 0,0$ df = 4	$\chi^2 = 15,4$ $\alpha = 0,0$ df = 4	$\chi^2 = 10,3$ $\alpha = 0,0$ df = 4

* Breakdown of tables 17 and 18 by individual topics.

women tend to talk in the context of their life histories (narration), while men tend to describe situations (circumstance). Members of the working class relate scenically, in other words, out of context but very spontaneously and emotionally. In certain groups of topics (1, 2, 4, 5, 6) there are slight sex-specific differences in women, while in men the class variable is obviously of great relevance throughout. This is an important result, particularly with reference to the priority (or even exclusiveness) of the variables of class and sex. This result is evident throughout the study and can be explained in the light of fundamental common aspects of female socialization. The male role, contrastingly, appears to be much more strongly determined by class. In women the class-specific results are particularly significant with reference to the private sphere (children, parents, relationships), but not to the public sphere, where they all first have to gain and fight for positions.

Social dimensions are thus dependent to a significant degree on linguistic categories (previous sociolinguistic studies have been limited mainly to the sociophonological level). We are therefore justified in assuming class- and sex-specific strategies in problem presentation in group therapy. This also offers evidence for our theory of text planning (SPTT) and for the text types realized by a cognitive text-planning strategy depending on social and psychological parameters (3.9.3).

4.3.1.2. Text length

As far as the length of the text passages is concerned, there are no class- and sex-specific differences. This, too, is an interesting and surprising result. The quantity (number of clauses in a turn) is not affected by class or sex. This finally proves the expedience of qualitative parameters. It also confirms that the purely quantitative dimensions used by Bernstein are not warranted—they are not derived from any linguistic theory and do not tell us anything about sociolinguistic issues (2.4.1.1). The interesting differences can be measured meaningfully only at the sentence and text levels using qualitative parameters.

4.3.1.3. Problem solving

Problem solving is one of the most important indicators that can be used to test all the hypotheses. According to prevailing opinion, the results that can be expected here should be that members of the middle class are more likely to have strategies for problem solving than members of the working class and that because of their "rational" behavior, men are more likely to have them than women. Yet this is not confirmed by the results. Very strongly differentiated class- and sex-specific results are obtained particularly in this category. The topic of a problem presentation also plays a major role. We shall therefore subsequently break down the results by class, sex, and topic (tables 20–25) (for statistical reasons, objectivity and solution had to be considered together).

The following results are particularly striking:

1. There is no difference between working-class men and women; in all other classes women proffer considerably more solutions than men, particularly in the lower middle class.
2. When all men and women are grouped together, there are significant class-specific differences in both groups, and here again, lower-middle-class women are remarkable: this group has considerably more solutions than ambivalence compared to the other classes. In every class men proffer fewer solutions than women.

TABLE 20

PROBLEM SOLVING/SEX/WORKING CLASS

Problem solving		Sex		Row total
		Male 1.	Female 2.	
Penetration	1.	9	12	21
		42.9	57.1	8.7
		6.6	11.4	
Ambivalence	2.	100	73	173
		57.8	42.2	71.5
		73.0	69.5	
Objectivity, solution	3.	28	20	48
		58.3	41.7	19.8
		20.4	19.0	
Column Total		137	105	242
		56.6	43.4	100.0

$\chi^2 = 1.77$ $\alpha = .4116$ $df = 2$

TABLE 21
PROBLEM SOLVING/SEX/LOWER MIDDLE CLASS

Problem solving		Male 1.	Female 2.	Row total
Penetration	1.	8 53.3 5.6	7 46.7 4.8	15 5.2
Ambivalence	2.	125 60.7 88.0	81 39.3 55.9	206 71.8
Objectivity, solution	3.	9 13.6 6.3	57 86.4 39.3	66 23.0
Column Total		142 49.5	145 50.5	287 100.0

$\chi^2 = 44.35$ $\alpha = .0001$ df $= 2$

TABLE 22
PROBLEM SOLVING/SEX/MIDDLE CLASS

Problem solving		Male 1.	Female 2.	Row total
Penetration	1.	46 57.5 28.7	34 42.5 7.6	80 13.2
Ambivalence	2.	104 24.7 65.0	317 75.3 71.2	421 69.6
Objectivity, solution	3.	10 9.6 6.3	94 90.4 21.1	104 17.2
Column Total		160 26.4	445 73.6	605 100.0

$\chi^2 = 55.46$ $\alpha = .0001$ df $= 2$

TABLE 23

CLASS/SEX/TOPIC/PROBLEM SOLVING
SUMMARY OF RESULTS OF THE INDIVIDUAL χ^2-TESTS OF INDIVIDUAL CALCULATIONS

Sex		Topic								
	Contact	Work	Medications	Group metalevel	Group activities	Illness	Children	Parents	Relationships
Male	$\chi^2 = 21,3$ $\alpha = 0,01$ df = 4	$\chi^2 = 10,43$ $\alpha = 0,01$ df = 4	$\chi^2 = 10,23$ $\alpha = 0,01$ df = 4	$\chi^2 = 3,0$ $\alpha = 0,5$ df = 4	$\chi^2 = 20,16$ $\alpha = 0,01$ df = 4	$\chi^2 = 26,4$ $\alpha = 0,01$ df = 4	$\chi^2 = 2,6$ $\alpha = 0,6$ df =	$\chi^2 = 8$ $\alpha = 0,01$ df =	$\chi^2 = 7,36$ $\alpha = 0,1$ df = 4
Female	$\chi^2 = 6,4$ $\alpha = 0,1$ df = 4	$\chi^2 = 1,3$ $\alpha = 0,8$ df = 4	$\chi^2 = 6,4$ $\alpha = 0,1$ df = 4	$\chi^2 = 6,0$ $\alpha = 0,04$ df = 4	$\chi^2 = 7,46$ $\alpha = 0,1$ df = 4	$\chi^2 = 4,3$ $\alpha = 0,3$ df = 4	$\chi^2 = 23,3$ $\alpha = 0,0$ df = 4	$\chi^2 = 7,2$ $\alpha = 0,1$ df = 4	$\chi^2 = 28,5$ $\alpha = 0,01$ df = 4

* Breakdown of tables 24 and 25 by individual topics.

TABLE 24
PROBLEM SOLVING/CLASS/WOMEN

Problem solving		Class			Row total
		Working 1.	Lower middle 2.	Middle 3.	
Penetration	1.	12 22.6 11.4	7 13.2 4.8	34 64.2 7.6	53 7.6
Ambivalence	2.	73 15.5 69.5	81 17.2 55.9	317 67.3 71.2	471 67.8
Objectivity, solution	3.	20 11.7 19.0	57 33.3 39.3	94 55.0 21.1	171 24.6
Column Total		105 15.1	145 20.9	445 64.0	695 100.0

$\chi^2 = 23.60$ $\alpha = .0001$ $df = 4$

TABLE 25
PROBLEM SOLVING/CLASS/MEN

Problem solving		Class			Row total
		Working 1.	Lower middle 2.	Middle 3.	
Penetration	1.	9 14.3 6.6	8 12.7 5.6	46 73.0 28.7	63 14.4
Ambivalence	2.	100 30.4 73.0	125 38.0 88.0	104 31.6 65.0	329 74.9
Objectivity, solution	3.	28 59.6 20.4	9 19.1 6.3	10 21.3 6.3	47 10.7
Column Total		137 31.2	142 32.3	160 36.4	439 100.0

$\chi^2 = 59.46$ $\alpha = .0001$ $df = 4$

3. When differentiated by topic, class, and sex, there are significant class-specific differences in men in all topics, with the exception of group metalevel and children. As far as group metalevel is concerned, only members of the working class proffer solutions, a result that is particularly surprising and interesting. Among men, middle-class men predominate with regard to the topic of children, as they are more preoccupied with the problem of bringing up children, because of the high frequency of small and nuclear families in this class. When families only consist of the partners and one or two children, and both partners work and have jobs, the man has to participate in the education of the children and also in the organization of housework (he shares). Otherwise, the partnership breaks (there is statistical evidence for this for the town of Vienna). Upper class families, working class families and rural population depend more on groups, large families (grandparents, etc.) and on personnel (naturally only upper class). Thus, child education remains a "female" topic. The differences with regard to relationships are not highly significant ($p = 10$ percent); men proffer remarkably few solutions to this topic. Among women, however, there are significant differences only with the topics group metalevel, children, and relationships (exactly opposite the situation with men). With group metalevel, among women the middle class predominates (again in contrast to men); with children and relationships the lower middle class predominates—in other words, socially upwards mobile women who are perhaps most obliged to find solutions in the sphere of career, marriage, and children, while searching for a new identity (with regard to both class and the new roles of the sexes).

4. If we compare the first and last sessions with regard to the expected increase in the number of solutions proffered (as an indicator of therapeutic effect), we notice a rising tendency, with the exception of the last two sessions, in which there was a sudden drop in response to the treatment of a new topic (sexuality) (table 26).

The results of the case studies support the conclusions listed above.

TABLE 26

PROBLEM SOLVING/SESSION

Problem solving		Session							Row Total
		1–4	5–8	9–12	13–17	18.	19.	20.	
Penetration	1.	29	33	8	25	11	3	7	116
		25.0	28.4	6.9	21.6	9.5	2.6	6.0	10.2
		15.7	12.2	3.4	12.6	10.8	3.4	13.5	
Ambivalence	2.	136	185	174	104	85	84	32	800
		17.0	23.1	21.7	13.0	10.6	10.5	4.0	70.5
		73.5	68.5	73.4	52.3	83.3	94.4	61.5	
Objectivity, solution	3.	20	52	55	70	6	2	13	218
		9.2	23.9	25.2	32.1	2.8	.9	6.0	19.2
		10.8	19.3	23.2	35.2	5.9	2.2	25.0	
Column Total		185	270	237	199	102	89	52	1134
		16.3	23.8	20.9	17.5	9.0	7.8	4.6	100.0

$\chi^2 = 102.034$ $\alpha = .0001$ df $= 12$

4.3.1.4. Defense mechanisms

The results of the analysis of defense mechanisms (tables 27, 28) confirm the assumptions made: middle-class men clearly tend to rationalize, working-class men to regress, women to turn against themselves, men to project (the groups had to be put together for quantification). With the exception of the topic of contact, the results remain constant even on differentiated analysis (by specific topics). The topic contact deviates because there is particularly low involvement of the lower middle class, and not enough data for projection and turning against the self. In tables 27 and 28, negation and denial had to be pulled together with rationalization.

4.3.1.5. Affectivity

Affectivity depends to a significant extent on the topic under discussion and on class and sex: men tend to display anger, shame, and spite, women guilt and fear. This, too, is in line with the hypotheses that middle-class men tend to display most anger, working-class women, joy, love, shame, spite. Lower-middle-class men are

TABLE 27

DEFENSE MECHANISMS / CLASS / MEN

Defense mechanisms		Class			Row total
		Working 1.	Lower middle 2.	Middle 3.	
Rationalization	1.	59	40	103	202
		29.2	19.8	51.0	57.4
		49.2	39.2	79.2	
Regression	3.	52	42	15	109
		47.7	38.5	13.8	31.0
		43.3	41.2	11.5	
Projection	5.	6	17	10	33
		18.2	51.5	30.3	9.4
		5.0	16.7	7.7	
Turning against the self	6.	3	3	2	8
		37.5	37.5	25.0	2.3
		2.5	2.9	1.5	
Column Total		120	102	130	352
		34.1	29.0	36.9	100.0

$\chi^2 = 52.46$ $\alpha = .0001$ $df = 6$

TABLE 28
DEFENSE MECHANISMS / CLASS / WOMEN

Defense mechanisms		Class			Row total
		Working 1.	Lower middle 2.	Middle 3.	
Rationalization	1.	22	62	169	253
		8.7	24.5	66.8	45.8
		26.8	52.5	48.0	
Regression	3.	51	46	148	245
		20.8	18.8	60.4	44.4
		62.2	39.0	42.0	
Projection	5.	4	2	15	21
		19.0	9.5	71.4	3.8
		4.9	1.7	4.3	
Turning against the self	6.	5	8	20	33
		15.2	24.2	60.6	6.0
		6.1	6.8	5.7	
Column Total		82	118	352	552
		14.9	21.4	63.8	100.0

$\chi^2 = 17.06$ $\qquad$ $\alpha = .0091$ $\qquad$ df = 6

most likely to display fear. Among women, class-specific differences are also significant, but smaller. Middle-class women have a particularly marked tendency to display feelings of guilt (3.10.2.2) (see also Wodak and Schulz 1984).

There are significant differences between men and women only with regard to the topics of group activities, children, and relationships. It is interesting to note that women display more anger than men when discussing the topic relationships.

The expression of emotions is very closely connected with affectivity: fear and anger are significantly more dissociated than other emotions: joy, love, shame, and spite being most admissible, fear and love slightly sublimated (tables 29–34).

4.3.1.6. The expression of affects

Tremendous class- and sex-specific differences are encountered here (the connection with affectivity and thus with topic has already been presented and explained) (3.10.2.3).

TABLE 29
AFFECTIVITY / CLASS / MEN

		Class			
Affectivity		Working 1.	Lower middle 2.	Middle 3.	Row total
Rage	1.	17 14.7 13.4	43 37.1 31.4	56 48.3 42.7	116 29.4
Guilt	2.	24 38.1 18.9	10 15.9 7.3	29 46.0 22.1	63 15.9
Fear	3.	64 37.6 50.4	66 38.8 48.2	40 23.5 30.5	170 43.0
Joy, love	4.	11 61.1 8.7	2 11.1 1.5	5 27.8 3.8	18 4.6
Shame, spite	5.	11 39.3 8.7	16 57.1 11.7	1 3.6 .8	28 7.1
Column Total		127 32.2	137 34.7	131 33.2	395 100.0

$\chi^2 = 56.33$ $\alpha = .0001$ $df = 8$

Once again, women hardly display class-specific differences, with the exception of members of the lower middle class, who consciously keep their language (and their affects) under control. They overadapt, as described in our theoretical assertions (2.4.1).

Members of the middle class dissociate, displace, and hesitate significantly more than members of the working class and lower middle class. Women admit and express significantly more feelings, as well as sublimate more (a conclusion that is not entirely in line with traditional psychotherapeutic theory). Within each sex, the class-specific differences among men are again very considerable; they are smaller among women. Moreover, there is only a slight difference between working-class men and women, men being more liable to admit their feelings. The same observation applies even more extremely to the lower middle class, where women dissociate more strongly than men. In the middle class, however, women clearly tend to admit some feelings.

TABLE 30
AFFECTIVITY / CLASS / WOMEN

		Class			
		Working	Lower middle	Middle	Row
Affectivity		1.	2.	3.	total
	1.	36	32	138	206
Rage		17.5	15.5	67.0	33.8
		37.5	27.4	34.8	
	2.	20	20	96	136
Guilt		14.7	14.7	70.6	22.3
		20.8	17.1	24.2	
	3.	26	50	133	209
Fear		12.4	23.9	63.6	34.3
		27.1	42.7	33.6	
	4.	7	7	24	38
Joy, love		18.4	18.4	63.2	6.2
		7.3	6.0	6.1	
	5.	7	8	5	20
Shame, spite		35.0	40.0	25.0	3.3
		7.3	6.8	1.3	
Column		96	117	396	609
Total		15.8	19.2	65.0	100.0

$\chi^2 = 22.40$ $\alpha = .0042$ $df = 8$

TABLE 31
TOPIC / AFFECTIVITY / SEX
SUMMARY OF RESULTS OF THE χ^2-TEXTS OF INDIVIDUAL CALCULATIONS

Topic			
Contact	$\chi^2 = 5,06$	$\alpha = 0,28$	$df = 4$
Work	$\chi^2 = 14,09$	$\alpha = 0,01$	$df = 4$
Medications	$\chi^2 = 0,62$	$\alpha = 0,8$	$df = 4$
Group metalevel	$\chi^2 = 4,9$	$\alpha = 0,2$	$df = 4$
Group activities	$\chi^2 = 30,3$	$\alpha = 0,01$	$df = 4$
Illness	$\chi^2 = 4,5$	$\alpha = 0,03$	$df = 4$
Children	$\chi^2 = 10,69$	$\alpha = 0,03$	$df = 4$
Parents	$\chi^2 = 6,9$	$\alpha = 0,19$	$df = 4$
Relationships	$\chi^2 = 29,9$	$\alpha = 0,01$	$df = 4$

TABLE 32

AFFECTIVITY/EXPRESSION OF AFFECTS

		Expression of affects					
		Disso-ciation	Hesita-tion	Displace-ment	Admis-sion	Subli-mation	Row total
Affectivity		1.	2.	3.	4.	5.	
Rage	1.	105	7	12	191	7	322
		32.6	2.2	3.7	59.3	2.2	32.1
		33.5	33.3	46.2	31.6	17.5	
Guilt	2.	61	4	8	123	3	199
		30.7	2.0	4.0	61.8	1.5	19.8
		19.5	19.0	30.8	20.4	7.5	
Fear	3.	142	9	4	206	18	379
		37.5	2.4	1.1	54.4	4.7	37.7
		45.4	42.9	15.4	34.1	45.0	
Joy, love	4.	1	1	1	43	10	56
		1.8	1.8	1.8	76.8	17.9	5.6
		.3	4.8	3.8	7.1	25.0	
Shame, spite	4.	4	0	1	41	2	48
		8.3	.0	2.1	85.4	4.2	4.8
		1.3	.0	3.8	6.8	5.0	
Column Total		313	21	26	604	40	1004
		31.2	2.1	2.6	60.2	4.0	100.0

$\chi^2 = 100.04$ $\alpha = .0001$ $df = 20$

Finally, calculations were made to determine how the expression of affects changed over the course of the sessions—in other words, whether there was any noticeable positive therapeutic effect (an increase in admission and sublimation). There is indeed a significant correlation between session and expression of affects. Dissociation decreases (a fact that is particularly evident in the eighteenth session), admission and sublimation increase. There is a break at the eighteenth session, which results from the introduction of the new topic of sexuality in sessions nineteen and twenty. In no psychotherapeutic method can one observe the steady growth of such indicators (this depends on theory and technique). This indicator also plays an important role in our case studies (tables 35–38); for statistical reasons it has been necessary to group several subcategories together in some instances.

TABLE 33
Expression of Affects/Class/Men

Expression of affects		Working 1.	Lower middle 2.	Middle 3.	Row total
Dissociation	1.	17	30	111	158
		10.8	19.0	70.3	36.0
		12.4	21.1	69.4	
Hesitation	2.	1	0	10	11
		9.1	.0	90.9	2.5
		.7	.0	6.3	
Displacement	3.	1	0	10	11
		9.1	.0	90.9	2.5
		.7	.0	6.3	
Admission	4.	112	110	28	250
		44.8	44.0	11.2	56.9
		81.8	77.5	17.5	
Sublimation	5.	6	2	1	9
		66.7	22.2	11.1	2.1
		4.4	1.4	.6	
Column Total		137	142	160	439
		31.2	32.3	36.4	100.0

$\chi^2 = 189.07$ $\qquad$ $\alpha = .0001$ $\qquad$ df = 10

4.3.1.7. The intensity of affective expression

The intensity of affective expression (whether verbal or nonverbal) is also an indicator of the admission and assimilation of feelings, in this instance in particular, of the intensity (3.10.2.4). Here, too, as in the previous categories, significant class- and sex-specific differences can be observed. Members of the middle class tend to remain neutral; members of the working class and lower middle class have a tendency to use violent speech and gestures. Women (with the exception of the lower middle class) are inevitably more violent in both speech and gesture, and the class-specific differences are considerably smaller, although still significant. Once again, this depends on the topic, and feelings are more likely to be revealed when discussing problems with illness and parents. Correlation with the course of the sessions shows a significant tendency up to the eighteenth session, with neutrality diminishing significantly and being replaced by violence (tables 39–41).

TABLE 34

EXPRESSION OF AFFECTS / CLASS / WOMEN

Expression of affects		Class			Row total
		Working 1.	Lower middle 2.	Middle 3.	
Dissociation	1.	13 6.7 12.4	42 21.6 29.0	139 71.6 31.2	194 27.9
Hesitation	2.	4 33.3 3.8	0 .0 .0	8 66.7 1.8	12 1.7
Displacement	3.	5 17.9 4.8	3 10.7 2.1	20 71.4 4.5	28 4.0
Admission	4.	74 17.7 70.5	87 20.8 60.0	258 61.6 58.0	419 60.3
Sublimation	6.	9 21.4 8.6	13 31.0 9.0	20 47.6 4.5	42 6.0
Column Total		105 15.1	145 20.9	445 64.0	695 100.0

$\chi^2 = 24.94$ $\alpha = .0016$ $df = 8$

4.3.1.8. Sex of intervention

In this category we are interested in whether interventions are made by one or both sexes and whether such interventions can be classified by topics (3.10.3.1).

Without differentiating among topics, one finds initially significant class- and sex-specific differences: men tend to intervene more with women and members of the lower middle class and middle class, while women tend to intervene with members of the working class. (This is connected with the fact that far more working-class men relate problems than working-class women).

When the individual topics are considered separately, the following areas are remarkable: medications (significant bisexual intervention), group activities (monosexual), children (bisexual), parents (bisexual as well as monosexual), relationships (bisexual). This can be explained by the fact that most of the contributions on the topics children, parents, and relationships were from women,

TABLE 35
EXPRESSION OF AFFECTS/SEX/WORKING CLASS

Expression of affects		Male 1.	Female 2.	Row total
		Sex		
Dissociation	1.	17 56.7 12.4	13 43.3 12.4	30 12.4
Hesitation	2.	1 20.0 .7	4 80.0 3.8	5 2.1
Displacement	3.	1 16.7 .7	5 83.3 4.8	6 2.5
Admission	4.	112 60.2 81.7	74 39.8 70.5	186 76.9
Sublimation	5.	6 40.0 4.4	9 60.0 8.6	15 6.2
Column Total		137 56.6	105 43.4	242 100.0

$\chi^2 = 12.61$ $\qquad$ $\alpha = .0274$ $\qquad$ df = 5

whereas men found it easier to intervene than to talk about themselves. As far as the topic medications was concerned, the other sex found it easier to assume a supporting role in each case. Finally, there were various sex-specific interests with regard to the topic of group activities, and these were also supported by interventions. (Tables 42 and 43 provide an overview of nature of intervention, sex of intervention, and topic.)

4.3.1.9. The nature of intervention

The result that there is no significant connection between narrative structure and intervention is particularly relevant. Interventions tend to correlate with the topic (table 43), not so much with formal presentation and class. This means that all patients receive the same treatment, regardless of the class-specific nature of the problem

TABLE 36

EXPRESSION OF AFFECTS/SEX/LOWER MIDDLE CLASS

Expression of affects		Male 1.	Female 2.	Row total
			Sex	
Dissociation	1.	30 41.7 21.1	42 58.3 29.0	72 25.1
Displacement	3.	0 0 .0	3 100.0 2.1	3 1.0
Admission	4.	110 55.8 77.5	87 44.2 60.0	197 68.6
Sublimation	5.	2 13.3 1.4	13 86.7 9.0	15 5.2
Column Total		142 49.5	145 50.5	287 100.0

$\chi^2 = 15.72$ $\qquad \alpha = .0013 \qquad$ df = 3

presentation. Sex is more likely to play a role in the nature of the intervention (table 44). There is thus no discrimination against working-class patients and women in this therapy.

The results in the category correspond to traditional stereotypes. These indicate that men tend to make interpretations and to intervene aggressively (using rejection and obstruction, for example), while women are more likely to respond with questions and analog problem presentations. However, the tremendous influence of the problem covered is evident when one considers the individual topics (3.10.3.2).

1. Contributions from women tend to be followed by questions, interpretations, consolation, and advice, contributions from men by rejection and problem presentations.
2. Men comment, interpret, support, advise, and reject more frequently than women, who mainly proffer questions and analog problem presentations.

TABLE 37
EXPRESSION OF AFFECTS/SEX/MIDDLE CLASS

Expression of affects		Male 1.	Female 2.	Row total
Dissociation	1.	112 44.6 70.0	139 55.4 31.2	251 41.5
Hesitation	2.	10 55.6 6.3	8 44.4 1.8	18 3.0
Displacement	3.	10 33.3 6.3	20 66.7 4.5	30 5.0
Admission	4.	27 9.5 16.9	258 90.5 58.0	285 47.1
Sublimation	5.	1 4.8 .6	20 95.2 4.5	21 3.5
Column Total		160 26.4	445 73.6	605 100.0

$\chi^2 = 100.06$ $\qquad$ $\alpha = 0.0001$ $\qquad$ $df = 5$

3. With the topic work, men mainly intervene, while women predominate with analog problem presentations; with the topic group metalevel, women ask considerably more questions; with the topic children, men interpret, comfort, and advise a great deal; with the topic relationships, men ask more questions than normal and interpret less. This is the only topic where women also interpret quite a lot and also display rejection (tables 43, 45).

4. The nature of the intervention has a significant effect on the patient's reaction ($\chi^2 = 341.78$, $\alpha = 0.0001$, $df = 48$). Analog problem presentations mainly produce obstructions; comments and questions produce insight and the description of new aspects; interpretations are obstructed or accepted, as are support and advice (help is often accepted with difficulty); obstructions are followed by massive conflict (table 46).

TABLE 38

Expression of Affects/Session

Expression of affects		1–4	5–8	9–12	13–17	18.	19.	20.	Row total
					Session				
Dissociation	1.	71 20.2 38.4	70 19.9 25.9	67 19.0 28.3	54 15.3 27.1	16 4.5 15.7	43 12.2 48.3	31 8.8 59.6	352 31.0
Hesitation	2.	6 26.1 3.2	8 34.8 3.0	1 4.3 .4	1 4.3 .5	1 4.3 1.0	0 .0 .0	6 26.1 11.5	23 2.0
Displacement	3.	5 12.8 2.7	7 17.9 2.6	9 23.1 3.8	9 23.1 4.5	3 7.7 2.9	5 12.8 5.6	1 2.6 1.9	39 3.4
Admission	4.	98 14.6 53.0	174 26.0 64.4	147 22.0 62.0	118 17.6 59.3	82 12.3 80.4	41 6.1 46.1	9 1.3 17.3	669 59.0
Sublimation	5.	5 9.8 2.7	11 21.6 4.1	13 25.5 5.5	17 33.3 8.5	0 .0 .0	0 .0 .0	5 9.8 9.6	51 4.5
Column Total		185 16.3	270 23.8	237 20.9	199 17.5	102 9.0	89 7.8	52 4.6	1134 100.0

$\chi^2 = 134.96$ $\alpha = .0001$ df = 30

TABLE 39

INTENSITY OF AFFECTIVE EXPRESSION/CLASS/MEN

Intensity of affective expression			Class			
			Working 1.	Lower middle 2.	Middle 3.	Row total
Verbal: Nonverbal: } Neutral		1.	21 12.0 15.3	29 16.6 20.4	125 71.4 78.1	175 39.9
Verbal: Violent Nonverbal: Neutral		2.	116 44.6 84.7	109 41.9 76.8	35 13.5 21.9	260 59.2
Verbal: Nonverbal: } Violent		3.	0 .0 .0	4 100.0 2.8	0 .0 .0	4 .9
Column Total			137 31.2	142 32.3	160 36.4	439 100.0

$\chi^2 = 161.31$ $\alpha = .001$ df = 4

TABLE 40

INTENSITY OF AFFECTIVE EXPRESSION/CLASS/WOMEN

Intensity of affective expression			Class			
			Working 1.	Lower middle 2.	Middle 3.	Row total
Verbal: Nonverbal: } Neutral		1.	22 9.6 21.0	51 22.4 35.2	155 68.0 34.8	228 32.8
Verbal: Violent Nonverbal: Neutral		2.	78 17.2 74.3	90 19.9 62.1	285 62.9 64.0	453 65.2
Verbal: Nonverbal: } Violent		3.	5 35.7 4.8	4 28.6 2.8	5 35.7 1.1	14 2.0
Column Total			105 15.1	145 20.9	445 64.0	695 100.0

$\chi^2 = 13.03$ $\alpha = .0111$ df = 4

TABLE 41
INTENSITY OF AFFECTIVE EXPRESSION/SESSION

Intensity of affective expression		1–4	5–8	9–12	13–17	18.	19.	20.	Row total
1. Verbal: } Neutral Nonverbal:		79 19.6 42.7	82 20.3 30.4	75 18.6 31.6	68 16.9 34.2	17 4.2 16.7	46 11.4 51.7	36 8.9 69.2	403 35.5
2. Verbal: Violent Nonverbal: Neutral		103 14.4 55.7	181 25.4 67.0	157 22.0 66.2	128 18.0 64.3	85 11.9 83.3	43 6.0 48.3	16 2.2 30.8	713 62.9
3. Verbal: } Violent Nonverbal:		3 16.7 1.6	7 38.9 2.6	5 27.8 2.1	3 16.7 1.5	0 .0 .0	0 .0 .0	0 .0 .0	18 1.6
Column Total		185 16.3	270 23.8	237 20.9	199 17.5	102 9.0	89 7.8	52 4.6	1134 100.0

$\chi^2 = 65.25$ df $= 12$ $\alpha = .0001$

TABLE 42

NATURE OF INTERVENTION/SEX OF INTERVENTION

Nature of intervention		Sex of intervention			Row total
		Male 1.	Female 2.	Mixed 3.	
None	0.	3 60.0 .6	1 20.0 .2	1 20.0 .9	5 .5
Commentary	1.	196 52.5 37.8	134 35.9 31.6	43 11.5 40.2	373 35.5
Question	2.	11 44.0 2.1	12 48.0 2.8	2 8.0 1.9	25 2.4
Analog problem presentation	3.	96 38.6 18.5	139 55.8 32.8	14 5.6 13.1	249 23.7
Interpretation	4.	76 54.7 14.6	54 38.8 12.7	9 6.5 8.4	139 13.2
Support	5.	56 47.1 10.8	41 34.5 9.7	22 18.5 20.6	119 11.3
Advice	6.	21 55.3 4.0	13 34.2 3.1	4 10.5 3.7	38 3.6
Obstruction	7.	50 64.9 9.6	20 26.0 4.7	7 9.1 6.5	77 7.3
Rejection	8.	10 40.0 1.9	10 40.0 2.4	5 20.0 4.7	25 2.4
Column Total		519 49.4	424 40.4	107 10.2	1050 100.0

$\chi^2 = 53.89$　　　　$\alpha = .0001$　　　　$df = 16$

4.3.1.10. Intervention by the therapist

The interventions by the therapist display only slight class- and sex-specific differences, which should be judged with caution because of the limited number of interventions (107). Questions tend to be put more to working-class patients (who are thus motivated to

TABLE 43

NATURE OF INTERVENTION/SEX OF INTERVENTION/TOPIC
SUMMARY OF THE RESULTS OF THE χ^2-TESTS OF INDIVIDUAL CALCULATIONS

	Topic							
Contact	Work	Medications	Group metalevel	Group activities	Illness	Children	Parents	Relationships
$\chi^2 = 7,13$ $\alpha = 0,01$ df $= 10$	$\chi^2 = 29,31$ $\alpha = 0,01$ df $= 16$	$\chi^2 = 9,89$ $\alpha = 0,6$ df $= 12$	$\chi^2 = 27,55$ $\alpha = 0,01$ df $= 12$	$\chi^2 = 12,61$ $\alpha = 0,3$ df $= 12$	$\chi^2 = 12,69$ $\alpha = 0,6$ df $= 16$	$\chi^2 = 42,91$ $\alpha = 0,01$ df $= 14$	$\chi^2 = 9,08$ $\alpha = 0,8$ df $= 14$	$\chi^2 = 44,03$ $\alpha = 0,01$ df $= 14$

TABLE 44

NARRATIVE STRUCTURE/NATURE OF INTERVENTION

Narrative structure		Nature of intervention								Row total
		Commentary 1.	Questions 2.	Analog problem presentation 3.	Interpretation 4.	Support 5.	Advice 6.	Obstruction 7.	Rejection 8.	
Narration	1.	166	13	98	53	45	21	30	11	437
		38.0	3.0	22.4	12.1	10.3	4.8	6.9	2.5	41.8
		44.5	52.0	39.4	38.1	37.8	55.3	39.0	44.0	
Scene	2.	95	7	77	38	39	8	20	3	287
		33.1	2.4	26.8	13.2	13.6	2.8	7.0	1.0	27.5
		25.5	28.0	30.9	27.3	32.8	21.1	26.0	12.0	
Circumstance	3.	112	5	74	48	35	9	27	11	321
		34.9	1.6	23.1	15.0	10.9	2.8	8.4	3.4	30.7
		30.0	20.0	29.7	34.5	29.4	23.7	35.1	44.0	
Column Total		373	25	249	139	119	38	77	25	1045
		35.7	2.4	23.8	13.3	11.4	3.6	7.4	2.4	100.0

$\chi^2 = 14.33$ $\alpha = .4253$ df = 14

TABLE 45

NATURE OF INTERVENTION/SEX

Nature of intervention		Sex		Row total
		Male 1.	Female 2.	
None	0.	46 51.7 10.5	43 48.3 6.2	89 7.8
Commentary	1.	128 34.3 29.2	245 65.7 35.3	373 32.9
Question	2.	4 16.0 .9	21 84.0 3.0	25 2.2
Analog problem presentation	3.	106 42.6 24.1	143 57.4 20.6	249 22.0
Interpretation	4.	42 30.2 9.6	97 69.8 14.0	139 12.3
Support	5.	45 37.8 10.3	74 62.2 10.6	119 10.5
Advice	6.	9 23.7 2.1	29 76.3 4.2	38 3.4
Obstruction	7.	40 51.9 9.1	37 48.1 5.3	77 6.8
Rejection	8.	19 76.0 4.3	6 24.0 .9	25 2.2
Column Total		439 38.7	695 61.3	1134 100.0

$\chi^2 = 44.57$ $\alpha = .0001$ df $= 8$

speak) than to lower-middle-class and middle-class patients, where therapists tend to interpret and reject. Men tend to be obstructed more than women. Interventions are not related to topic. Both male and female therapists lead the groups in an entirely constant manner. The appraisal of the therapists by the patients is dealt with in detail in the qualitative analysis of the in-depth interviews (6.4).

TABLE 46
NATURE OF INTERVENTION/REACTION OF PATIENTS

Nature of intervention		Reaction							Row total
		None 0.	Rejection 1.	Repetition 2.	New aspect 3.	Counter-question 4.	Conflict 5.	Insight 6.	
None	0.	1 1.1 100.0	32 36.0 9.4	11 12.4 9.0	9 10.1 3.6	4 4.5 17.4	2 2.2 2.5	30 33.7 9.4	89 7.8
Commentary	1.	0 .0 .0	50 13.4 14.7	30 8.0 24.6	124 33.2 49.4	9 2.4 39.1	11 2.9 13.7	149 39.9 46.9	373 32.9
Question	2.	0 .0 .0	0 .0 .0	1 4.0 .8	5 20.0 2.0	3 12.0 13.0	1 4.0 1.3	15 60.0 4.7	25 2.2
Analog problem presentation	3.	0 .0 .0	138 55.4 40.7	41 16.5 33.6	27 10.8 10.8	3 1.2 13.0	17 6.8 21.2	23 9.2 7.2	249 22.0
Interpretation	4.	0 .0 .0	35 25.2 10.3	10 7.2 8.2	32 23.0 12.7	2 1.4 8.7	20 14.4 25.0	40 28.8 12.6	139 12.3

	1	2	3	4	5	6	7	Row Total
5. Support	0 .0 .0	33 27.7 9.7	10 8.4 8.2	27 22.7 10.8	2 1.7 8.7	3 2.5 3.8	44 37.0 13.8	119 10.5
6. Advice	0 .0 .0	13 34.2 3.8	1 2.6 .8	8 21.1 3.2	0 .0 .0	3 7.9 3.8	13 34.2 4.1	38 3.4
7. Obstruction	0 .0 .0	28 36.4 8.3	14 18.2 11.5	16 20.8 6.4	0 .0 .0	16 20.8 20.0	3 3.9 .9	77 6.8
8. Rejection	0 .0 .0	10 40.0 2.9	4 16.0 3.3	3 12.0 1.2	0 .0 .0	7 28.0 8.8	1 4.0 .3	25 2.2
Column Total	1 .1	339 29.9	122 10.8	251 22.1	23 2.0	80 7.1	318 28.0	1134 100.0

$\chi^2 = 341.78$ df $= 48$ $\alpha = .0001$

Quantitative Analysis

TABLE 47

REACTION OF PATIENTS / CLASS / MEN

Reaction of patients		Class			Row total
		Working 1.	Lower middle 2.	Middle 3.	
Rejection	1.	17 13.6 12.4	61 48.8 43.0	47 37.6 29.4	125 28.5
Repetition	2.	29 46.0 21.2	15 23.8 10.6	19 30.2 11.9	63 14.4
New aspect	3.	27 45.0 19.7	24 40.0 16.9	9 15.0 5.6	60 13.7
Counterquestion	4.	0 .0 .0	3 100.0 2.1	0 .0 .0	3 .7
Conflict	5.	19 33.3 13.9	20 35.1 14.1	18 31.6 11.2	57 13.0
Insight	6.	45 34.4 32.8	19 14.5 13.4	67 51.1 41.9	131 29.8
Column Total		137 31.2	142 32.3	160 36.4	439 100.0

$\chi^2 = 69.71$ $\alpha = .0001$ $df = 10$

4.3.1.11. The reaction of patients

There are both significant class- and sex-specific differences with regard to the reactions of patients, and a dependence on the nature of the intervention is also detectable (tables 47, 48).

1. Male members of the working class repeat and provide new aspects; members of the lower middle class mainly pose counterquestions, obstruct, and argue; members of the middle class usually have the greatest insight. The marked readiness of the lower middle class to enter into conflict is particularly linked with their strong tendency to rationalize; the ease with which the middle class acquires insight is linked

TABLE 48
REACTION OF PATIENTS / CLASS / WOMEN

Reaction of patients		Class			Row total
		Working 1.	Lower middle 2.	Middle 3.	
None	0.	0 .0 .0	0 .0 .0	0 100.0 .2	1 .1
Rejection	1.	36 16.8 34.3	59 27.6 40.7	119 55.6 26.7	214 30.8
Repetition	2.	31 52.5 29.5	10 16.9 6.9	18 30.5 4.0	59 8.5
New aspect	3.	9 4.7 8.6	39 20.4 26.9	143 74.9 32.1	191 27.5
Counterquestion	4.	3 15.0 2.9	6 30.0 4.1	11 55.0 2.5	20 2.9
Conflict	5.	3 13.0 2.9	4 17.4 2.8	16 69.6 3.6	23 3.3
Insight	6.	23 12.3 21.9	27 14.4 18.6	137 73.3 30.8	187 26.9
Column Total		105 15.1	145 20.9	445 64.0	695 100.0

$\chi^2 = 99.19$ $\alpha = .0001$ $df = 12$

to their adaptation to situations of authority.

2. Working-class women repeat most; middle-class women have most insight but are also most ready to engage in conflict.

3. Generally speaking, men tend to enter into conflict, while women tend to acquire insight and introduce new aspects.

4. Repetition occurs particularly in the case of the topic illness, new aspects in the case of the topic parents, counterquestions in the case of the topic work. All the above-mentioned reactions are also typical of the topic relationships.

4.3.1.12. Topic of problem presentation in group therapy

The dependence of topic choice on class and sex has already been emphasized in detail. The general results are summarized here: members of the middle class tend to talk about children, parents, and relationships, while members of the working class prefer the topics contact and group metalevel (3.7).

Women deal with the topics relationships, parents, children, medications, and illness significantly more than men. This is completely in line with our assumptions on class- and sex-specific socialization (tables 49, 50).

4.3.2. Women relate, men report. . . .

Broken down individually, the results have confirmed most of the hypotheses but have also differentiated them in several respects.

1. For the first time it has been possible to give differentiated treatment to the factors of class and sex. Different priorities became apparent, depending on the category. It has proved absolutely essential to apply both categories at the same time, however. In this context it is particularly important that class-specific differences are smaller among women and even nonexistent with certain groups of topics. (This can be explained by the common features of female socialization.) At the same time, it was shown how essential it is to differentiate between topics.

2. The form of the narrative structure does not determine the nature of the intervention. This is more likely to depend on sex and topic. This means that problem presentations by patients from all classes receive equal treatment.

3. It is very surprising to find that working-class males are most likely to talk about metacommunicative problems, while at the same time, they have strategies of problem solving on hand. This contradicts all previous assertions on metacommunication as well as the assertion that members of the working class are restricted and unable to cope with the therapeutic situation because of the reflection of relationships required.

TABLE 49

Topic/Class

Class		Contact	Work	Medications	Group metalevel	Group activities	Illness	Children	Parents	Relationships	Row total
Working class	1.	23 9.5 43.4	26 10.7 15.7	14 5.8 23.7	23 9.5 43.4	17 7.0 14.7	59 24.4 31.9	13 5.4 16.9	23 9.5 16.0	44 18.2 15.7	242 21.3
Lower middle class	2.	10 3.5 18.9	53 18.5 31.9	19 6.6 32.2	10 3.5 18.9	39 13.6 33.6	38 13.2 20.5	15 5.2 19.5	19 6.6 13.2	84 29.3 29.9	287 25.3
Middle class	3.	20 3.3 37.7	87 14.4 52.4	26 4.3 44.1	20 3.3 37.7	60 9.9 51.7	88 14.5 47.6	49 8.1 63.6	102 16.9 70.8	153 25.3 54.4	605 53.4
Column Total		53 4.7	166 14.6	59 5.2	53 4.7	116 10.2	185 16.3	77 6.8	144 12.7	281 24.8	1134 100.0

$\chi^2 = 84.97$ $\alpha = .0001$ df = 16

TABLE 50

TOPIC/SEX

Sex		Contact	Work	Medications	Group metalevel	Group activities	Illness	Children	Parents	Relationships	Row total
							Topic				
Men	1.	33	86	19	32	67	87	28	12	75	439
		7.5	19.6	4.3	7.3	15.3	19.8	6.4	2.7	17.1	38.7
		62.3	51.8	32.2	60.4	57.8	47.0	36.4	8.3	26.7	
Women	2.	20	80	40	21	49	98	49	132	206	695
		2.9	11.5	5.8	3.0	7.1	14.1	7.1	19.0	29.6	61.3
		37.7	48.2	67.8	39.6	42.2	53.0	63.6	91.7	73.3	
Column Total		53	166	59	53	116	185	77	144	281	1134
		4.7	14.6	5.2	4.7	10.2	16.3	6.8	12.7	24.8	100.0

$\chi^2 = 132.36$ df = 8 $\alpha = .0001$

4. Women and members of the working class are more emotional and spontaneous than the members of other classes.

5. Lower-middle-class women are conspicuous for their over-adaptation and high degree of control. This corresponds with some sociolinguistic theories, which, however, have rarely been subjected to close empirical examination, as they have normally been produced as speculative byproducts (2.4.1.3).

6. Members of the middle class only admit their emotions later in the course of the therapy.

7. Women of all classes consistently introduce their life histories.

8. Explicit linguistic proof was provided for assumptions from psychotherapeutic theory (relating to affectivity and defense mechanisms), and empirical evidence was provided of their dependence on the class and sex of the patient and the topic of the problem presented.

4.3.3. Predictions

With the help of Goodman's log-linear model (1972), it was possible to calculate the dependence and correlation of one variable on two others, making predictions possible. No conventional correlations could be produced, as we were dealing with qualitative parameters. These results represent an initial attempt to describe linguistic variation explicitly. Three correlation models were made: (1) narrative structure/class/sex; (2) defense mechanisms/topic/class/sex; and (3) reaction of patients/nature of intervention/sex.

Narrative structure/class/sex

Several results are presented below by way of illustration. It is not necessary to present every possible combination of the variables in each case. The calculation was effected with the programming language ECTA. In layman's terms we calculated the relationships of variables to one another, or odds, such as 1:4 for the probability of working-class males using the text type scene. An exact description of this correlation model for qualitative parameters (without standard distribution) can be found in Goodman (1972) (tables 51, 52).

TABLE 51

NARRATIVE STRUCTURE / CLASS / SEX
PREDICTABLE RELATIONSHIPS BETWEEN THREE VARIABLES

V1	V3 V2	M (1) WC (1)	LMC (2)	MC (3)	F (2) WC (1)	LMC (2)	MC (3)
Narration		19 21.61	58 55.95	80 79.46	31 28.39	74 76.06	206 206.54
Circumstance		34 31.39	62 64.06	72 72.54	22 24.61	54 51.94	113 112.46
Σ		53	120	152	53	128	319
Ωij		0.688 1	0.873 1	1.095 1	1.153 1	1.464 1	1.836 1
P (Narration)%		40.77	46.61	52.27	53.57	59.42	64.75
P (Circumstance) = 1-P% (Narration)		59.23	53.39	47.73	46.43	40.58	35.25

LEGEND:

M = M(ale)/F = F(emale)/WC = W(orking) C(lass)/LMC = L(ower) M(iddle) C(lass)/MC = M(iddle) C(lass)/V = V(ariable)

$V1$ = variable$_1$ = narrative structure (for statistical reasons, only two subcategories are selected; see table 52).

$V2$ = variable$_2$ = class (WC = working class, LMC = lower middle class, MC = middle class).

$V3$ = variable$_3$ = sex (M = male, F = female).

The first three lines contain the actual and expected values.

Ω = omega represents the ratio (odds), i.e., the relationship of the value to one another. Probability P (N) results from $\dfrac{\Omega ij}{1 + \Omega ij}$ (e.g. $\dfrac{0.688}{1.688} = 0.4077 = 40.77\% =$ P (N) for working-class males).

The predictable probabilities of the occurrence of narration or circumstance for a given class and given sex of speaker are listed under P (N) and P (C).

Defense mechanisms/topic/class/sex

The relationship between four variables was calculated in this model. The variables had to be condensed from the original coding system as the model would otherwise have become too complicated. We were thus able to calculate the systematic dependence of the occurrence of certain defense mechanisms (linguistically operationalized) on the class and sex of the patient and on the text topic (table 53).

TABLE 52

NARRATIVE STRUCTURE / SEX / CLASS
PREDICTABLE RELATIONSHIPS BETWEEN THREE VARIABLES

V1	V3 V2	M WC	M MC	F WC	F MC
Narration (1)		19 21.93	58 55.07	31 28.07	74 76.93
Scene (2)		84 83.01	22 22.99	52 52.99	17 16.01
Circumstance (3)		34 32.06	62 63.94	22 23.94	54 52.06
Σ		137	142	105	145
Ω (1 → 2)		0.264 / 1	2.395 / 1	0.530 / 1	4.805 / 1
P (1) %		20.90	70.55	34.63	82.77
P (2) %		79.10	29.45	65.37	17.23
Ω (1 → 3)		0.684 / 1	0.861 / 1	1.173 / 1	1.478 / 1
P (1) %		40.62	46.27	53.97	59.64
P (3) %		59.38	53.73	46.03	40.36

LEGEND:

V1 = variable$_1$ = narrative structure (with three subcategories).

V2 = variable$_2$ = class (in this instance only working class [WC] and middle class [MC]).

V3 = variable$_3$ = sex (M = male, F = female).

When Ω (1 → 2) the relationship between scene and narration is calculated, when Ω (1 → 3) that between circumstance and narration (for statistical reasons, one point of reference must be kept constant).

If the class and sex of the speaker are known, the predictable probabilities can now be read off (e.g., P = 0.8 that a male working-class speaker will produce a scenic problem presentation).

The significant results calculated (4.3.1) are again reflected here.

As is already obvious from the other results, here, too, we find confirmation of the tendency for the working class and middle class to diverge less for women than for men. The dependence on the topic is also clearly apparent.

The weighting of the individual variables also becomes clearer when this differentiated method is used. The occurrence of the defense mechanisms projection and turning against the self is

TABLE 53
Class/Sex/Topic/Defense Mechanisms
Predictable Relationships Between the Variables

Sex V4	M						F					
Class V3	WC			MC			WC			MC		
Topic V2	I	II	III	I	II	III	I	II	III	I	II	III
Defense Mechanisms V1												
Rationalization (1)	25,5 / 25,46	31,5 / 31,21	3,5 / 3,84	43,5 / 43,54	5,5 / 5,79	55,5 / 55,16	8,5 / 8,54	3,5 / 3,80	11,5 / 11,16	48,5 / 48,46	30,5 / 30,20	91,5 / 91,48
Regression (2)	31,5 / 31,99	17,5 / 17.06	4,5 / 4,45	11,5 / 11,01	0,5 / 0,94	4,5 / 4,55	6,5 / 6,01	5,5 / 5,94	40,5 / 40,55	22,5 / 22,99	47,5 / 47,06	79,5 / 79,45
Projection (3)	2,5 / 2,07	4,5 / 4,77	0,5 / 0,66	7,5 / 7,93	0,5 / 0,23	3,5 / 3,34	0,5 / 0,93	1,5 / 1,23	3,5 / 3,34	8,5 / 8,07	1,5 / 1,77	6,5 / 6,66
Turning against the self (4)	3,5 / 3,48	0,5 / 0,96	0,5 / 0,05	2,5 / 2,52	0,5 / 0,04	0,5 / 0,95	2,5 / 2,52	1,5 / 1,04	2,5 / 2,95	3,5 / 3,48	0,5 / 0,96	17,5 / 17,05
Σ	63	54	9	65	7	64	18	12	58	83	80	195
Ω (1 → 2)	$\frac{0,8}{1}$	$\frac{1,83}{1}$	$\frac{0,86}{1}$	$\frac{3,95}{1}$	$\frac{6,16}{1}$	$\frac{12,12}{1}$	$\frac{1,42}{1}$	$\frac{0,64}{1}$	$\frac{0,28}{1}$	$\frac{2,11}{1}$	$\frac{0,64}{1}$	$\frac{1,15}{1}$

P (1) (RAT) %	44,31	64,66	46,32	79,81	86,03	92,38	58,69	39,01	21,58	67,82	39,09	53,51
P (2) (REGR) %	55,69	35,34	53,68	20,19	13,97	7,62	41,31	60,99	78,42	32,18	60,91	46,49
Ω (3 → 4)	$\frac{0,59}{1}$	$\frac{4,97}{1}$	$\frac{13,2}{1}$	$\frac{3,15}{1}$	$\frac{5,75}{1}$	$\frac{0,37}{1}$	$\frac{1,18}{1}$	$\frac{1,13}{1}$	$\frac{2,32}{1}$	$\frac{1,84}{1}$	$\frac{0,39}{1}$	
P (3) (PRO) %	37,3	83,25	93	75,89	85,19	77,86	26,96	54,18	53,1	69,87	64,84	28,01
P (4) (TURN) %	62,7	16,75	7	24,11	14,81	22,14	73,04	45,82	46,9	30,13	35,16	71,99

LEGEND:

Defense Mechanisms: rationalization (RAT), regression (REGR), projection (PRO), turning against the self (TURN) = (V1)

Topic was divided into three groups (V2): (1) contact, work, group metalevel, group activities (I); (2) medications, illness (II); (3) children, parents, relationships (III)

Class: working class (WC) and middle class (MC) = V3

Sex: male (M) and female (F) = V4

In the interests of clarity, the relationships and probabilities of [Ω (1 → 3), Ω (1 → 4)] are not listed. These values can easily be calculated from the absolute and expected frequencies given in the table, however. For example, the table gives the probability of the occurrence of rationalization in the case of a middle-class man with topic group I as P = 0.7981. A second example: P = 0.7199 for the occurrence of turning against the self in the case of a middle-class woman with topic group III.

strongly dependent on the text topic. The factor of class is of primary relevance (more so than sex), except in the case of the third group of topics, children, parents, and relationships. It is therefore possible to make much more accurate predictions on the basis of this calculation.

Sex/nature of intervention/reaction of patients

In this case the reaction of the patient is the dependent variable, which, on the basis of the results in 4.3.1.11, is distributed mainly according to sex. Once again, the formulation of the categories had to be condensed in order to enable us to make forecasts (table 54).

In this correlation model, the differences are not as marked as it seemed after the first statistical computation. The factors of class and topic obviously have a decisive effect.

TABLE 54
SEX/NATURE OF INTERVENTION/REACTION OF PATIENTS
PREDICTABLE RELATIONSHIPS BETWEEN THE VARIABLES

V3		M		F	
V1	V2	I	II	I	II
Rejection		90	56	117	60
Conflict (1)		92,25	53,75	114,75	62,25
Repetition		44	28	70	51
New aspect (2)		41,75	30,25	72,25	48,75
Σ		134	84	187	111
Ω (1 → 2)		2,21	1,78	1,59	1,28
		1	1	1	1
P (1) %		68,84	63,99	61,36	56,08
P (2) %		31,16	36,01	38,64	43,92

LEGEND:

Reaction (V1): rejection, conflict (1); repitition, new aspect (2)

Nature of Intervention (V2): analog problem presentation, support, advice (I); interpretation, rejection, obstruction (II)

Sex (V3): male (M), female (F)

In this case, for example, the probability of the occurrence of rejection or conflict with a male patient following an intervention of group I (support, advice, analog problem presentation) can be read off as P = 0.6884.

The results of sociopsychological variation (see also Wodak and Schulz 1984) presented here enable us to predict the occurrence of variables such as narrative structure, defense mechanisms, and re-action under exactly defined conditions. One category was deliberately chosen from each group for this calculation (3.10). More exact weightings of the factors of class, sex, and topic are then possible. These predictions are of particular relevance for practical application: on the basis of such explicit linguistic analyses and predictions, therapists can forecast (with an exactly determinable degree of probability) the way in which patients will behave. This, in particular, may well be a decisive aid in practical therapeutic work and may also prove a valuable addition to the theory of therapeutic technique.

4.4. Case studies

Six case studies have been selected (patients 2, 3, 7, 10, 13, 16) to illustrate the therapeutic effect (2.5). It was not the "brightest" or "best behaved" patients who were selected, but, rather, those who made regular contributions, thus allowing not only qualitative analysis but also quantitative comparison of the sessions.

The most important indicators of therapeutic effect (this has already been theoretically derived in the section on the individual categories) are alterations in the narrative structure (transition from circumstantial reports to narrations or scenes, or to a new, mixed text type; see 5.5), in the elaboration of problems (acceptance of strategies for problem solving) (3.10.1.3, 4.3.1.3), in the defense mechanisms (reduction of rationalizations, turning against the self, and so on) (3.10.2.1, 4.3.1.4), in affective expression (admission of emotions) (3.10.2.3, 4.3.1.6), and finally, in reaction patterns (increased introduction of new aspects and more insight) (3.10.3.4, 4.3.1.11). Several indicators are quantified for each patient by way of example. At the same time, the selected passages (or references to texts already reproduced) are designed to illustrate qualitative changes in the presentation of one and the same problem. Several problem presentations were also selected which reflect the patient's positive self-assessment particularly strongly. Self-assessment is dealt with in greater detail in the analysis of the focused interviews (6.4).

Middle-class woman (patient 2)

This patient's main problem was her divorce. She had to learn to cope with the new situation and to fend for her three children alone. She came to the crisis center with an acute nervous breakdown and severe depression. The indicators problem solving, affectivity, and expression of affects clearly show positive changes, as does the interview.

Defense mechanisms/session:

$$\chi^2 = 12.3$$
$$df = 6$$
$$\alpha = 0$$

The patient rationalizes significantly less.

Affective expression/session:

$$\chi^2 = 7.9$$
$$df = 4$$
$$\alpha = 0$$

The patient dissociates significantly less.

To begin with the patient was in a very bad state (text 40). In the course of two years, she became a central figure in the group, assuming a motherly role. She finally learned to organize her free time together with the members of the group, began to work, and overcame her grief at the breakup of her marriage and the loss of her husband. She was able to fight out her divorce, give her aggressions free rein, and devote herself to her children again. She was touchingly concerned about new members of the group and spoke out for the liberation of women in view of her own unfortunate experiences (texts 31, 39).

Text 61. Session 18, patient 2 (W). Subject: support.

M: Yes, I must do that. But I find that really difficult. And I'll just have to learn to do it. I'll have to learn to live again. In fact I'll have to learn to live.

W: I think so, too—you will find a person who will be to you—of course, they'll not be able to give you what you've got behind you, but if you could find a person who would be kind to you, who could give you a home in some way or at least help you a lot in these things.

Text 62. Session 19, patient 2 (W1).

W1: I just wanted to add something, because you pulled me to pieces because I had bad luck with my husband. It's just that one should look after one's own interests in life more, stand on one's own two feet, and not just be dependent on one's parents, and now, when somebody says, well, she has a husband who earns well, that's fine, and she has her security anyway, but one should really look after oneself, find out for oneself what one—

W2: I don't want to depend on parents, anyway!

W1: One must be an egoist; in the present times, one must be a sort of egoist, because when things go wrong, one must stand on one's own two feet and see to it that one can earn one's way; then nobody will question you. I never approached marriage with that attitude, but I have paid for it now after twenty years, and now my attitude is that I will never again be dependent on a man.

Middle-class woman (patient 3)

This patient suffered from never effecting a complete break from her parents, who tyrannized her greatly (text 8). She suffered from severe depression, had attempted suicide, and had been an inpatient at the psychiatric clinic for a considerable length of time.

Her parental problems were closely associated with her job, as she was employed in the family business. This patient's problem was dealt with in the section on problem discussion in the group (3.8.5). At the time she was very deeply involved. Text A and text B (assimilation and solution of family conflict) indicate the tremendous change that this patient had undergone. These two texts are reproduced and subjected to qualitative analysis in chapter 5 (5.4, 5.5).

Problem solving, defense mechanisms, and reaction thus illustrate the far-reaching change, as does the interview, which is dealt with later (6.2).

Problem solution/session:

$$\chi^2 = 31.28$$
$$df = 6$$
$$\alpha = 0$$

The patient finds significantly more solutions.

Defense mechanisms/session:

$$\chi^2 = 28.56$$
$$df = 12$$
$$\alpha = 0$$

The patient rationalizes significantly less.
   Intensity of affective expression/session:

$$\chi^2 = 10.78$$
$$df = 6$$
$$\alpha = 0$$

The patient is significantly more emotional toward the end of the therapy.
   Her role in the group also changed considerably. To begin with, she suffered from feelings of inferiority; a year later she often embodied hope by describing her successes in the group (5.5).

Working-class woman (patient 7)

This patient came to the group with serious parental and relationship conflicts as well as psychosomatic symptoms. She was also susceptible to severe depression, nourished mainly by feelings of guilt about her aging mother living in the country. At the same time, she was waging a struggle for emancipation with and against her husband. She wanted to go out to work, while he wanted her to stay at home (texts 28, 46). The conflict began to be resolved in the fifth session (a year later). She wept through an entire session, and the problem came to light. At the end of the second year, she had found a job and had increased self-assurance and confidence; she also viewed her mother more objectively. She, too (like patient 2), became a central figure in the group. She comforted and helped many members, even in their everyday lives (a part of her symptom, yes, she was too helpful, motherly, masochistic already), and was always present for recreational activities. She could also manage her children better.

Problem solving/session:

$$\chi^2 = 7.7$$
$$df = 3$$
$$\alpha = 0$$

The patient finds significantly more solutions.
Defense mechanisms/session:

$$\chi^2 = 13.64$$
$$df = 6$$
$$\alpha = 0$$

The patient rationalizes significantly less, and her turning against the self has also decreased.

Lower-middle-class female patient (patient 10)

This patient came to the group in an acute relationship crisis. She had been divorced for a long time and had fended for her children alone (one of them was handicapped). Although she had a nice companion, she wanted to break off the relationship even at the risk of being entirely on her own again. The group helped her survive this period. At the same time, she was having difficulties in her career, where she felt overtaxed. She solved her problems comparatively quickly, her hypercorrect language being replaced by much more spontaneous affective expression.
Affective expression/session:

$$\chi^2 = 9.56$$
$$df = 3$$
$$\alpha = 0$$

The sample texts provide evidence of the patient's process of emancipation (texts 12, 48).

Middle-class man (patient 13)

This patient needed a very long time before opening up to the group. For almost a year he acted as counselor and comforter, assuming the group role of the superego, of bolstering morale, and giving the impression of the stereotype of a decent civil servant. His long-suppressed problem finally came to light, however: he was married to a foreigner who had been unable to cope with the move to Vienna. He also had a psychically unstable daughter who took drugs. The patient was uncertain whether he should try to save the marriage or seek a divorce. The group showed great involvement in this problem. The important change in the patient was his acquisition of the ability to suffer openly and to learn to solve problems. There are changes in both problem solving and reaction.

Narrative structure/session:

$$\chi^2 = 11.83$$
$$df = 2$$
$$\alpha = 0$$

The patient changes from circumstance to narration.

Problem solving/session:

$$\chi^2 = 22.77$$
$$df = 2$$
$$\alpha = 0$$

The patient finds significantly more solutions.

Reaction/session:

$$\chi^2 = 34.10$$
$$df = 3$$
$$\alpha = 0$$

The patient replies significantly more frequently.

Text 63. Session 20, patient 13 (male).

M: I'd like that, and my wife has also talked about it, but the problem for me is by no means solved. Then it starts all over again, with her finding friends here, her getting to know people here who like her and whom she can also like—that is, I think, the difficult problem, even if she comes back, that would still . . .

Text 64. Session 20, patient 13 (M).

M: Of course I have some feelings of guilt, because I have not made any decision in such an important situation for myself, for my wife, and for our marriage, actually because I am afraid to.

W: Well, I mean that rather now [inaudible].

M: On the contrary, it has been a great help to me, the fact that I have said it myself at all. I have been aware of the problem for a very long time now. And you have helped me to say it out loud. That was the help you gave me.

Working-class man (patient 16)

This patient underwent an astonishing change in his symptoms and in his life. To begin with, he was still severely depressed and had terrible nightmares. He became more self-assured, began a new job (as a male nurse), tried out alternative ways of life (living with other patients), broke out of his difficult marriage, and in spite of his social improvement, did not lose sight of the fact that he came from the working class. On the contrary, this is a clear example of the fact that therapy does not mean *adaptation* in the sense so often assumed. A stable and balancing identity seems assured in this instance. Text samples illustrate the change even more clearly, particularly the acquisition of metacommunicative abilities (texts 4, 24, 26, 32, 43, 47).

Problem solving/session:

$$\chi^2 = 18.03$$
$$df = 3$$
$$\alpha = 0$$

Significantly more problem solutions occur toward the end of the therapy.

Affective expression/session:

$$\chi^2 = 7.9$$
$$df = 4$$
$$\alpha = 0$$

The patient admits to significantly more emotions.

From the role of the young (but very amusing) failure, the patient assumes a new group role: the role of adviser, the individual who has already been through a lot, the experienced and cured patient. (I shall subsequently examine the rather unfortunate position of some‾working-class members of the group, who play what could be euphemistically referred to as the clown's role; see 6.4, 6.5.)

4.5. Summary

A considerable therapeutic effect has been demonstrated in these small qualitative and quantitative case studies, either through changes in indicators or through the self-assessment of the patients themselves. This information will be supplemented by the interviews (6.4). The requirement of anonymity prevents me from going into the case studies in great detail, yet they do give particular insight into the complexity of the group events. Each patient develops differently against the background of his unique life history (2.3.4). Tendencies may, however, be similar, thus making it possible to forecast development. Conflicts become transparent and predictable. Each of the patients introduced here reaches another stage in his development and experiences his ups and downs. Therapy can never be regarded as a uniformly rising curve, but as a continuous up-and-down process with several level plateaus. In chapter 5, the limits of quantitative analysis must therefore be plumbed to enable us to include self-assessment in the qualitative analysis of the interviews (with both patients and therapists), thus rounding off the study (6.4, 6.5).

5
The Limits of Quantitative Analysis

5.1. Introduction

Quantitative analysis has verified most of the hypotheses and brought to light—in a tentative form—previously unknown facts. The results on the weighting of the variables of class and sex are of particular importance, as is the successful proof of the therapeutic effect (4.3, 4.4).

A great deal was achieved with the aid of quantitative methods, and important correlations were calculated and used to test hypotheses. Nevertheless, these did not provide an adequate means of recording the complexity, variety, and uniqueness of the therapeutic process. The following factors were not explicitly dealt with:

1. the session context of problem presentations;
2. the context of each problem presentation (what happened immediately before and after);
3. the uniqueness of every session and every problem presentation;
4. the levels of meaning of problem presentations (analysis of the unconscious content);
5. the motives of the patients in presenting a problem and in the subsequent treatment of it;
6. the relevance of problem presentations in a therapeutic context;
7. the nonverbal level.

In section 5.2 I shall go on to include several of the factors listed above in the light of a detailed qualitative analysis of two problem presentations, thus illustrating the three-level model (2.3).

5.2. Qualitative methods of text analysis

Previous analysis of therapeutic communication (and even of communication in other everyday situations) has been mainly qualitative (1.3). This has been because, on the one hand, of the explorative nature of these investigations, which have usually been based on limited linguistic corpora (Martens 1974; Frankenberg 1976), and, on the other hand, because of the nature of the material. Colloquial language is diverse and full of vague meanings and can only be interpreted in the light of the overall context and a large amount of background knowledge, which the researcher acquires by participation.

Such analysis must of necessity remain subjective, being based on everyday knowledge and on internalized values.

As we have already seen in the theoretical considerations (2.3), therapeutic communication is characterized by its particular complexity, and the vague and diverse meanings acquire particular relevance in this situation. This very complexity, however, can be adequately qualitatively analyzed because of the restrictedness of the situation and because of the specific setting. Psychotherapeutic theories offer a framework of categories suitable for the description of deeper levels of meaning (2.3.3). In the following analysis of two problem presentations, I shall therefore be proceeding from the categories introduced in 3.10, which also allow us to establish a reference to the entire context of the session and to the motivational and affective structure of the speaker. A detailed utterance-by-utterance analysis of the problem presentations is also intended to illustrate the linguistic categories (3.9).

In concord with the "objective hermeneutics" of Oevermann and his colleagues (1979:352 ff.), I am of the opinion that "assessing the validity of an interpretation is mainly a function of the explicitness of the criteria used" (p. 387).

For this reason the explicit introduction and definition of the categories used were particularly important. These are not simply applied to the text, however, but are used heuristically, their suitability being tested in tiny steps (p. 392). An attempt is made to extract as many meanings as possible with regard to the overdetermination of social interactions, as proposed in psychotherapy (there is never a single motive or one meaning for speech acts; there is instead a variety of often-conflicting attitudes and impulses that precede actions).

In view of the fact that we are dealing here with the text class of problem presentation, there seems to be justification for the use of the linguistic categories introduced in 3.9 and 3.10. Speech-act analysis is applied only to the interventions and reactions—in other words, to typical dialogue. Even the greatest proponents of speech-act analysis, such as Wunderlich, admit that in the case of complex turns (such as problem presentations) "speech act theory is not able to contribute anything significantly new. In this instance the analyst must largely make use of primary syntactic and semantic methods" (Wunderlich 1979:301 ff.).

The problems of allocating individual speech acts to categories of speech-act analysis are considerable even with simple turns (Ballmer 1979:247 ff.). Wunderlich (1979:321 ff.) mentions six problems that must necessarily occur in the application of speech-act analysis. The problems of delimitation, identification, and classification are most important. For this reason, only clearly defined speech-act categories are applied in the classification of interventions and reactions of patients. They are therefore allocated to categories using Wunderlich's classification (1976:175 ff.) and Labov and Fanshel's taxonomy of "actions" in a therapeutic situation which are realized by "speech acts" (1977:59 ff.).

In contrast to some analyses of therapeutic communication (Klann 1979:135 ff.; Frankenberg 1976; Goeppert and Goeppert 1975), it is not my intention to mix up categories relating to different levels of communication and different perspectives (sociological, linguistic, pragmatic, psychoanalytical). Instead, each level of meaning in the three-level model will be placed in a separate frame. (Linguistic, psychoanalytical, and sociological categories were introduced, their linguistic manifestation demonstrated in 3.10.)

The theoretical considerations of 3.9.3 will be applied in the analysis of the text structure of problem presentation. In this respect the present analysis differs from previous investigations of complex turns (from the "classical" Labov and Waletzky schema [1967] and its elaborations, from Norman and Rumelhart's event model [1975] and Kallmeyer and Schütze's compulsive moves [1976]).

The application of linguistic categories seems imperative in view of the corpus and borders on other "purely" hermeneutic interpretations of therapeutic sessions (Beutin 1972; Pagès 1974; Slater 1978).

5.3. Technical information

The description of the nonverbal level is only an outline and is based on my own impressions of the session, which were noted down. Comments provide additional important information during the verbalization of the text (actions of members of the group, tone of voice). The texts were transcribed using the method of Gumperz and Herasimschuk (1972), as well as that of Ehlich and Switalla (1976:89 ff.) (3.7.3). Each contribution is defined as a unit (turn) with the change of speaker. Both texts come from the same female (patient 3), whose problems have already been dealt with in detail in a case study (4.4). In contrast to the qualitative analysis in Wodak-Leodolter (1977:46 ff.), the latent level of meaning is not analyzed using linguistic categories (such as that of indirect speech act).

I have already mentioned elsewhere that it is impossible to describe this level using speech-act analysis (2.3.2.1). The topic of both texts is the same problem encountered by a female patient: it is the patient's extremely difficult and disturbed relationship with her parents, with her father in particular. The second presentation of this problem in group therapy was recorded exactly a year after the first and shows the change in the patient particularly well. The qualitative analysis is therefore intended not only to illustrate the technique of interpretation and discuss the difficulties and limits of quantification but also and above all to prove the hypothesis of the therapeutic effect.

5.4. Text A: The problem is acute[1]
5.4.1. Text A

1 F: *Wenn irgendein, eben so ein Problem in einem steckt, da geht's am*
       If there's some—well if you have a problem, you feel
       [door opens, a woman enters, sound of chairs being moved]

2   *so, dass man, dass ma so beinander ist, dass man gar net glaubt*
       so awful, you just wouldn't believe it,

3   *und dass man mit dem Problem z.B. net fertig geworden ist,*
       and that you haven't managed to cope with the problem. For example,

4   *z.B. ja—ich hab g'sagt, es geht ma gut—letztes Mal—dass es so, also*
       for example, yes—I already said, everything's fine—last time—that it was;

5   *ich bin wieder zu ruhig, obwohl—aber, das Problem, was in einem Menschen*

I am too calm again, although—but the problem of what is inside you,

6   *drinnen steckt, dass, was ma mit der Geburt mitkriegt, oder wie einen*
what you have in you from birth on, or how

7   *die Eltern erzogen haben oder—I wāss net, wie ich da heute sagen soll, aber—*
your parents bring you up or—I don't know how I should say this today, but—

8   *bled, dass das gerade heute aufgenommen wird, i hab mit meinem Vater*
silly, that this is being recorded, today of all days. I talked to my father,

9   *gesprochen, also er gibt mir immer die Schuld, also, dass ich*
and he always blames me, and after all [cough]

10   *schliesslich und endlich erst dreiund dreissig Jahre alt bin; i kann—es geht heut*
I am only thirty-three years old; I can—I can't do it

11   *net.*
today.

12 M: *No redens aus!*
No, finish what you were saying!

13 F: *I red z'viel.*
I talk too much.

14 M: *I red ā viel.*
I talk a lot, too!

15 F: *Na, aber, na i wāss schon, dass i net a Stunde jetzt red—aber aber—dass*
No, well, I know I haven't been talking for hours, but, but—

16   *i halt net so viel mitgemacht hab, wie er. Dass i net im Krieg war, dafür*
I haven't been through as much as him. It's not my fault that

17   *kann i ja nix, i kann ja nix dafür, dass i erst so alt bin und dass i*
I wasn't in the war; I can't help being as old as I am and that I—

18   *bis jetzt—no kā Krieg war, na? Oder, bei uns ist es so, wir haben einen*
that there's been no war so far. In our case we had a

19   *Familienbetrieb und er hält mir eben vor, dass er—also gestern hab'ma*
family business and he reproaches me that he—only yesterday we

20   *g'sprochen—i möcht das nur zu Ende bringen noch—telefoniert hab'ma—*

talked—I'd just like to get this over with—we spoke on the
phone

21 *ganz nett, ruhig ang'rufen, und dann ist das immer—und also, er
hält*
quite nicely, all calm, and then it is always—and so he
accuses me,

22 *mir vor, er mänt, er hätte vor zehn Jahren in Pension gehen
können,*
he says he could have retired ten years ago,

23 *konnte aber nicht gehen, weil ich krank war, also seit zwölf
Jahren die*
but couldn't because I was ill, as for twelve years I've had

24 *Depressionen hab, und i mān, des halt er mir immer vor. Er
sagt, "Ja, wenn*
depressions, and he never lets me forget it. He says, "Yes, if

25 *Du net krank gewesen wärst, da waret i schon in Pension und
kriegert*
you hadn't been ill, I would already have retired and would get
my—"

26 *jedes Monat mei—also—was er halt von der Pension kriegt,
net—*
you know, whatever he gets from his pension insurance, every
month.

27 *vielleicht wirkt das gar nicht so, wenn ich das so erzähle, aber in*
Perhaps that doesn't sound much, as I tell it to you, but inside

28 *mir, also—kann gar net reden drüber—so hab i mi
aufg'regt, den*
me, I can't even talk about it. I got so excited that I

29 *Hörer hab i hing'haut, also, und da sagt er, "Ja, die
Bekannten, die*
threw down the receiver, and then he said, "Yes, our friends,
the one

30 *ma haben, der is schon zehn Jahr, der is scho zwei und zwanzig
Jahr"—sag i—"Erzähl*
has already been retired ten years, the other twenty-two years,"
and I say, "Don't

31 *ma kan Blödsinn, der is—wäss i—achtund sechzig Jahr und
kann net jetzt schon*
talk rubbish, he's only—I don't know—sixty-eight years old and
can't have

32 *zwei und zwanzig Jahr in Penison—kann nicht sein." Aber i
mein, i hab des schon*
been retired for twenty-two years." But I think I have already

33   *abgebaut, in mir ja, so wie Sie das letzte Mal erklärt haben, Ihr*
      Vater
      got rid of that, as you said last time, your father,

34   *net—i wäss net—i glaub, Sie waren das, ja? Sie sollen so viel*
      yes—I don't know—I think it was you? They say you smoke
      such a lot,

35   *rauchen und die Diät, net, also—er immer wieder an mich*
      heran—also,
      and the diet, and so on—he always comes to me, you see,

36   *mit, wie er halt mänt, also und so; i kann ihn nit amal mehr*
      sehen, obwohl
      and as he says, and so; I can't stand the sight of him any more,
      although

37   *er net schlecht is, ja; er tut alles für mich, er war immer für mi*
      he's not bad; he does everything for me, he has always been
      there for me;

38   *da und—i hab schon amal g'sagt, i bin net zwölf Jahr zum Arzt*
      'gangen und
      and I said to him once, I haven't been going to the doctor for
      twelve years, and

39   *wenn i eing'stellt wäre, i bringert meinen Vater um, i halt des*
      nimmer
      if I had a job, I'd kill my father. I just can't stand it any more,

40   *aus, das Seelische, i hab so drüber nach'denkt, hab i von ihm—*
      Jahrzehnte
      this mental—I thought about it, he drilled it into me for
      decades:

41   *des eindrillt 'kriegt; "Zuerst denken, na zuerst schalten—zuerst*
      denken, schalten,
      "First think, then act—first think, then act,

42   *dann sprechen." Also so hab i des immer. Wenn i den Mund*
      aufg'macht hab,
      then speak." That's what I always got. Whenever I opened my
      mouth,

43   *hab i immer, "zuerst denken, dann schalten, dann sprechen." I*
      män, so
      I heard, "first think, then act, then speak." I mean, I'm

44   *dumm bin i sicher net, aber aber—des is, voriges Jahr hab i des*
      certainly not so stupid, but, but—that is, last year I was

45   *Glück g'habt, also Gott sei Dank, dass i an die Klinik 'kommen*
      bin, zwei ein halb
      lucky, thank heavens, that I came to the clinic two and a half
      months

46   *Monat. Und drüber war i dann so selig, und die haben mich*
      g'sund g'macht,
      months. And I was so happy about it then, and they made me
      healthy,

47   *mit Medikamenten und da hab i 'glaubt, i hab das abgebaut,*
      also es ist weg
      with medications, and I thought I had got rid of it, that it was
      gone.

48   *von mir und seit—wāss i—a paar Monat oder paar Wochen*
      schleichen
      And since a couple of months or a couple of weeks—I don't
      know how long—

49   *sich langsam diese Depressionen an und jetzt—na, des halt i net*
      durch.
      these depressions have been creeping up, and now—well, I can't
      stand it.

50   *War beim Herrn Dr. _____ , hab—hat er mir a anderes Mittel*
      geben und des
      I went to Dr. _____ , and he gave me another medicine and that

51   *is ja eh guat, aber—Man sollte so sagen: Mit dem Menschen, der*
      einen
      was fine, but—perhaps I should put it like this: the person who

52   *immer wieder in das hineintreibt, warum man ja die*
      Depressionen hat, dass
      repeatedly forces you into that, why, you have depressions, so
      that

53   *man mit dem nie wieder in Kontakt gehen soll. Wie kann man*
      denn das, wann
      you don't want to see him again. How can you do that if

54   *das so a Mensch in der Familie is, na der Vater?*
      such a person is a member of your family, your own father?

55 M: *Na, habens durch eahm die Depressionen 'kriegt, oder hat er . . .*
      Was it because of him that you got depressions, or did he . . .

56 F: *Na ja, "Des kannst net, des wirst nie können, für des bist zu*
      bled"—
      Well, "You'll never be able to do that, because you're too
      stupid"—

57   *bin immer schon so gehemmt gewesen, dass i, wann ma so, wāss*
      i, mit der
      I've always had such inhibitions, that I, if we, I mean, when we

58   *Firma von meinem Mann fort'gangen san, hab i kein Wort*
      gesprochen,
      went out with my husband's firm, I never said a word

59   *weil i mi net 'traut hab, den Mund aufzumachen, dass ich*
      vielleicht
      because I was afraid to open my mouth, in case I
60   *irgendwas sag, was blöd wär.*
      said something stupid.

5.4.2. The context of the session

The patient presents her problem shortly after the commencement of the session (this session was also taken as an example of problem elaboration in 3.8.5). One has the feeling that she "explodes": the problem breaks out, although she has many inhibitions about talking, particularly as the tape recorder was placed within sight for the first time. It is immediately obvious that the presence of the tape recorder is not subsequently a hindrance; she speaks openly and honestly in a very excited and emotional manner about her problem. The problem is subsequently discussed almost until the end of the session, and many new aspects become apparent (see 3.8.5.3). The interventions come mainly from a young working-class man (patient 16) who described his problem with his father in the previous session and who also opened this session with a description of his dreams. The group is very emotionally involved. When the tape was played back in the presence of the therapist, he explained that he had allowed the problem to be discussed in such detail because many patients had troubled relationships with their parents and could therefore benefit from the discussion.

5.4.3. The colloquial level

Narrative structure

The limits of quantitative evaluation are reached even in the first category. Although this is certainly a true story, containing the narration of a telephone call and the resulting conflicts (an "event" in the narrative past with interspersed direct speech, in the definite personal speaker's perspective see 3.10.11), it also includes both scenic moments (lines 41–43) and descriptions of symptoms (lines 32, 45–51). Classification with the aid of Labov and Waletzky's categories is fairly obvious: orientation (lines 1–19), complication (lines 19–32) and scenic element (lines 40–43), evaluation (lines 33–40), (resolution coda, lines 47–51 and lines 44–46).

Orientation: The patient begins with a description of how difficult it is to talk about her problem. She withdraws (lines 10–11) and continues only after encouragement (lines 12–14), beginning with a part of the conflict: reproaches of her father (lines 16–17), in the face of which she justifies her actions, and a further assurance that she will not speak for too long. It is particularly interesting to note the change from the impersonal *one* in the introduction (lines 1–3, 5–6), with the personal interjection in line 4, to the definite personal speaker's perspective in the remainder of her problem presentation.

Complication: The event (line 20) of the telephone call is not described coherently, but in brief, chopped sentences, repeatedly interrupted by the scenic description of the conflict in direct speech (reproaches of her father, justifications) and the description of her feelings (line 28).

Evaluation: Evaluation and self-reflection begin with the speech act *ich mein* ("I think") (line 32). Initially she addresses the working-class patient from whose account she appears to have learned something. Anger and aggression then explicitly come to light, with restrictions (line 37). The primary scene—her memory of the "drill"—is also interwoven in the narration (lines 41–43).

Resolution: The resolution in this case is very brief and coincides partly with the evaluation and the coda. It is condensed (between lines 44 and 46) and changes into evaluative speech acts, and disappointments, as in the coda.

Coda: She describes the conclusion of her therapeutic "career" and again mentions the main problem, namely, that it is impossible to avoid one's own father, that a solution to the conflict must be found (lines 47–51), although this is a person who always hurts her. Part of the coda remains a description of the symptoms by the use of the descriptive present. Her explicit addressing of the therapist (line 50)—a sort of cry for help—is also typical.

There is a striking difference in style between complication and the evaluation and coda, from very excited, hurried, and emotional speech (sociophonological style 1—see Feldstein et al. 1963; Leodolter 1975a:260), to the assessment, which is relatively consistent in explicit, evaluative speech acts, and to the descriptive coda. This is reminiscent of Labov and Fanshel's description of "frame shifts"

(1977:35 ff.) ("so hab' i mi aufg'regt, den Hörer hab i hing'haut" (28/29), "hab so drüber nach'denkt, hab von ihm jahrzehnte des eindrillt 'kriegt" (40/41), "'da hab i 'glaubt, i hab das abgebaut, also es ist weg von mir . . . " (47/48)—"I got so excited, I threw down the receiver, and thought about it, he drilled it into me, and then I thought I had got rid of it, that it had left me . . .").

Text length

The problem presentation is fairly long, which is typical of the patient's high degree of involvement and of her willingness to talk. She suffers a great deal and must admit this (although she intends not to talk for too long, out of consideration for the group and because of her own insecurity [line 15]).

Problem solving

This problem presentation is typical of ambivalence, of vacillation and involvement in one problem field (3.10). Several topics are touched on and outlined (life history, childhood, illness, therapy), heuristic aspects mentioned (break with her father [line 53], as well as the existing tie "although he's not bad; he does everything for me" [lines 36–37]). Hate and anger are interspersed with feelings of guilt and justifications. She goes through the entire conflict. Her disappointment that she has still not managed to find a satisfactory solution to this problem (lines 3–5, 46–48) is apparent. She tries to justify her anger to the group, which is why we find a large number of justifications (lines 16, 17, 31, 41–44). Her involvement is particularly apparent from the degree of emotionality in the playing of the scene. One has the feeling of actually being present because of the strong vernacular, which is typical of excitement. (The patient normally uses elevated colloquial language.) The fact that we are dealing here with ambivalence and not with penetration is evident from the evaluation, the setting, and the patient's clear insight that it is her problem.

Defense mechanisms

Here, too, we reach the limits of quantification. We encounter not simply a single type of defense mechanism but at least three. The regression is particularly striking, however, especially in the scenic reproduction, which has therefore been coded. The adult woman (she is over thirty years old) falls back completely into the childish conflict mechanism with her father, using the reproach-justification schema and unable to analyze the reproaches. Her scenic recollection (lines 41–43) and childish patricidal fantasy (line 39) can be allocated linguistically to childhood (family frame). Regarded objectively, the reproaches that she has not been through the war (line 16), that she is only "so" old (line 17), that her father cannot retire because of her (line 22), and so on, are absurd, but they are also typical of the double bind and conflict and subjectively certainly terribly embarrassing. The reaction of anger ("threw down the receiver," line 29) is certainly not an adequate mechanism to act out the conflict. But other defense mechanisms are also apparent: tremendous feelings of guilt are manifest, as the reproaches would not otherwise fall on such fertile ground (line 17). She even feels guilty toward the group (projection of feelings of guilt) (lines 13, 15, 20) and uses quasi-excuses, modifications, and rationalizations ("he's not bad" [lines 37, 38]; "that was fine" [lines 50–51]; "I have already got rid of that" [line 33]). These represent attempts to solve the conflict intellectually, to suppress it and reduce its magnitude. Rationalization is particularly clear in line 37, for it is followed soon after by the childish fantasy "I'd kill my father."

Affectivity

In this instance, it is relatively easy to allocate affective conditions to utterances because of the explicit verbalization of affects. Anger, aggression, and hatred (directed at the father) are in the foreground (mainly in lines 28–29 and 39 ff.). The problem presentation was thus allocated to this category. Here, too, however, there are explicit and latent mixed emotions. Feelings of guilt follow the internalized reproaches of the father, indicated by the whining tone and the falling intonation in lines 16 through 18. Sorrow and disappointment might be expected in lines 47 and the following but are partly suppressed, as she does not dare to reproach the therapist openly.

The expression of affects

In connection with the previous category, one can detect admission of feelings in this problem presentation (with the exception of disappointment). This is evident from several indicators (such as have already been mentioned when the category was introduced) (3.10). Several feelings are explicitly mentioned (line 28: "I got so excited"; line 36: "I can't stand the sight of him any more"; lines 39–40: "I just can't stand it any more"; line 49: "I can't stand it"). Yet this by itself is not sufficient to detect the admission of feelings. Intellectual insight and emotion are often separate, particularly in cases of dissociation (expressions of anger in a neutral tone). The mode of speech and suprasegmental and sociophonological features are therefore of greater importance.

The problem presentation is characterized by short, chopped, often incomplete sentences (line 20), hesitations (line 36), repetitions ("I mean, I don't know"), parentheses, and short breaks attributable to excitement and agitation (Goldman-Eisler 1961, 1968; Scherer 1979). Switching has already been mentioned, and depends on topic and frame (i.e., reflexion or recollection). There is also significantly frequent use of sociolinguistically marked phonological variables (change of input and variable rules) (3.7.3, 3.10.2.3). The fact that this is indicative of affective speech in the case of this patient is based on a comparison of this text with other verbalizations and with the interview (4.4, 6.4).

The intensity of affective expression

Apart from the verbally violent, emotional quality of the problem presentation, the patient is also very active nonverbally. She has a tendency to jump up from her chair, gesticulating wildly; conflict is also strongly reflected in mimicry.

Sex of intervention

As has been mentioned, the patient is supported at the beginning of her problem presentation by a male working-class patient. She partly identifies, or at least sympathizes, with him (note the recourse to the previous session in lines 33–34). The working-class male intervenes again after the problem presentation. In the subsequent course of the session, women also intervene, but male intervention is predominant. The males offer very rational, factual solutions and advice but do not consider the patient's affects.

The nature of the intervention

Three interventions occur: in lines 12 and 14, we find support in the form of explicit encouragement and observation. The man gives the patient courage, taking up her latent request (lines 10–11) to ask her explicitly, thus relieving her feelings of guilt about taking up too much time. (As mentioned above, this is a case of projection, a continuation of lines 8–9.)

In line 55, the member of the working class actually poses a question (a closed either-or question). This, however, encourages the patient to continue, because of its incompleteness (the question is incomplete, even though the patient does not interrupt him). At the same time, this intervening question also fulfils another function: that of an interpretation, a summary of the conflict ("Was it because of him that you got depressions, or did he . . . "). The male speaker is almost impatient that she is still in doubt, is still ambivalent.

The reaction of the patient

It is understandable that the patient does not take up the explicit question, preferring instead the indirect interpretation. She confirms the interpretation with a further recollection (line 56) and with further evidence of her symptom (inhibition, fear), which has been caused by her father's upbringing. Her reaction can therefore be classified both as introduction of new aspects and as insight, although the main aspect is again selected for quantification.

5.4.4. The level of the group meaning

Text A has several functions and meanings in the transference within the group. It is not by chance that precisely this problem is verbalized in the session. As mentioned above, the woman patient continues from the previous session, during which the working-class patient spoke about his relationship with his father. At the same time, she attaches her verbalization to a dream described by the same patient and addresses him explicitly (lines 34–35); she is supported (lines 12, 14) and interpreted (line 55) by him. There is, therefore, identification and solidarity; a brother-sister relationship exists between them.

The content of the father problem—the problem of authority—is not a matter of chance, either. In reality, the entire problem presentation should be interpreted as a censure of the therapist's authority, as disappointment that the therapy has not yet helped her to solve her problem. This is conclusively apparent from the resolution (44 ff.), particularly in the coda in her direct address of the therapist (lines 49–50). She still suffers from depression, although he has prescribed medications for her (if she didn't take them, she would kill her father, line 39). Her massive feelings of guilt for taking up too much time stem, on the one hand, from her father's aggression toward her (lines 8–9, 36–37, 53–54), and on the other, from her (unconscious) censure of the therapist. For this reason the coda also contains rationalizations ("es is eh guat," line 51; —"and that is fine," "the therapy must work").

The group gives the patient the opportunity to settle ambivalences; to begin with, she assumes both roles in the dialogue (those of her internalized father and of herself). These functions are subsequently assumed by members of the group, and the conflict with authority is acted out, but not directly against the therapist. The patient's mention of an extremely authoritarian upbringing in a scenic recollection (lines 41–42, 56) and the frequent repetition of reproaches (lines 16–17) bring out similar associations in many members of the group. The patient's explicit mention of her father's parents opens them to interrogation; only several sessions later the group discusses the meaning of the therapy, a discussion certainly initiated in part by the latent disappointment of this patient.

5.4.5. The individual private language level

This problem presentation in group therapy is the patient's first large outbreak in the group. She has been receiving treatment for some time, partly as an inpatient, and has been calmed by medication. The patient's central conflict with her parents comes to light here: the difficulty of breaking away because of her massive feelings of guilt vis-à-vis her parents. (Only her father is mentioned in the current problem presentation. It subsequently becomes apparent, however, that her mother has exemplified for her the suffering, self-sacrificing woman's role and is also involved; she may indeed play even a more important role, for example with respect to sex identification.) Important scenes are verbalized together with the relevant feelings and connotations, and the first steps are taken toward understanding her symptoms. In spite of her inhibitions (lines 58–60), the patient manages to describe her problem in detail, but she needs help, which she implicitly requests (lines 11–15). Addressing other members of the group, particularly the males, is typical and quite understandable as a result of her relationship with her father. Only relatively late in the course of the therapy does she also deal with women. In spite of her feelings of guilt and attacks on her own person (self-aggression), this outbreak in the group represents a great step forward. For the first time, she admits her aggressions, her fantasies, and her recollections of her strict father (not an unusual fate for a woman, though it is certainly singular). There is much that conforms with recent psychoanalytical concepts of women (Windhoff-Heritier 1976): The bond with the therapist is very strong, a fact that is revealed not only in this text. Her father's drill has driven her to depression. In this context she also shows a strong urge to work, she rushes herself, is a perfectionist (all this is subsequently mentioned in the discussion). The scenic recollection, the repressed language games (1.2.3, 1.2.6) are very clear in this problem presentation. Lines 43 and 56 certainly have quite specific connotations in connection with the patient's father (2.3.5). Only through assimilation of her past history can she come to terms with the present and find a solution to the conflict. I cannot go any further into the patient's life history without endangering her anonymity; the text is self-explanatory.

5.5. Text B: The problem is solved
5.5.1. Text B

Subtext I

1 F1: *Na ja gut. I wäss ja, jetzt . . . und i wollt eh mit*
    Alright. I know now, . . . understandable and I wanted to make
2   *Herrn Dr. _____ an Termin ausmachen. Da red'i nur über*
    mein Vater.
    an appointment with Dr. _____ [the therapist]. Then I only
    talk about my father.
3   *Jetzt wäss i ä, was is und was is und wieso der Grund is und*
    warum er des
    Now I know what's what, and what the reason is, and why he
4   *immer macht, was er da g'macht hat. Lang hat's ja 'dauert.*
    always does that, what he has done. It's taken a long time,
    though.

5   F2:   *I bewunder' Dich eigentlich immer, dass Du immer no bei Deine Eltern*
          I always think it's great, actually, that you still work

6   *arbeitst, also.*
          with your parents.

Subtext II

7   F1:   *Na ja, na wo soll i hingehn, was anders, weil i ma ja doch irgendwie im*
          Well, where should I go, something different, because somehow inside me I

8   *Innersten do net zutrau, dass i wo acht Stunden den ganzen Tag beschäftigt*
          don't really dare, because if I were employed for eight hours, the whole day,

9   *bin, ununterbrochen steh und und doch, net, i mān, halbtags täglich*
          and had to stand the whole time, and, well, I mean, half-days,

10   *sicher, aber den ganzen Tag is ja doch, dass i wāss, ich a Stund, dass i nix*
          of course, but the whole day is rather—I know, an hour during which I

11   *tu oder so. Aber dafür hol i des dann wieder auf, dass i oft halt kā*
          don't do anything. But I make up for it later, as I often don't have

12   *Pause hab oder oft halt—so halt; aber aber wohin gehen und— sag ma—dort ar-*
          a break, or often—that's it; but going somewhere and—say— working

13   *beiten, des wāss i net, ob i—aber um des gehts ja jetzt gar net. I*
          there, I'm not sure whether I—but that's not the problem. I

14   *wāss, warum mei Vater immer so war.*
          know why my father was always like that.

15   M1:   *Du, entschuldigen, i weiss net, ob's Dir so unangenehm is, aber mich würd*
          I'm sorry, I don't know whether it's so unpleasant for you, but I would

16   *des aus dem Grund interessieren, weil ja so ähnlich die Lage is vielleicht*
          like to know about it, because my situation may be similar,

17　　*bei mir und wenn Du auf was draufkommst, hätt i ā gern*
　　　g'wusst, was
　　　and if you realize something, I'd also like to know what
18　　*Du da machst.*
　　　you do then.
19　F1:　*Auf was ich drauf'kommen bin?*
　　　What I realized?
20　M1:　*Ja.*
　　　Yes.

Subtext III

21　F1:　*Auf eh ganz was Harmloses. Also mei Vater is furchtbar*
　　　eifersüchtig auf
　　　Something quite harmless. You see, my father is terribly jealous
22　　*mi, und dass er halt nur in der Werkstatt is und sunst nix tut*
　　　und i eigentlich
　　　of me, as he's only in the workshop and doesn't do anything
　　　else, and I
23　　*mit der Mutter eigentlich alles mach, net, das G'schäft und des*
　　　and mother actually do everything, you see, the business and
24　　*alles, net. Des is halt a, is halt a Pech, wann der Chef*
　　　nimmermehr halt
　　　everything, you know. That's bad luck, when the boss is no
　　　longer
25　　*so kann. I mān, i sehs ja ein. Er is siebzig, er hat halt in seinen*
　　　früheren
　　　able to do everything. I mean, I accept it. He is seventy, he
　　　produced his achievements
26　　*Jahren des geleistet, und jetzt gehts halt nimmer, net und wann*
　　　er in die
　　　when he was young, and now he can't manage any more, and
　　　when he
27　　*Werkstatt kommt, sagt er, "da, scho wieder 1.500—*
　　　Ö. S. Reparatur,
　　　comes into the workshop, he says, "There now, another repair
　　　for 1,500 Austrian shillings
28　　*scho wieder 3.000—," und wann'st das zählst, sans drei*
　　　Reparaturen um 90—Ö. S.
　　　another S 3,000," and if you count it up, that makes three
　　　repairs for S 90,
29　　*net, und sagen tut er 1.500—, net. Na, da redst halt nix und,*
　　　weil er

you know, and he says S 1,500. Well, you don't say anything,
and because he

30 *hat die Kunden—und so. Die Mutti erzählt immer,*
has got the customers—and so on. Mummy always tells me,

31 *"na Jessasna," s'is ihr scho zuviel und des tuts und des machts
und jetzt, san*
"my word," it's too much for her and this and that, and now

32 *da, seit Tagen hat er so einen Zorn und eine Wut und eine
Aggression auf*
for days he has been so angry and so cross and so aggressive
toward

33 *mi g'habt, und die hat er mi dann halt vorigen Freitag wieder
spüren*
me, and he let me feel that again last Friday,

34 *lassen, net; aber es is, Gott sei Dank, nimmermehr so tief
'gangen, dass i*
you see; but thank heavens it wasn't so bad that I

35 *im Betrieb umg'fallen bin, net. I war nur a bissl halt—war i
unsicher,*
collapsed at work, you see. I was just a bit—I was unsteady,

36 *hab i ma 'denkt, "Jessas-Maria, wenn i jetzt wieder tiefer g'falln
bin, wie*
and I thought, "My God, if I fall so low again, how will I ever

37 *komm i da wieder auf," net. Aber i bin: nach drei Tag wars
wieder vorbei*
get up again," you see. But I did: three days later it was all
over

38 *und vergessen, net. Und er hat auf d'Nacht scho wieder g'lacht
und hat*
and forgotten, you see. And that night he laughed again and
said,

39 *g'sagt, "Schau, weh tuts ja mir, weil i schrei mit Dir und i reg
mi auf;*
"Look, it hurts me, because I shout at you and get excited;

40 *Dir tut ja des gar net so weh—i leid ja, net Du." Also müsste*
it doesn't hurt you so much—I suffer, not you!" [laughs] So

41 *ich*
I'd have to

42 M2: *I glaub, beide leiden bei so an Streit.*
I think both parties suffer in such a quarrel

43 F1: *Ja, des is ma ja eh jetzt scho egal.*
Yes, well it's all the same to me now.

44 M1: *Es is angenehm, wenn ma's weiss, net, die Zusammenhänge.*

But it's nice if you understand the connections.
45 F1:   *Na ja sicher, wenn ma einmal weiss.*
Yes, of course, once you know.

5.5.2. The context of the session

This session focuses on the work problem. Several patients describe their difficulties in detail, in particular a male middle-class patient, a civil servant. Even the therapist intervenes, pointing out how the male patient always goes around in circles. All the other patients in the group are bored; it becomes apparent that the female middle-class patient—(this session was recorded exactly a year after text A)—wants to say something. She begins by addressing the therapist directly and announces that she has discovered the solution to her problem.

5.5.3. The selection of the text

A problematic text has deliberately been chosen here: it actually consists of three problem presentations (by formal definition; see 3.9) that together make up one problem presentation in view of the fact that subtexts I and II can be regarded as introductions to subtext III, which contains both an account and a problem solution. This is the knowledge acquired by the patient, which has enabled her to see things in their proper perspective. This type of immanently coherent problem presentation in group therapy must be regarded as rather an exception and was selected for interpretation with this in mind. Most problem presentations in group therapy—as the many published examples show (Wodak 1981*a*, *b*, *c*)—are complete, even if the problem continues to be dealt with after verbalization (3.8.5). The limits of quantification are thus particularly clear in this instance. Three problem presentations have to be classified from the necessarily restrictive definition of the contribution to the discussion (determined by change of speaker), although intrinsically and thematically, the texts belong together. It is thus very difficult to assign them to categories, because all three text types occur. Subtexts I and II are descriptions of circumstances (3.10.1.1); in subtext III an "event" with scenic elements is interwoven in the problem solution (Cicourel 1975, Quasthoff 1979). In subtext III in particular, however, the value of the story is of secondary importance.

Subtext I (lines 1–6) can be assigned to the category of circumstance, although it contains a definite speaker's perspective, an active genus, and factual mode, which point rather to scene and narration.

Subtext II (lines 7–20) in this instance can definitely be assigned to the category of circumstance. The description of everyday life at work is passive. It must be regarded as a strategy of justification, however, as an answer to the implicit reproach in lines 5 and 6. (The fact that every typology involves abstraction and idealization is discussed in 3.9.3.5.)

As far as interpretation is concerned, subtext III is a parable[2]: a little story illustrates the nature of the problem solution, representing this and the newly acquired strategies for coping with the conflict.

It must therefore be assumed that this is a mixed type (with regard to narrative structure). Circumstance (problem solving and narration are interwoven and occur simultaneously (Wodak 1981b).

The success of the therapy is thus manifest not only in the context of the successful problem solving but also in the form, in a new text type that contains elements of all three basic types: Circumstantial, scenic, and narrative elements occur without special priority being given to any one component; this is therefore a *mixed type*.

In the context of the session and group dynamics, subtexts I and II pave the way for subtext III (and can be interpreted as strategies for awakening curiosity). Subtext III is therefore mainly used in the qualitative analysis, as an example of the effect of therapy on the form (and naturally also content) of problem presentation in group therapy!

5.5.4. The colloquial level

Narrative structure

The problematics of this classification have already been mentioned: first, subtext II contains an introduction to a circumstantial description, which is abruptly interrupted in line 13. Second, the core of the problem presentation is the problem solution (lines 21–31), with a narration inserted by way of illustration. The text was classified as a mixed type mainly after a playback with the therapist. The patient is naturally very concerned about the renewed conflict with her father, but she is now in a position to relate it differently, against the background of a problem solution.

The question remains as to whether the suggested problem solution can be considered a rationalization or a purely intellectual solution of the problem. Polemically one could argue that the patient has only acquired a new language and that nothing else has changed. A new language would by itself not be an indication of therapeutic success if the usual meaning of *language* is taken. This interpretation is strengthened by the patient's subsequent reluctance to admit that she suffers in the conflict, although she certainly must. Nevertheless, the validity of the problem solution is strongly supported by other factors, by the patient's distance—both verbal and emotional—and by her quite different and new manner of coping with the conflict. An interpretation as rationalization is thus refuted by the strong emotional involvement. This means that all three levels of language behavior have undergone a change. As is so often the case in therapeutic communication, various motives and interpretations can be applied, many of them conflicting.

Introduction: The introduction is very long (lines 1–4, 7–14, 21). The patient begins twice, mainly because intervention (lines 5/6) forces her briefly into a circumstantial description, which is also related in another linguistic style. Conflict and ambivalence can be felt here (short incomplete sentences, pauses, hesitations, expletives). She announces her knowledge of her problem and makes the group curious, as she says she only wants to tell the therapist about her insight. Subtext II is thus a renewed description of everyday life at work, presented in justification of the internalized (and not explicitly verbalized) reproach of her father that she does not work enough. It follows the intervention (lines 5/6), however, which she obviously misinterprets, perceiving it as reproach instead of praise. Only the intervention in lines 15/18 induces the patient to describe her solution.

Problem solving: Lines 21/32 must be classified as an evaluation, a metacommunicative, reflexive speech act (strategies for problem solving are metacommunicative acts—see 2.3.2.2). She interprets the conflict and sets the frame in which the "event" (Cicourel 1975), the complication, must be seen. It is this consistent, calmly presented evaluation in particular that indicates the speaker's new perspective. The linguistic style is significantly different from that used in subtext II of text B and text A. She outlines her father and has seen through him.

Narration: The actual incident only comes to light in line 32, an incident (she almost collapsed) that is dealt with very briefly. The speaker merely mentions the incident in a subordinate clause (line 35, "dass i im Betrieb umg'fallen bin"). The speaker relates feelings and reactions and how she copes with the conflict (lines 35–37): this is again evaluative. Although the incident was certainly subjectively terrible, her language is also consistent here (there is a definite personal speaker's perspective: she is excited, but there is a significant difference from text A).

Resolution: The summary of the problem presentation is partly narrative, partly evaluative. She describes her strategy for coping with the conflict and at the same time assesses her condition, expressing pleasure at her successful strategy. A scenic moment is also woven in as a sort of conclusion (lines 39–41). This is her father's realization (and her own) that he is actually the one who suffers most from this conflict.

Text length

The entire text is long, testifying to the patient's readiness to talk. Subtext I (which is a complete introduction and is, at the same time, exhortative) is relatively short, but she waits for the intervention (an implicit invitation).

Problem solving

The entire problem presentation can be regarded as an explicit description of a strategy for problem solving. To begin with, the solution is announced (lines 1–4, 14). This is followed by a description of the insight leading to the successful solution of the conflict, by an explanation of the patient's relationship with her father (lines 23–31), and finally, by her strategy for coping with the problem (lines 35–38). This is illustrated by the narration of an incident and its solution. There is no sign here of an ambivalent attitude with the relevant linguistic indicators.

Defense mechanisms

We find negation in the foreground of subtext II (line 13); part of the symptom not yet mastered emerges (lines 8–12) but is explicitly suppressed. The entire father problem will remain unsolved as long as the problems at work are not mastered as well. Her new strategy of conflict thus represents a first step forward. Thus it seems logical to interpret lines 21/31 as rationalization: the insight gained still conceals other, unsolved problems. Regression also occurs in the description of everyday life (lines 30–31) and in the scenic recollection (lines 39–40). The childish tie to the mother ("Mummy," line 30) is still present. Once again, we reach the limits of quantification, as we would have to allocate the text hierarchically to several categories.

Affectivity

The prevalent affect that we would expect—and that is also expressed—is joy. This is evident in the patient's self-assured declaration that she at last knows the solution (lines 1–4), all the way through to the description of how the conflict was overcome (lines 37–41). The quotation from the father is meant as an anecdote, a joke, and the patient laughs while telling it. The feeling of guilt (lines 7–12) is obstructed.

The expression of affects

As mentioned above, the patient expresses her joy; she admits it— a joyful excitement is evident. The narration is astonishingly coherent when one compares it with the previous text. She wants to tell her group about her success. The mood explicitly imparted is that of harmony—even her strict father laughed after the conflict (lines 38–39). Only from lines 8/13 is there a trace of the whining tone of childish self-justification. This part is also interspersed with repetitions and hesitations.

The intensity of affective expression

The patient's gestures and mimicry are not nearly as marked as in text A. This is exactly the indication of a more objective approach to the problem. In the regressive elements, there is a significant switch to another style (family frame). The affect is fully admitted. This is testified by the personal manner of speech (this is not a neutral description). There are many sociophonological indicators expressing excitement (in this instance, joyful excitement). The scenic description of her father (lines 24–30) is particularly indicative of strong affective involvement. This description is virtually equivalent to an anecdote (she has seen through him).

Sex of intervention

Apart from intervention (lines 5/6, Subtext I), the other interventions are by males. In this case a middle-class man with similar problems intervenes, though he is not yet in a position to describe them independently.

The nature of the intervention

The first intervention (line 5) is a statement of fact, a commentary. Yet this intervention in particular has multiple implicit meanings. It also contains a reproach (the group realized long ago that the patient should no longer work for her father), and indeed, the intervention is almost cynical, intended perhaps as an incursion against the patient's obvious self-confidence. At the same time, it can be paraphrased as an interpretation as follows: "What about your job problem; have you already solved it? This is actually one of your main problems—don't forget!"

The patient's reaction (a justification) clearly shows that these implicit meanings have been accepted. The intervention in lines 15 to 18 is an exhortation to the patient to talk and is meant to provide support, as the first intervention has put the patient off.

The intervention in line 44 is again meant as support, backing down because the patient has not responded to line 42. It contains implicit praise for the patient because she has obviously realized the important connections.

The reaction of the patient

The reaction (lines 7–14) to the first intervention is a justification in response to the implicit reproach in line 5. New aspects and a different topic are described.

Reaction 19, a counterquestion, is mainly an invitation for affirmation that she should actually tell her story. This is reminiscent of a similar strategy in text A but is by no means as blunt.

The reaction in line 43 is an obstruction; the patient is unwilling to admit unpleasant feelings but wishes to continue delighting in her joy.

The reaction in line 45 is a repetition of the intervention, a confirmation that she does in fact know about the connections. Note the contrast between "I don't know (7, 34) and "I know" (lines 3, 45) in texts A and B.

5.5.5. The level of the group meaning

This problem presentation is extremely interesting with regard to group dynamics. The patient wishes to describe her success to the group and to be praised (expectations such as are otherwise directed at the family). At the same time, she wants to make the group particularly curious and even jealous by initially addressing the therapist directly (line 2). She has "made it," while the others have not. The group immediately takes its revenge in the first intervention (line 5); the hidden problem, which the patient did not want to mention at all, comes to light. The group reproaches her with not always having solved her job problem, so she need not think she is any better, or that she is loved. One can feel the terrible dread that somebody could be better off than oneself, could be more advanced in the therapy. The female patient who intervenes is heavily dependent on the therapist (lines 5–7); competition, even for the therapist's attention, can therefore be regarded as a self-justification, laden with feelings of guilt even vis-à-vis the group. The intervention of line 15 shows interest and helps the patient to drop the unpleasant subject, showing solidarity and a willingness to learn. The patient in particular is very pleased to have his problem dealt with by others, so that he can act as a listener and interpreter, a role which he also assumes here. Praise for the account is not immediately forthcoming, whereupon the patient withdraws, disappointed. She has not received what she wanted; the group has not behaved in the way that she unrealistically expected. Nobody likes to see obvious success. It is clear that the mechanisms in the group are similar to those in everyday life. The patient subsequently assimilates her disappointment and in doing so acquires a slightly more realistic viewpoint.

5.5.6. The individual private language level

For the first time the patient is able to feel pleasure, to feel pleased at her success. The terrible ambivalence and conflict situation have been cleared up; she can now see things in a realistic perspective and is better able to cope with any conflicts that may occur. She also dares to admit her pleasure publicly, something that she was previously unable to do, in keeping with her socially imposed, suffering female role. The fact that she is still unstable is shown by her rapid retreat after the intervention in line 5, her regressive tendencies (lines 30–31), and her great disappointment (line 43) when praise is not forthcoming. She can now tackle other problems—above all, her job problem and her relationship with her mother—on the basis of her new perspective, her first resolution of a conflict. The entire narrative mode has changed (as shown by the linguistic indicators). She describes the strategy used to solve her problem self-confidently and coherently. There is also a far higher degree of explicit, verbalized self-reflection: she is no longer torn between different values; she has found her own standard, establishes her own evaluative frame, puts forward arguments and explanations. The differences from text A are obvious. They provide evidence of the effect of the therapy, which is linguistically apparent (mixed type). The patient can by no means be regarded as cured, but her progress is unmistakable, as seen in her renewed pleasure in life, which is finally expressed in this joyous outcry:

> You're so glad you've made it, that you, that you realize how happy you are, and I have to say, my God, the beautiful, well, the day is beautiful and—excuse me if I just say this quickly: I have such a wonderful view from my living room; I look out into the woods and now—when I was just feeling so happy and my father says, "nothing to do"—well, just for a moment, I—I didn't quite realize what he had said, I was so intent on the view. My husband immediately looked at me: "Please don't say anything, please, otherwise there'll be trouble again." But inside me, I needed that again, such things; life is wonderful, life is worth living!

6

The Self-assessment of Patients and Therapists

6.1. Introduction

There are several reasons for my decision to carry out semistructured interviews with some of the patients:

1. In many cases sociolinguistic studies (Labov 1966; Trudgill 1974; Dressler et al. 1972) have already shown that there are significant differences between self-assessment and outside appraisal, particularly with regard to the individual's own (language) behavior. The tape recordings in a different situation (in most cases I visited the patients in their homes) allowed me to make a comparison between two situations, thus making it possible to analyze, evaluate, and understand the group interaction better (the "purely" sociolinguistic aspect is dealt with in Wodak 1981b).

2. The interviews were used to obtain social data that enabled me to allocate each patient to the appropriate class, especially in the case studies (I tried to interview these patients in particular).

3. I intended to test the hypotheses on class- and sex-specific differences (2.4) in the light of the patients' subjective assessment, as well as to obtain further information about prejudices.

4. I wanted to differentiate further my assumptions on the therapeutic effect (2.5) on the basis of the patients' subjective assessment of the therapy and therapeutic success. It was not my intention to attempt quantification (Till 1977: 58 ff., 100 ff.); individual utterances are judged in their own right (4.4).

5. I hoped that a more intimate knowledge of individual patients in their accustomed environments would make it easier for me to understand their behavior in the group.

6. Criticism, praise, and the expressed wishes of the patients with regard to the Vienna Crisis Intervention Center made it easier for me to assess the effectiveness of the institution and to put forth postulates for new forms of psychiatric practice. Apart from determining linguistic styles in other situations, the interviews with the therapists were intended to establish their attitudes toward the patients, the group, and the hypotheses. It was also important to discover the therapists' motives for using the technique of group therapy and at the same time to find out their assessment of possible therapeutic effects (3.7.1).

6.2. The interviews

The interviews lasted an average of one hour. The duration depended on the readiness of the patients or therapists to talk. Some patients were comparatively brief, while others forced me into the role of therapist and used the interview to describe to me their current emotional state and their problems. When I visited the patients in their homes, I was treated as an important guest and entertained; the patients did not regard the interview as a nuisance but as an honor; they considered it a privilege that they had been selected to give their opinions. Only one female patient declined to give an interview (she didn't specify a reason).

The impression that I obtained from the patients' living conditions and from this intensive conversation opened up new perspectives to me in many aspects of the investigation. My subjective assessments of the patients on the basis of their problem presentations during the group sessions were in many cases relativized and objectified: the people before me were no longer "patients" in the restrictive therapeutic situation, but human beings in their accustomed environments.

6.3. The method of the focused interview

This method of interviewing has many advantages (Till 1977: 47 ff.; Friedrichs 1973:224 ff.) compared to standardized forms of interrogation (Tausch 1970). When questionnaires are sent out by mail, experience has shown that only about half of them are returned (Strupp et al. 1969). A standardized interview with uniform questions represents such a formal, restrictive situation that inter-

viewees normally only give the answers that they think the interviewer wants to hear (Filstead 1971). Only a focused interview
provides the opportunity of overcoming these restrictions and of
getting to know the interviewee. The interviewer leaves the course
of the discussion to the interviewee, subtly attempting to keep a
consistent thread without provoking obvious breaks in the conversation. This was an easy matter for me, as I was already familiar
with the patients. Many unconsciously forced me into the role of
therapist; as a result, I certainly heard more "truths" and opinions
than would an unknown interviewer (Dittman and Wynne 1961;
Cremerius 1962; Hersko and Winder 1958).

The interview began initially with questions as to social status
(age, profession, education, income, parents, reading habits, media
and leisure activities). The last questions are mainly useful for sociolinguistic classification. Patients were also asked about their motives for visiting the group, how long they had gone, and the effect
of the group (what had changed, what problems had been solved).
They were also asked to evaluate the differences between women
and men and between working class and middle class in the group,
and about their preferences for a certain therapist. Some of these
questions were designed to determine a patient's attitude toward
the group mechanisms (who had their own way, who was popular,
which role did the interviewee assume within the group) and finally
to provoke criticism and praise (or appraisal) of the institution.
Finally I asked two further questions about the language used in
the group. These related to a patient's evaluation of his own language, his attitude to dialect, the use of dialect at school, and the
current "dialect craze" in the media (there is now a general trend
in Austria toward producing plays, records, and so on in local
dialect). The therapists were interviewed in a similar manner (to
glean social data) and were questioned as to their motivation for
becoming therapists and about the possibilities and limitations of
therapy. I was also interested in the way in which they handled
speakers of dialect and whether they thought that there were class-
and sex-specific differences in the group. The goals of the therapy
were also discussed (emancipation or adaptation). The therapists
were also asked to express their criticism, praise, or satisfaction
with the crisis intervention center. Once again, the interview ended
with questions regarding the therapists' appraisal of their own language behavior.

6.4. The analysis of the interviews—the patients

The interviews were subjected to qualitative analysis: it would have been pointless to carry out a quantitative analysis with the small number of patients interviewed. This qualitative analysis contributed yet another dimension to the overall investigation: that of control by means of self-evaluation. The interviews were broken down into groups of questions, individual text passages being selected for illustration. A more detailed sociophonological analysis is unnecessary in this context, as the interviews in the present investigation were designed to ascertain the subjects' self-evaluation and self-appraisal. A sociophonological analysis—for example, a comparison of two problem presentations from two situations—would not serve this purpose. This has been done elsewhere (Wodak 1981*b*). The qualitative analysis of the interviews with the therapists also serves as an introduction to the final remarks.

6.4.1. The therapeutic effect

The most important factors contributing to a positive therapeutic effect are the relief of isolation, the establishment of new friendships, the opportunity of moving in a new social sphere, the insight that one is not alone with one's problems, the experience of alternative ways of life, advice, consolation, and solidarity. In all cases the group was experienced as a "free zone" in which—in contrast to the outside world—it was possible to speak openly and be honest.

Each individual also realized that in the final analysis, one can only help oneself, as there is no such thing as a pat solution. Two patients expressed their regrets that the therapists did not give more opinions and were not more authoritative.

Explicit mention was also made of the function of the group as a substitute family in which one could again find security and through which one could learn to grow up (2.2.4).

An important contribution to success was also made by contacts and meetings outside the sessions, such as visits to restaurants and other activities (excursions, dances) (3.8.4).

At the same time, there was also a hint of regret that meetings with members of the group had recently become more difficult and less frequent because of the reduced number of group sessions, patients no longer needing the therapy as much.

Text 66. Patient 9 (female).

As I said, I am glad, and [have] the feeling that I can go somewhere, and there will be somebody there for me.

Text 67. Patient 21 (male).

Yes, I went there for about six months, was very nervous there, and hardly ever spoke at all; you won't believe that, because you know me a bit from the group, well, and then I didn't go for six months; the group was important for me, and I also said that in the group, so to speak, a fear of aggression [was relieved], a free zone, and where several people can sit together. It is also—even if I don't use it, the knowledge that I can go there at any time is decisive.

Text 68. Patient 23 (male).

Well, actually I saw time and time again that I was not alone with my problem, or on the other hand, sometimes I was even able to help somebody. Naturally that helps a lot, too.

Text 69. Patient 16 (male) (W-interviewer).

M: Let's say I have learned—I mean, my problem is still there: some have been added to it, some have disappeared, and so on, but simply, simply living with the problem, you know; and I think it's much better now than when I came here years ago. My whole—

W: Yes, how does the group actually help you, what's it like, as it were? [short break, coughing] Does it change in the course of time, I mean your particular problem, taking Valium? [short break]

M: Actually, well, I was, I can talk about problems spontaneously and in the group and they are usually accepted, too, and and are dealt with; things that one simply can't say outside, and that simply helps me a lot, too, when something happens. I can't think of a concrete example, but when something goes wrong, and I can tell anyone in the group, I can at least tell them about it. And I say it, too, and that helps me a step further, you know. Apart from that, I think that people quite, some of them quite like me, and I think that's also good for you.

Text 70. Patient 9 (female).

W: I had plenty of time that Friday, and then I also appreciated the fact that one could talk with the people there, because all of them have also had problems and listened to you, you know. One could talk to them about it, when you had some problem or other, when you would find nobody else who might listen to us, you know. Or you don't want to confide in people who know you better, because they would say, for example, "well, what you've got, actually, other people have the same problem, too"; but there one can talk about one's problem in peace without anybody ripping you to pieces, you know.

Text 71. Patient 15 (M) (W-interviewer).

W: And had anything changed for you during the last few years?

M: Well, how shall I put it—the situation has changed to the extent that I no longer take it so seriously, I mean, these blows of fate that afflict me, you know, that's the only thing, and that is nevertheless an advantage, you know, as I was already just about to flip my top, you know—sooner, yes, when something like that happened, you know; but now these things leave me more or less cold, you know.

W: And what has the group actually done for you? I mean, have you made friends, or what?

M: Yes, the group used to be very wonderful, doctor, you know; I also had a large group of friends in the group, and we all got on well together, you know, Frau _____ and Herr _____ : yes, my, what fun that was. And then there were others, too, Frau _____ , for example; we were a small group, you see, and we got on so well together, and she, she, she was always such fun in the restaurant, you know, and then, when she'd had a bit to drink, she'd give each of us a kiss, and she was very generous, you know, and, well, we also came out of our shells a bit, you know; and for, I don't know how long, for some time now, for a year or two, this cozy—yes, I think I'd call it that—this cozy atmosphere has no longer existed in the group. Perhaps it's because of the fact that new people are continually joining the group, so somebody has destroyed the good group spirit, do you understand?

6.4.2. Class and sex

There were considerable differences in the tendency to prefer male or female therapists. Two patients considered the sex of the therapist immaterial, while the other six expressed preference for a therapist of their own sex (it was easier to talk "man to man" or "woman to woman"; one could expect greater understanding and intuition—more empathy, in other words). Nevertheless, the visit to the group was often less dependent on the choice of therapist than on when it was scheduled. The early session on Friday afternoon was more popular with many patients than the late evening sessions (3.8.2).

In response to the question as to whether they felt there were sex-specific differences in the group, two patients (a man and a woman) replied that they had noticed none, while six mentioned noticeable differences. Four patients thought that women were more likely to have problems with their partners and men more likely to have worries at work. Women were also regarded as more open. One male patient also thought that pretty young women received preferential treatment; another man remarked on the obvious dominance of women, which formed a wall, a barrier against the men (Wodak 1981c).

On the other hand, class-specific differences played a much less important role in the patients' subjective perception. Only three patients admitted that they had noticed such tendencies; three others refused to answer, saying they did not understand the question, that they were all on an equal footing, and that they were all in a bad way. One middle-class woman said that some members of the group had been too vulgar for her liking; a middle-class male patient felt that others envied his position, and a lower-middle-class patient observed the formation of cliques on the basis of social criteria. In principle, however, all the patients stressed that there were no differences in the group and that all patients were suffering equally and in need of help. One working-class patient described the initial difficulties he had experienced: when he came to the group, he was thrown together in sessions with a number of intellectuals. He had initially felt himself inferior, but this feeling had disappeared in the course of the therapy (text 47).

6.4.3. Group roles and group mechanisms

The questions as to "who gets his own way most" and "who is most popular" were rejected by almost every patient, that is, they were misunderstood. Some patients took this as a reproach for being too dominant (not without good reason perhaps) and justified their own actions; others associated their personal difficulties and contacts with members of the group. These descriptions made it apparent for the first time what a lively social life the members of the group led. Subgroups had formed that met and telephoned one another at regular intervals. At the time of the interviews, however, these ties had loosened slightly; the patients met one another less frequently, with the exception of a couple that had met in the group.

The most popular were "kind" patients who showed patience and willingness to help. Hardly any names were mentioned.

In response to the question as to their own roles in the group, only two men provided an answer, a working-class man and lower-middle-class man. The working-class man was aware of his role as a joker and humorist (a role he did not enjoy) (6.5). The lower-middle-class patient regarded himself as a cotherapist, a perception that coincided with my own observations. He did not usually talk much about his own problems, enjoyed dealing with others, and gave advice and interpretations.

The other patients found this question disquieting (insisting that "we are all the same"); they prevaricated or obstructed the question completely.

6.4.4. Awareness of language

All patients were comparatively aware of their language, and all had a positive attitude toward dialect (or colloquial language), although this positive attitude was sometimes qualified. While one middle-class female patient associated dialect with vulgarity, she knew that she herself often spoke dialect. A second middle-class female patient had a positive attitude toward dialect but instructed her youngest daughter to speak High German (an apparent contradiction that corresponds with the results of other sociolinguistic investigations).

All patients were fully aware that they changed their language depending on the situation and the partner with whom they conversed. One lower-middle-class patient was particularly concise on this subject. He precisely characterized the typical difficulties of social advancement, and the lack of and loss of identity expressed in and through language:

Text 72. Patient 21.

M: On the one hand is the language that I speak from my upbringing, and on the other is the language I would like to speak, but which I do not speak out of protest, which I only speak when I have an argument with somebody, a superior, for example, who is not in the same class as me; then I naturally speak his language, and that is one of the reasons why I practice at least a bit, because I quite simply wanted to leave behind the [déclassé social status] of my family that I have experienced, and that is probably my problem. It is always easier for somebody who remains in his social class.

Not only is this patient's precison remarkable, one can also notice the switch quite clearly: the patient uses another style as soon as feelings are admitted. There is also marked phonological and syntactic hypercorrection ("wenn ich z.B. also mit an Oberen, mit an . . . sprech ich natürlich seine Sprache / Es ist jederzeit leichter, einer der in seiner Schicht bleibt").

6.4.5. Conclusions

Analysis of the interviews with the patients provides important corroboration of our hypotheses (2.4, 2.5, 4.2). Each patient felt considerably more at ease than at the beginning of the therapy and was satisfied with the group. Several aspects were added to the quantitative and qualitative analysis (4.3, 4.4, 5.4, 5.5). The experience and knowledge of the patients' lives, which I gained from conversations in a different situation, enabled me to judge and understand the patients better. Their strong rejection of some questions (6.4.2, 6.4.3) verifies the hypothesis on the difference between self-assessment and outside appraisal.

Scarcely any criticism was expressed, with the exceptions of a desire sometimes felt to split the group in two when too many patients were present and the desire for more "recipes for success." Apart from being objectively legitimate, both wishes are quite understandable in psychotherapeutic terms. The first expresses a desire for more attention and interest, the second illustrates a typical frustration with the therapeutic method (2.2.2). Generally speaking, tremendous gratitude and affection were expressed for this institution; these sentiments far outweighed any minor criticism.

6.5. Interviews with the therapists

I interviewed four therapists, two women and two men. One man and one woman were the therapists whose group sessions had been recorded on tape; I had observed sessions held by the other two. My decision to interview two further members of the team was intended to objectify the statements made by the first two. Each of the interviews lasted about an hour and was carried out on the premises of the crisis intervention center and at the university psychiatric clinic. Here, too, I offered a guarantee of anonymity, as the remarks made would otherwise certainly not have been candid. Three of the therapists had been members of the team since the establishment of the crisis intervention center, while one female therapist had only worked there for three years. The persons interviewed also reflected the hierarchy at the crisis intervention center: one was a social worker, one was a psychiatrist, and two were psychologists.

6.5.1. The profession of therapist:
Is there such a thing as an individual therapeutic style?

The therapists' motives for choosing their profession were all very similar in nature: they all wanted to help and had arrived at this choice of profession as a result of different personal experiences. The most important reasons given were a desire to assume the role of helper or the role of rescuer, curiosity, pleasure in teaching, and an interest in the unconscious, in human behavior, and in communication. Only one interviewee was not completely satisfied with his choice of profession and could imagine being a craftsman instead.

They each were of the opinion that they possessed a specific therapeutic style but were only able to characterize this vaguely (where explicit descriptions [4.3, 5.4, 5.5] can contribute much to the clarification of theoretical and practical considerations). The descriptions revolved around such expressions as "neutral," "let things take their course," and "activation." All four also stressed that their style was strongly dependent on the group situation in each case: sometimes it was worth asking a patient for further details and interpreting them, and in other cases, communication and contact among all members of the group were of greater importance. They also stressed that the group took priority over the individual. The basic aim was to provide an opportunity for expression, and the group had to develop its insights by itself.

The two female therapists did not see any difference between the handling of the group by men and women, while the men saw a marked difference: women responded better to them. This is in complete contradiction to the patients' own observations (6.4.2). How should this self-assessment be interpreted? Are male therapists more narcissistic?

6.5.2. The goals of group therapy

When asked about the goals and aims of group therapy, the main answers were communication, relief of isolation, establishment of contact, and integration. They all rejected or avoided the concept of healing, preferring instead to talk about the "workings" of the human being, and hoped the therapy would enable patients to work and love. An improved ability to cope with problems was by no means an indication that the patient was already healthy. Each of the therapists knew that the course of the group therapy was symptom oriented and that far-reaching change was not possible in this setting. Regarding the problems of choosing between the two extremes of emancipation and adaptation, the therapists expressed the view that the objective of the therapy depended entirely on the patient. It was not possible to force anybody to become emancipated (i.e., to develop partly without consideration for the environment). Conversely, pure adaptation was undesirable if it meant being overcautious and ceasing to delve into social problems. *Adaptation* means realistic behavior based on an awareness of reality. The emphasis was placed on therapy as a means to developing awareness, an opportunity for self-reflection and adaptation (in the sense that one should accept from society what one can get—in other words, the patient should be enabled to make decisions, to do what is best for himself).

6.5.3. Class and sex

Sex-specific differences in language behavior were generally recognized and noticed. These were to be found in the choice of topic, and feelings were expressed more by women. Women's increased awareness of authority was also mentioned ("they look at me more directly, expecting something from me") (2.4.2). The therapists judged the problems of class to be more important. One therapist rejected the concept of class, replacing it with the phrase "previous experience," that is, experience with therapeutic establishments, with psychotherapeutic theory. Yet it was not apparent to him that in fact, this previous experience was extremely class specific (see Hollingshead and Redlich 1975). Working-class patients were regarded as more aggressive; in many cases they were forced into the role of clowns because of their "super lingo," a role that naturally caused them embarrassment (6.4.2). They also emphasized the difficulty of giving therapeutic treatment to intellectual middle-class patients. This group of patients was the most difficult to deal with (they put up the greatest resistance, especially verbally), and their integration within the group was not a simple matter either, because of their inhibitions and suppressed feelings (this observation was very surprising only initially). Lower-middle-class patients were best suited for therapy. The fact that their problems were often different, as well as possibly incomprehensible to others (unemployment, compared to a middle-class problem, such as students' writing difficulties), was of less importance. The essential thing was that a problem should be accepted as such. The most successful patients were the "well-behaved" ones: those who attended the sessions regularly, were ready to help, eager to learn, and obliging.

6.5.4. Attitudes toward the institution of crisis intervention

All the therapists gave evasive answers when questioned about their satisfaction with the team. Nobody was really satisfied. They noticed the hierarchy between doctors and the others, and irregular working hours and the occasional impossibility of contacting members made their work more difficult. They found the work itself, dealing with seriously ill patients, strenuous, but no more so than in other jobs. The mechanisms in a therapy group carried out by the team under supervision were not fundamentally different from the groups of patients observed, with the exception that "we are more ingenious." Several possible improvements to the center's offerings were mentioned, such as psychodrama, groups with drawing, pantomime, painting (not just verbalization), and family therapy.

6.5.5. Awareness of language

It was also interesting to note the therapists' attitudes to language, to their own language behavior, and to dialect. All therapists maintained that they spoke colloquial German and adapted their language to the patients. Talking dialect was positively rated as being more emotional, as well as an indication of the elimination of fear ("people dare to talk dialect").

Text 73. Therapist.

T: You have to be tremendously, you have to be very careful in therapy not to set a sort of linguistic standard, indicating to patients that they should talk with me in this manner, so as not to inhibit their entire expression from the start, although I think that particularly with our aim, which is actual crisis intervention, dealing with people undergoing crises, that it is just as important to find out about a patient's feelings, that he can confront himself with his feelings in front of me, something which he cannot normally do, . . . that he should be able to express these using words with which he is familiar, which he is accustomed to use to express such a thing, often even without words.

6.6. Summary and outlook

The analysis of the interviews with the therapists supplements our mosaic of the therapeutic situation and communication. A comparison of their aims, values, and ideas with the objective results of our investigation is particularly profitable and by no means incongruous. On the contrary, many of the hypotheses were also confirmed here (2.3, 2.4, 4.2). It is surprising how the sex-specific factor, the differentiated interplay of class and sex, is underrated. The assessment of the possibilities and objectives of group therapy and of the institution seems very realistic. It is also astonishing to note the tremendous awareness of language and the therapists' self-reflection on their own language and the language behavior of their patients. In fact, I never had the impression that there was a language barrier between therapists and patients (2.4.1.2).

This concludes the discussion of the interviews with the therapists. I shall now propose several postulates based on the results of this study:

1. The existing class-specific differences (2.4.1, 4.3, 4.4) call for *more information about the therapy and therapeutic facilities* and for the reduction of prejudices. Attitudes toward this treatment and the institutions practicing it are strongly determined by previous experience. The "intellectual" middle-class patient and the "clown" role of working-class patients (6.5.3) are phenomena that scientists and therapists will have to examine in theory and in practice. The explicit objectification and linguistic analysis of these factors rep-

resents a first step in this direction (1.3) (Nedelman and Horn 1976; Candlin et al. 1976).

2. During their training, therefore, therapists should be informed about class- and sex-specific phenomena in the (language) behavior of the group (e.g., the use of different problem presentations—see 3.9, 3.10), and they should adopt various styles, and even outlooks, in order to achieve more empathy. These findings should also be incorporated into *therapeutic technique.*

3. More *therapeutic facilities* of different kinds are required. Some of the alternatives and additional possibilities, such as a combination of group and individual therapy, were mentioned by the therapists interviewed. Communication and integration in the group should not restrict the individual's interpretation and the progress associated with it. Communes of therapists and patients undergoing severe crises would ensure the survival of the patients during this period and give them comprehensive care and maximum understanding. This does, however, require a tremendous amount of work on the part of the therapists. Family therapy as an additional form of treatment is also desirable and efficient. The individual's crisis cannot be regarded out of context from his environment, and a treatment that also affects his immediate surroundings would seem to be much more expedient (2.2.4). More accessible possibilities for supplementary therapy and more intensive individual therapy must be provided (2.4.1.2). This is the only means of guaranteeing emancipation that goes beyond the mere treatment of symptoms (1.2.6).[1]

The results of the present psycholinguistic and sociolinguistic study are of tremendous relevance, not only for the *theory* and *practice* of *psychotherapy* but for *basic research* in *linguistics* and its *interdisciplinary fields* as well.

The study has shown that *there are class- and sex-specific differences* even in the therapeutic situation and that these differences manifest themselves in language behavior. Recently developed quantitative and qualitative linguistic methods have made it possible to demonstrate these differences explicitly (2.4.1, 2.4.2, 4.3, 4.4).

For the first time, both qualitative and quantitative analysis of the text class of *problem presentation in group therapy* and of the text types used to realize it have proved empirically that members of the middle class prefer *narration* and *circumstantial description*, while members of the working class tend to use *scenes*. Members of the lower middle class, particularly women, tend to overadapt, and circumstantial description is encountered particularly frequently in this class (2.4.1.3). Significant differences between women and men were also established: women tend to use narration and scenes, men, descriptions of symptoms.

A change in the mode of presentation was established as the main effect of development and therapy (5.5). Elements of all three text types are interwoven, resulting in a *mixed type* that contains not only problem solutions but also feelings expressed in a narrative and scenic way. As far as the psychologically oriented categories used are concerned, the hypotheses on class- and sex-specific differences were further elaborated (3.10.2). *Forecasts* based on explicit linguistic analysis make it possible to predict the occurrence of *certain defense mechanisms* and *reactions by patients*, depending on the class and sex of the speaker and the topic selected (4.3.3).

The *choice of topic* also proved to be strongly dependent on class and sex and was also influenced by the phase of the therapy (3.7.4, 4.3.1.2). This result confirmed the hypotheses on socialization (2.4). Finally, case studies proved that the *therapeutic effect* (4.4) and the development of individual patients could be demonstrated both qualitatively and quantitatively, thus verifying the hypotheses on therapeutic effect (2.5).

Such comprehensive results could be achieved only by the use of a full range of new quantitative and qualitative linguistic methods; thus, a valid picture of the therapeutic situation investigated was provided. Qualitative linguistic parameters were also analyzed quantitatively for the first time; this has justified the large amount of text material used (3.3, 3.5). Even so, qualitative linguistic analysis (5.4, 5.5) proved suitable for the diversity and complexity of therapeutic communication (2.3). The comparison of *self-assessment* and *outside appraisal* (6.4, 6.5) served to extend the research perspective and to reduce the observer paradox and the ethical dilemma (3.4).

In spite of significant linguistic differences, it was evident that there was no connection between the nature of the intervention and the formal linguistic narrative structure (3.9, 4.3). Members of the working class, the lower middle class, and the middle class all acquire new speech strategies in the course of a therapy based mainly on verbalization. New dimensions of affective expression open up, and alternative strategies for problem solving are proffered (4.4, 5.4, 5.5), tending to produce a *balancing identity* (2.4.2.2).

The myth and the prejudice that *members of the working class* are not capable of dealing with the therapeutic situation (2.4.1) have been shown to be false, as has the ideology that *women* could only be helped by groups of women or by female therapists (2.4.2).

The tremendous benefit to potential suicide candidates also became apparent in the course of the longitudinal study of this open group (4.4, 5.5, 6.4). This has decisive consequences for psychiatric and psychotherapeutic practice. Psychotherapy should receive much greater publicity in the media, and by means of public relations, it could serve as an important aid for people in distress. It can no longer remain the exclusive domain of a small class of people but should, instead, be embodied in institutions.

The results have also boosted basic research in psycholinguistics, text linguistics, and sociolinguistics (2.3, 2.4). A new theory on meaning in therapeutic discourse (three-level model), a sociopsychological theory on text planning and comprehension, and a text model for the description of problem presentation in group therapy were developed following analysis of the extensive amount of text material (3.9, 3.10).

It is to be hoped that any unanswered questions may provide an incentive for further research in this field in the interests of a humanitarian social science.

Notes

1: Interdisciplinary research

1. See Hager et al. (1977), Moersch (1976), Lorenzer (1970, 1976, 1977), Wolff (1974), Ricoeur (1974), and Lacan (1975: 71 ff.) on the discussion of symbols. Piaget's contribution is important from a nonpsychoanalytical point of view: He carries out an empirical investigation of the development of symbols and speech in childhood (1969). The book by Piro (1967) is worth mentioning in connection with schizophrenic speech behavior.

2. Yet, etymology must above all avoid considering only the one extreme (root etymology at the remotest period of time) or the other (derivation of words without inquiring as to their origin). It should endeavor, rather, to unite both aspects and thus consider in detail the derivation of the word concerned, taking into account not only the facts of phonetic history and the derivation of the word but also its meaning; it must trace the connections with the object described and explain the motivation of the word—in other words, its relationship to associated derivations and the position of the word within an entire or partial vocabulary, nor must it exclude considerations of linguistic geography, and so on (Schmitt 1977, foreword:4). It is obvious that etymology involves only words, and not texts or scenes (see also Lord 1966:201 ff., 209 ff.).

3. In this context, see the psycholinguistic discussion of automation processes (Van Lancker 1972*a,b*).

4. The discussion in Grewendorf (1979) is of importance. The papers collected here deal above all with the difficulties of allocating individual utterances to categories of speech-act taxonomies. Searle (1971, 1975) also falls into this category. The qualitative methods of text analysis are dealt with in detail in 5.2.

5. Ethnomethodology continues the tradition of Schütz (1960). To begin with, the text is checked for rules of everyday routine, without recourse to a theoretical background. See also Sudnow (1972) on this point.

2: Formation of hypotheses

1. After the development of group therapy and its peculiarities is outlined, many aspects are then reintroduced into my own theoretical considerations so that they can be reinterpreted and described from a linguistic point of view. There is a lot to be said for this procedure, although there is a risk of mentioning the same thing twice from different perspectives. I am naturally interested mainly in psycholinguistic and sociolinguistic analysis of therapeutic communication in the group (although in a different form, the proposed model is also applicable to individual therapy). Nevertheless, in order to avoid any misunderstanding of the processes occurring in groups that may be attributable to everyday knowledge, psychotherapeutic concepts and terms offer a starting point and a support. For a sociologist, it is interesting to note the dialectic between conventional concepts and their reformulation (reinterpretation) in light of linguistic considerations. Many aspects that have fallen prey to the polemics of various schools turn out to be insignificant from the layman's point of view. As a result of my research, greater importance is attached to others that have been of little significance in conventional theories. I believe this to be extremely fruitful methodologically. Self-evident facts are questioned, problematical aspects initially ignored, thus jolting scientific discussion out of its rut and opening the way for new perceptions.

2. Klann (1977:150 ff.), Menninger and Holzman (1973: 15 ff.), and Becker (1975:178 ff.) provide impressive descriptions of the psychotherapeutic setting. Several things need to be added in the present study, as we are dealing with group, not individual, therapy.

3. In the extensive literature on family psychology and sociology, some important publications, by way of example, are Cazden (1966), Kohn (1962–1963), and Ruth (1966); they have dealt with these problems from a sociolinguistic perspective. Hess and Handel (1975), Anderson (1973), and Bateson et al. (1969) deal with "sick" families, with psychogenic and pathogenic mechanisms. Walter (1973) offers a firm theory of socialization. Not many authors have tackled the working-class family. They are Dinitz et al. (1975), Miller and Riessman (1961), John (1963), Whyte (1973), and Peisach (1965). The differences between the working class and the middle class with regards to the type of family and socialization

are of particular relevance to the development of sociolinguistic theory.

4. See also Wygotski's concept of the inner language (1971: 312 ff.).

5. Text semantics also represent a context-free concept of meaning and are also of importance in this context to the extent that they are derived from Chomsky's theory (1965) (Petöfi 1973: 208 ff.). See also Beaugrande and Dressler (1980:40 ff.) on text semantics.

6. The 'Meaning ↔ Text' model developed in the Soviet Union is also of significance: "The proposed model is translative (= transformative), rather than a generative system; its purpose consists in establishing correspondences between any given meaning and (ideally) all synonymous texts having this meaning. We assume here that we can formally describe meaning as an invariant of a set of equisignificant texts, that analysis of meaning as such lies outside the model, and that the 'Meaning ↔ Text' model (MTM) is a fragment of the more general model 'Reality ↔ (Meaning ↔ Text) ↔ Speech'" (Mel´čuk 1974). See also Žol'kovskij and Mel´čuk (1967) and Mel´čuk (1976) on this subject.

7. In this context, it is also worth mentioning Jakobson's six functions of speech (1971, II:703), which differentiate Bühler's threefold classification (3.9.2.1).

8. Like Heigl-Evers (172), Foulkes (1965) differentiates between three phases in the group process, while Wolf and Schwartz (1962) mention six phases.

9. These investigations were based on a criticism and extension of Bernstein's theories (1962*a*,*b*, 1970*a*), particularly his assertions relating to the "elaborated" and "restricted code." Dittmar (1973) presents a good summary of historical development. Labov (1966), Trudgill (1974), Leodolter (1975*a*, 1976), and Oevermann (1972) carried out precise empirical investigations of both individual speech situations and speech communities. It is generally accepted that Bernstein ignored the category of the speech situation as well as other social classes, such as the lower middle class (Brown and Fraser 1979, Leodolter 1975*b*).

10. A great deal of literature on psychiatry and psychiatric institutions has been published, particularly in recent years: Basaglia (1973), Goffman (1961, 1970), Horn (1972), Forster and Pelikan (1977), Gleiss et al. (1973), Cremerius (1975). Most sociologically

oriented studies have in common their criticism of the "psychiatric" institution. Alternatives are put forward, and even class-specific selection of type of therapy and institution is discussed.

11. The works of Thorne and Henley (1975), Dubois and Crouch (1976), West and Zimmermann (1975), OBST (1979), Lakoff (1975), Winitz (1959), Lüder et al. (1970), and Smith (1979) are interesting from a sociolinguistic point of view, although most of these investigations are of an exploratory nature only. The works of Beauvoir (1968), Anger (1973), Dräger (1968), Oevermann (1970), McCarthy (1953), Bönner (1973), Komarovsky (1946), Maccoby (1966), and Rubin (1972) are interesting from a sociological and psychological point of view. These authors put forward a wide range of viewpoints that cannot be discussed in detail. The independent approach will be introduced later (partly through discussion and criticism of existing studies) (Wodak-Leodolter 1979).

12. Chasseguet-Smirgel (1974), Moeller-Gambaroff (1977), Windhoff-Heritier (1976), and Franks and Burtle (1974) present some interesting approaches with regard to the development of the sex roles from a psychoanalytical point of view. These concepts can be regarded as an extension of Freud's theory.

3: Empirical investigation

1. The participatory observation method and the ethical dilemma associated with it have already been dealt with in detail by many authors. It is worth mentioning several important studies on this method of field research and on sociological research in general: Habermas (1977) offers a metatheoretical framework that contrasts with a positivistic research logic. Filstead (1971), Barnes (1971), Becker (1958, 1971), Becker and Geer (1957), Leodolter (1975a: 198 ff.) and Wodak-Leodolter (1980) make important contributions to the discussion of strategies regarding the ethical dilemma. Bales (1950), Berdan (1973), Guy (1976), and Overbeck et al. (1974) proffer other procedures for the analysis of group discussion: in some instances the ethical dilemma is reduced, although the observer paradox is certainly maximized. My reasons for deciding to use participatory observation have already been stated (3.2, 3.3).

2. *Translator's note:* this subchapter applies to the choice of the German word *Schicht* ("social stratum") in preference to the word *Klasse* ("social class"). As *class* is the term generally used in

English, this subchapter is of purely semantic interest in the English translation, although it represents a theoretical and political debate in the sociological paradigm.

3. Douglas (1967) provides a sociological analysis of suicide, Weiss (1954), a clinical investigation. Sacks (1966) gives the first ethnomethodological and linguistic analysis of telephone conversations from and with potential suicide candidates.

4. Classification by class was particularly problematical in this case for two reasons. Several details cannot be published or were not available because of the necessity of maintaining anonymity. Second, many patients had been torn away from their normal everyday lives and familiar environments by their mental crises (divorce, death, advancement, demotion, unemployment, inpatient treatment). To the extent that information was available, I therefore had to orient myself by patients' status before their illness. It was easiest to classify those patients interviewed, as I was able to gather more detailed social data during the interviews (6.4).

5. The tables contain the χ^2 (chi-square test) results for the parameters specified in each case. If four figures are given, the first refers to the absolute frequency, the second to the row frequency, the third to the column frequency, and the last to the relative frequency with reference to the entire sample. Each table designation consists of the qualitative parameters correlated with one another (for example, "narrative structure/class" means that the distribution of narrative types with reference to the three classes is examined for significant deviations) (Sachs 1969:152). Other abbreviations are α (= probability of error) and df (= degrees of freedom).

6. In the quantitative analysis (4.3), I have attempted to deal with individual categories both synchronically and diachronically. In other words, the existence (or absence) of class-specific differences was calculated for the entire text volume (synchronic). I then carried out a progressive investigation of individual parameters (expression of feelings, attitudes to problem solving) and made case studies that indicate the qualitative development. As a result, there are qualitative differences between the beginning and the end of the therapy in spite of the fact that there was not always a straight-line development. Because of the unique nature of every session, however, a minimum of four sessions had to be grouped together, as synchronic and diachronic comparisons would not otherwise have been meaningful. Observations (e.g., class/session for sessions

1–4 versus class/session for sessions 16–20) cannot be statistically evaluated because of the limited amount of data. Nevertheless, the case studies permit us to conclude, for example, that women and men approximate one another (balancing identity: 2.4.2).

7. A wide variety of classification is available for the analysis and classification of texts (Werlich 1975; Sandig 1975; Beaugrande and Dressler 1980:3 ff.; Gülich and Raible 1975:144–146). I myself use Gülich and Raible's definition of text class: "Text classes are systematic units the manifestations of which are the text itself. They should be described as configurations of text-external and text-internal features, i.e., as a definition of features" (1975:144 ff.).

I do not agree with the view that distinctive features must be used and feel that this involves factors constituting the text in the sense of speaker strategies (2.3.2.2). *Text type* can then be understood as a realization pattern from the principal text class and is related to the term *text sample* used by Sandig (1978:19 ff.). Problem presentation in group therapy as a separate text class is defined here mainly by functional description (3.9.2.2) and by qualitative parameters (3.10) that record the central dimensions.

8. Labov and Waletzky's schema (1967) offers a framework for the registration of spontaneous spoken texts and narratives. It was designed for the analysis of narratives of a central terrible thing (mortal fear) experienced by the speaker interviewed. As a result, every narrative is broken down into orientation (temporal and spatial background), complication (incident), evaluation (assessment of the incident), resolution, and coda (summary). Labov and Waletzky also provide a model for quantifying the complexity of the story (using the position and number of important "clauses"). This makes it possible to give formal definitions of various narrative patterns. Yet the schema is only suitable for "ideal," typical narratives and not for all lengthy monologue passages, as we shall see (3.10, 5.5).

9. More recently van Dijk has also incorporated the results of cognitive psychology in his reflections on text theory (3.9.3). Nonetheless, he is interested not so much in the generation of complete texts as in text reduction ("summarizing"). Yet the constitutive elements of his earlier theories still remain (macrostructure, proposition, etc.), so our criticism of this new development is still valid (see also van Dijk and Kintsch 1978:74 ff.).

10. At an epistemological level, Holenstein (1975, 1976) offers an analysis and justification of the phenomenological procedure in

linguistic description. He refers to Jakobson's structuralism (Jakobson 1971). His ideas can, however, be generalized as well as applied to our data.

11. It is possible to justify transferring the sociophonological register of styles from Leodolter (1975a:256 ff.) by the presence of an equally restrictive speech situation and the conflict with authority. Nevertheless, the therapeutic setting permits more spontaneous expression of feelings. The hierarchy in Leodolter (1975a:256) should therefore be regarded as a first approximation.

12. The use of the term *dissociation* does not correspond to that of Pagès (1974:194). Pagès (pp. 274 ff.), undertakes a classification by "affective languages" a strategy that in my opinion mixes up the real and latent language levels, verbal and nonverbal aspects, metacommunication and content; thus, the individual language levels remain undifferentiated.

13. See also Wunderlich (1976), Searle (1971), Martens (1974), Frankenberg (1976), Klann (1979), and Goeppert and Goeppert (1973, 1975) on this subject.

14. The literature on interpretation in psychotherapy is almost too extensive to review. The central work is still *The Interpretation of Dreams* (Freud 1976a, II/III). From a linguistic point of view, Trömel-Plötz (1978) is interesting in that she attempts a linguistic classification of types of interpretation. The debate in *Analytical Philosophy* on the terms *interpretation, explanation,* and *construction* is also of importance (Ekstein 1979).

15. Menninger and Holzman (1973) and Trömel-Plötz (1979) describe the difficulties in writing and analyzing interpretations. When does the correct moment arrive in a therapeutic session to enable one to give an interpretation? The linguistically explicit analysis of therapeutic discourse is the very thing to provide an answer (Flader 1979).

4: Quantitative analysis

1. See note 5 for chapter 3.

5: The limits of quantitative analysis

1. These two texts have been analyzed in such detail that both the original text and its translation have been reproduced. Also, it

may interest the reader to see an original text in the Viennese dialect (vernacular).

2. Sandig says the following on the use of such figures of speech as the metaphor, the parable, and the analogy: "The linguistic phenomenon described as a figure of speech is not dependent on its predominant features, but can only be described as stylistic when specifically used in text. The consequence of this is that any linguistic phenomenon can be a figure of speech" (1978:29 ff.).

6: The self-assessment of patients and therapists

1. It is naturally impossible in the present psycholinguistic and sociolinguistic study to draw conclusions about all the settings based on psychotherapeutic concepts (and the theories upon which each is based). The various schools define therapeutic effect differently, and its presence can therefore only be demonstrated initially within the specific setting investigated.

Bibliography

Abraham, K. 1969. Über die determinierende Kraft des Namens; Traum und Mythos. Eine Studie zur Völkerpsychologie. In *Psychoanalytische Studien I*. Ed. J. Cremerius. Frankfurt on the Main: Fischer (conditio humana).

Aebischer, V. 1979. Wenn Frauen nicht sprechen. *Osnabrücker Beiträge zur Sprachtheorie*, Beiheft 3:85–95.

Althusser, L. 1970. *Freud und Lacan*. Berlin: Luchterhand.

Ammon, G. (ed.). 1976. *Gruppenpsychotherapie*. Munich: Kindler.

Anderson, M. (ed.). 1973. *Sociology of the Family*. London: Penguin.

Anger, H. 1973. Männliches und weibliches Denken. In *Die Geschlechterrolle*. Ed. K. H. Bönner. Munich: Nymphenburger Texte zur Wissenschaft.

Anker, J., and Duffey, R. 1958. Training Group Psychotherapists: A Method and Evaluation. *Group Psychotherapy* 11, 4:314–326.

Argelander, H. 1972. *Gruppenprozesse*. Reinbek/Hamburg: Rowohlt.

_____. 1974. Die psychoanalytische Situation einer Gruppe im Vergleich zur Einzeltherapie. *Psyche* 4:310–327.

Austin, J. L. 1971. *How to Do Things with Words*. Oxford: Oxford University Press.

Autorinnengruppe Uni-Wien. (ed.) 1981. *Das ewige Klischee*. Vienna: Böhlau.

Bales, R. 1950. *Interaction Process Analysis*. New York. Holt, Rinehart and Winston.

Balkányi, C. 1964. On Verbalization. *International Journal of Psycho-Analysis* 45:64–74.

Ballmer, T. 1979. Probleme der Klassifikation von Sprechakten. In *Sprechakttheorie und Semantik*, ed. G. Grewendorf. Frankfurt on the Main: Suhrkamp.

Bally, C. 1930. *Traité de stylistique française*. Paris: Klinksreck.

Barnes, D., and Todd, F. 1977. *Communication and Learning in Small Groups*. London: Routledge and Kegan Paul.

Barnes, J. A. 1971. Some Ethical Problems in Modern Fieldwork. In *Qualitative Methodology. Firsthand Involvement with the Social World,* ed. W. D. Filstead. Chicago: Markham.

Bartlett, F. C. 1932. *Remembering: A Study in Experimental and Social Psychology.* Cambridge: Cambridge University Press.

Basaglia, F. (ed.). 1973. *Die negierte Institution oder "Die Gemeinschaft der Ausgeschlossenen."* Frankfurt on the Main: Suhrkamp.

Bateson, G., et al. 1969. *Schizophrenie und Familie.* Frankfurt on the Main: Suhrkamp.

Beaugrande, R. de, and Dressler, W. 1980. *Introduction to Text-Linguistics.* London: Longmans.

————. 1981. *Einführung in die Textlinguistik.* Tübingen: Niemeyer.

Beauvoir, S. de. 1968. *Das andere Geschlecht—Sitte und Sexus der Frau.* Reinbek/Hamburg: Rowohlt.

Becker, A. M. 1975. Psychoanalyse. In *Psychotherapie: Grundlagen, Verfahren, Indikationen.* Ed. H. Strotzka. Munich: Urban und Schwarzenberg.

————. 1979. Tiefenpsychologie. Manuscript. Vienna.

Becker, H. S., and Geer, B. 1957. Participant Observation and Interviewing. *Human Organization* 16, 3:28–32.

Becker, H. S. 1958. Problems of Inference and Proof in Participant Observation. *American Sociological Review* 23:652–663.

————. 1971. Whose Side Are We On? In *Qualitative Methodology. Firsthand Involvement with the Social World.* Ed. W. D. Filstead. Chicago: Markham.

Berdan, R. 1973. The Use of Linguistically Determined Groups in Sociolinguistic Research. *SWPL Educational Report* 26.

Bergin, A., and Strupp, H. H. 1972. *Changing Frontiers in the Science of Psychotherapy.* Chicago: Chicago University Press.

Bernstein, B. 1962*a*. Social Class, Linguistic Code and Grammatical Elements. *Language and Speech* 5:221–240.

————. 1962*b*. Linguistic Codes, Hesitation Phenomena and Intelligence. *Language and Speech* 5:31–46.

————. 1970*a*. Familiales Rollensystem, Kommunikation und Sozialisation. In *Soziale Struktur, Sozialisation und Sprachverhalten.* Ed. B. Bernstein. Amsterdam: De Munter.

————. 1970*b*. Soziale Schicht, System des Sprachgebrauchs und

Psychotherapie. In *Soziale Struktur, Sozialisation and Sprach-verhalten*. Ed. B. Berstein. Amsterdam: De Munter.

———. (ed.). 1970. *Soziale Struktur, Sozialisation und Sprachver-halten*. Amsterdam: De Munter.

Beutin, W. (ed.). 1972. *Literatur und Psychoanalyse*. Ansätze zu einer psychoanalytischen Textinterpretation. Munich: Kindler.

Bion, W. R. 1961. *Experiences in Groups*. London: Tavistock.

Birbaumer, N. (ed.). 1973. *Neuropsychologie der Angst*. Munich: Urban und Schwarzenberg.

Bolinger, D. 1978. Intonation across Languages. In *Universals of Human Language*. Ed. J. H. Greenberg. Stanford, Calif.: Stanford University Press.

Bönner, K. H. (ed.). 1973. *Die Geschlechterrolle*. Munich: Nymphenburger Texte zur Wissenschaft.

Boomer, D. S. 1965. Hesitation and Grammatical Encoding. *Language and Speech* 8:148–158.

Brekle, H. E. 1972. *Semantik*. Munich: Fink UTB.

Bremond, C. 1973. *Logique du récit*. Paris: Ed. du seuil.

Brody, E. B., and Redlich, F. C. (eds.). 1957. *Psychotherapy with Schizophrenics: A Symposium*. New York: International. University Press.

Brown, P., and Fraser, C. 1979. Speech as a Marker of Situation. In *Social Markers in Speech*. Ed. K. R. Scherer and H. Giles. Cambridge: Cambridge University Press.

Brown, P., and Levinson, S. 1979. Social Structure, Groups and Interaction. In *Social Markers in Speech*. Ed. K. R. Scherer and H. Giles. Cambridge: Cambridge University Press.

Buchinger, K. 1978. Gruppentherapeutische Methoden. Manuscript. Vienna.

———. 1979. Analytic Group Therapy and Group Dynamics. Some Problems. Manuscript. Vienna.

Bühler, K. 1934. *Sprachtheorie: Die Darstellungsfunktion der Sprache*. Jena: Fischer.

Cadow, B. 1977. Therapist Sex Differences in Empathy. Implications for Defining Empathy, Training and Client Selection. Ph.D. Dissertation. Florida State University.

Candlin, L., et al. 1976. Doctors in Casualty: Applying Communicative Competence to Components of Specialist Course Design. *International Journal in Applied Linguistics* 14, 3:245–253.

Carroll, L. 1965. *The Annotated Alice in Wonderland.* Harmonds-
worth: Penguin.
Cavell, S. 1976. Availability of Wittgensteins Later Philosophy. In
Must We Mean What We Say?, Ed. S. Cavell. Cambridge: Cam-
bridge University Press.
————. (ed.). 1976. *Must We Mean What We Say?* Cambridge:
Cambridge University Press.
Cazden, C. 1966. Subcultural Differences in Child Language: An
Interdisciplinary Review. *Merill-Palmer Quarterly* 12:185–219.
Ceplitis, L. K. 1974. *Analiz rečevoj intonacii.* Riga: Zinatne.
Chafe, W. L. 1977. Creativity in Verbalization and Its Implications
for the Nature of Stored Knowledge. In *Discourse Production
and Comprehension.* Ed. R. Freedle. Norwood, N.J.: Ablex.
Chassseguet-Smirgel, J. 1974. *Psychoanalyse der weiblichen Sexu-
alität.* Frankfurt on the Main: Suhrkamp.
Chesler, P. 1974. *Frauen-das verrückte Geschlecht.* Reinbek/Ham-
burg: Rowohlt.
Chomsky, N. 1969. *Aspekte der Syntax-Theorie.* Frankfurt on the
Main: Suhrkamp.
Cicourel, A. V. 1970. *Methode und Messung in der Soziologie.*
Frankfurt on the Main: Suhrkamp.
————. 1975. Discourse and Text: Cognitive and Linguistic Processes in Studies of Social Structure. Manuscript. La Jolla.
Cremerius, J. 1962. *Die Beurteilung des Behandlungserfolgs in der
Psychotherapie.* Berlin: Springer.
————. 1969. Schweigen als Problem der psychoanalytischen Tech-
nik. *Jahrbuch der Psychoanalyse* 6:69–105.
————. 1975. Schichtenspezifische Schwierigkeiten bei der An-
wendung der Psychoanalyse. *Münchener medizinische Wochen-
schrift* 117:1229–1232.
————. (ed.). 1969. *Psychoanalytische Studien* I. Frankfurt on the
Main: Fischer (conditio humana).
Cube, F. v. 1971. *Was ist Kybernetik?* Munich: Fink UTB.
Davitz, J. R. 1967. *The Communication of Emotional Meaning.*
Westport, Conn.: Greenwood Press.
Deese, J. 1973. Cognitive Structure and Affect in Language. In
Communication and Affect. Ed. P. Pliner et al. New York: Ac-
ademic Press.
Deutsch, H. 1977a. Some Forms of Emotional Disturbance and
Their Relationship to Schizophrenia. In *The World of Emotions.*

Ed. C. W. Socarides. Bloomington: Indiana University Press.

────── . 1977*b*. Absence of Grief. In *The World of Emotions*. Ed. C. W. Socarides. Bloomington: Indiana University Press.

Dijk, T. A. van. 1972. *Some Aspects of Text Grammars*. The Hague: Mouton.

Dijk, T. A. van, and Kintsch, W. 1978. Cognitive Psychology and Discourse: Recalling and Summarizing Stories. In *Current Trends in Textlinguistics*. Ed. W. U. Dressler. Berlin: De Gruyter.

Dinitz, S., et al. 1975. *Deviance*. Oxford: Oxford University Press.

Dittman, A. T., and Wynne, L. C. 1961. Linguistic Techniques and the Analysis of Emotionality in Interviews. *Journal of Abnormal Social Psychology* 63:201–212.

Dittmar, N. 1973. *Soziolinguistik*. Exemplarische und kritische Darstellung ihrer Theorie, Empirie und Anwendung. Frankfurt on the Main: Fischer Anthenäum.

Dogil, G. 1979*a*. On the Tonology of WH-Questions in Polish and English. *Wiener Linguistische Gazette* 20:15–30.

────── . 1979*b*. *Autosegmental Account of Phonological Emphasis*. Edmonton: Linguistic Research.

Dörner, D. 1979. *Problemlösen als Informationsverarbeitung*. Stuttgart: Kohlhammer.

Douglas, J. 1967. *The Social Meanings of Suicide*. Princeton: Princeton University Press.

Dräger, K. 1968. Übersicht über psychoanalytische Auffassungen von der Entwicklung der weiblichen Sexualität. *Psyche* 6:410–422.

Dressler, W. (ed.). 1978. *Current Trends in Textlinguistics*. Berlin: De Gruyter.

────── , et al. 1972. Phonologische Schnellsprechregeln in der Wiener Umgangssprache. *Wiener Linguistische Gazette* 1:1–29.

Dressler, W., and Wodak, R. 1982. Sociophonological Methods in the Study of Sociolinguistic Variation in Viennese German. *Language in Society*: 239–270.

Dressler, W., and Wodak-Leodolter, R. 1977. Language Preservation and Language Death in Brittany. In *Language Death. International Journal of the Sociology of Language*. Ed. W. U. Dressler and R. Wodak-Leodolter.

Dressler, W., and Wodak-Leodolter, R. (eds.). 1977. Language Death. *International Journal of the Sociology of Language* 12.

Dubois, B., and Crouch, L. (eds.). 1976. *The Sociology of the Lan-*

guages of American Women. San Antonio, Tex.: Trinity University Press.

Edelheit, H. 1969. Speech and Psychic Structure: The vocal-auditory Organization of the Ego. *Journal of the American Psychoanalytic Association* 16:233–243, 17:452–459.

Ehlich, K., and Rehbein, J. 1976. Praktisches Transkribieren. *Linguistische Berichte* 45:21–42.

Ehlich K., and Switalla, B. 1976. Transkriptionssysteme—eine exemplarische Übersicht. *Studium Linguistik* 2:78–106.

Ekstein, R. 1979. Further Thoughts Concerning the Nature of the Interpretative Process. Sigmund Freud House Bulletin 3, 1: 12–19.

Engel, G. L. 1963. Toward a Classification of Affects. In *Expressions of Emotions in Man.* Ed. P. Trapp. New York: International University Press.

Epstein, S. 1973. Versuch einer Theorie der Angst. In *Neuropsychologie der Angst.* Ed. N. Birbaumer. Munich: Urban und Schwarzenberg.

Erb, M., and Knobloch, C. 1979. Einige Bestimmungen therapeutischer Kommunikation. In *Therapeutische Kommunikation. Ansätze zur Erforschung der Sprache im-psychoanalytischen Prozeß.* Ed. D. Flader and R. Wodak-Leodolter. Königstein/Taunus: Scriptor.

Farberow, N. 1973. Group Therapy for Self Destructive Persons. Manuscript. Washington, D.C.

Feldstein, S., et al. 1963. The Effect of Subject, Sex, Verbal Interaction and Topical Focus on Speech Disruption. *Language and Speech* 6:229–239.

Filstead, W. D. (ed.). 1971. *Qualitative Methodology.* Firsthand Involvement with the Social World. Chicago: Markham.

Finger, U. D. 1976. *Sprachzerstörung in Gruppen.* Frankfurt on the Main: Fachbuchhandlung für Psychologie.

Flader, D. 1979. Techniken der Verstehenssteuerung im psychoanalytischen Diskurs. In *Therapeutische Kommunikation. Ansätze zur Erforschung der Sprache im psychoanalytischen Prozeß.* Ed. D. Flader and R. Wodak-Leodolter. Königstein/Taunus: Scriptor.

Flader, D., and Grodzicki, W. D. 1978. Hypothesen zur Wirkungsweise der psychoanalytischen Grundregel. *Psyche* 7, 32:545–594.

Flader, D., and Wodak-Leodolter, R. (eds.). 1979. *Therapeutische Kommunikation. Ansätze zur Erforschung der Sprache im psychoanalytischen Prozeß*. Königstein/Taunus: Scriptor.

Fliess, R. 1949. Silence and Verbalization. A Supplement to the Theory of the "Analytic Rule." *International Journal of Psycho-Analysis* 30:22–30.

Forster, R., and Pelikan, J. 1977. Krankheit als Karriereprozeß. *Österreichische Zeitschrift für Soziologie* 3, 4:29–43.

Foulkes, S. H. 1965. *Therapeutic Group Analysis*. New York: International University Press.

————. 1976. Über die Interpretation in der analytischen Gruppentherapie. In *Gruppenpsychotherapie*. Ed. G. Ammon. Munich: Kindler.

Frank, J. D. 1961. *Persuasion and Healing:* A Comparative Study of Psychotherapy. Baltimore: Johns Hopkins University Press.

Frankenberg, H. 1976. Vorwerfen und Rechtfertigen als verbale Teilstrategien der innerfamilialen Interaktion. Ph.D. Dissertation. Düsseldorf.

Franks, V., and Burtle, V. (eds.). 1974. *Women in Therapy*. New York: Brunner and Mazel.

Freedle, R. (ed.). 1977. *Discourse Production and Comprehension* Norwood, N.J.: Ablex.

————. (ed.). 1979. *New Directions in Discourse Processing*. Norwood, N.J.: Ablex.

Freedle, R., and Duran, R. 1979. Sociolinguistic Approaches to Dialogue with Suggested Applications to Cognitive Science. In *New Directions in Discourse Processing*. Ed. R. Freedle. Norwood: Ablex.

Freud, A. 1936. *Das Ich und die Abwehrmechanismen*. Munich: Kindler.

Freud, S. 1972. *Drei Abhandlungen zur Sexualtheorie*. Gesammelte Werke (GW) V, Frankfurt on the Main: Fischer.

————. 1973*a*. *Zur Psychopathologie des Alltagslebens*. GW IV, Frankfurt on the Main: Fischer.

————. 1973*b*. *Trauer und Melancholie*. GW X, Frankfurt on the Main: Fischer.

————. 1973*c*. *Über Triebumsetzungen, insbesondere der Analerotik*. GW X, Frankfurt on the Main: Fischer.

————. 1973*d*. *Vorlesungen zur Einführung in die Psychoanalyse*. GW XI, Frankfurt on the Main: Fischer.

Freud, S. 1973e. *Neue Folge der Vorlesungen zur Einführung in die Psychoanalyse.* GW XV, Frankfurt on the Main: Fischer.

———. 1976a. *Traumdeutung. Über den Traum.* GW II/III. Frankfurt on the Main: Fischer.

———. 1976b. *Das Interesse der Psychoanalyse für die nicht psychologischen Wissenschaften.* GW VIII, Frankfurt on the Main: Fischer.

———. 1976c. *Das Ich und das Es.* GW XIII, Frankfurt on the Main: Fischer.

———. 1976d. *Die Frage der Laienanalyse.* GW XIV, Frankfurt on the Main: Fischer.

———. 1976e. *Die Verneinung.* GW XIV, Frankfurt on the Main: Fischer.

———. 1976f. *Selbstdarstellung.* GW XIV, Frankfurt on the Main: Fischer.

———. 1976g. *Hemmung. Symptom und Angst.* GW XIV, Frankfurt on the Main: Fischer.

———. 1977a. *Studien über Hysterie.* GW I, Frankfurt on the Main: Fischer.

———. 1977b. *Zur Psychotherapie der Hysterie.* GW I, Frankfurt on the Main: Fischer.

Friedrichs, J. 1973. *Methoden empirischer Sozialforschung.* Reinbek/Hamburg: Rowohlt.

Fromkin, V. A. (ed.). 1973. *Speech Errors as Linguistic Evidence.* The Hague: Mouton.

Givon, T. (ed.). 1979. *Syntax and Semantics.* New York: Academic Press.

Gleiss, I., et al. 1973. *Soziale Psychiatrie.* Frankfurt on the Main: Suhrkamp.

Goeppert, H., and Goeppert, S. 1973. *Sprache und Psychoanalyse.* Reinbek/Hamburg: Rowohlt.

———. 1975. *Redeverhalten und Neurose.* Reinbek/Hamburg: Rowohlt.

Goffman, E. 1959. *The Presentation of Self in Everyday Life.* New York: Doubleday.

———. 1961. *Asylums: Essays on the Social Situation of Mental Patients and other Inmates.* New York: Doubleday Anchor.

———. 1970. *Stigma.* Harmondsworth: Penguin.

———. 1971. *Interaktionsrituale*—Über Verhalten in direkter Kommunikation. Frankfurt on the Main: Suhrkamp.

———. 1974. *Das Individuum im öffentlichen Austausch*. Frankfurt on the Main: Suhrkamp.

———. 1975. *Frame Analysis*. Harmondsworth: Penguin.

Goldman-Eisler, F. 1958. The Predictability of Words in Context and the Length of Pauses in Speech. *Language and Speech* 1:226–231.

———. 1961. A Comparative Study of Two Hesitation Phenomena. *Language and Speech* 4:18–26.

———. 1968. *Psycholinguistics*. London: Academic Press.

Goodman, L. 1972. A General Model for the Analysis of Survey. *American Journal of Sociology* 77:31–45.

Graupe, S. R. 1975. Ergebnisse und Probleme der quantitativen Erforschung traditioneller Psychotherapieverfahren. In *Psychotherapie: Grundlagen, Verfahren, Indikationen*. Ed. H. Strotzka. Munich: Urban und Schwarzenberg.

Green, H. 1974. *Ich habe Dir nie einen Rosengarten versprochen*. Stuttgart: Klett.

Greimas, A. J. 1966. *Sémantique Structurale*. Paris: Larousse.

Grewendorf, G. (ed.). 1979. *Sprechakttheorie und Semantik*. Frankfurt on the Main: Suhrkamp.

Grice, P. 1968. The Logic of Conversation. Mimeo.

Grindler, J., and Bandler, R. 1976. *The Structure of Magic*. Vol. 1, 2. Palo Alto, Calif.: Science and Behavior Books, Inc.

Grumiller, I. 1975. Therapeutische Grundkonzepte. In *Psychotherapie: Grundlagen, Verfahren, Indikationen*. Ed. H. Strotzka. Munich: Urban und Schwarzenberg.

Gülich. E., and Raible, W. 1975. Textsortenprobleme. In *Linguistische Probleme der Textanalyse. Jahrbuch 1973 des Instituts für deutsche Sprache*. Düsseldorf.

———. 1977. *Linguistische Textmodelle*. Stuttgart: UTB.

Gumperz, J. J., and Herasimchuk, E. 1972. The Conversational Analysis of Social Meaning. A Study in Class-Room Interaction. Manuscript.

Gunderson, K. (ed.). 1975. *Language, Mind and Knowledge*. Vol. VII. Minneapolis: University of Minnesota Press.

Guy, G. R. 1976. Variation in the Group and the Individual. *Pennsylvania Working Papers of Linguistic Change and Variation* 1/4.

Habermas, J. 1969. Systematisch verzerrte Kommunikation. Manuscript.

Habermas, J. 1971. Vorbereitende Bemerkungen zu einer Theorie der kommunikativen Kompetenz. In *Theorie der Gesellschaft oder Sozialtechnologie.* Ed. J. Habermas and N. Luhmann. Frankfurt on the Main: Suhrkamp.

———. 1977. *Erkenntnis und Interesse.* Frankfurt on the Main: Suhrkamp.

Habermas, J., and Luhmann, N. (eds.). 1971. *Theorie der Gesellschaft oder Sozialtechnologie.* Frankfurt on the Main: Suhrkamp.

Hager, F., et al. 1977. *Die Sache der Sprache.* Stuttgart: Metzler.

Hall, E., et al. 1977. Variations in Young Children's Use of Language: Some Effects of Setting and Dialect. In *Discourse Production and Comprehension.* Ed. R. Freedle. Norwood, N.J.: Ablex.

Halliday, M. A. K. 1976. System and Function. In *Halliday: System and Function in Language.* Ed. G. Kress. Oxford: Oxford University Press.

Heigl-Evers, A. 1972. *Konzepte der analytischen Gruppenpsychotherapie.* Göttingen: Vandenhoeck and Ruprecht.

Helm, J. (ed.). 1967. *Essays on the Verbal and Visual Arts.* Seattle, London: University of Washington Press.

Hersko, M., and Winder, A. E. 1958. Changes in Patients' Attitudes Toward Self and Others during Group Psychotherapy. *Group Psychotherapy* 11, 4:309–320.

Hess, R., and Handel, G. 1975. *Familienwelten.* Düsseldorf: Schwann.

Hofmannsthal, H. v. 1951. *Der Brief des Lord Chandos.* Gesammelte Werke in Einzelausgaben, Prosa II. Frankfurt on the Main: Fischer.

Holenstein, E. 1975. *Roman Jakobsons phänomenologischer Strukturalismus.* Frankfurt on the Main: Suhrkamp.

———. 1976. *Linguistik, Semiotik, Hermeneutik.* Plädoyers für eine strukturale Phänomenologie. (Roman Jakobson zum 80. Geburtstag). Frankfurt on the Main: Suhrkamp.

Hollingshead, A., and Redlich, F. 1975. *Der Sozialcharakter psychischer Störungen.* Frankfurt on the Main: Fischer.

Horn, K. (ed.). 1972. *Gruppendynamik und der "subjektive Faktor":* Repressive Entsublimierung oder politische Praxis. Frankfurt on the Main: Suhrkamp.

Jager, E. 1975. Die therapeutische Gemeinschaft. In *Psychotherapie: Grundlagen, Verfahren, Indikationen.* Ed. H. Strotzka. Munich: Urban und Schwarzenberg.

Jakobson, R. 1971. Language in Relation to other Communication Systems. *Selected Writings II.* (Word and Language.) The Hague: Mouton.

Janik, A., and Toulmin, S. 1973. *Wittgenstein's Vienna.* New York: Simon & Schuster.

Jappe, G. 1971. *Über Wort und Sprache in der Psychoanalyse.* Frankfurt on the Main: Fischer (conditio humana).

John, V. P. 1963. The Intellectual Development of Slum Children: Some Preliminary Findings. *American Journal of Orthopsychiatry* 33:813–822.

Junker, H. 1872. Erfahrungen aus der Ehepaargruppentherapie mit Patienten aus der oberen Unterschicht. *Psyche* 5:370–388.

Kallmeyer, E., et al. 1974. *Lektürekolleg zur Textlinguistik I.* (Einführung.) Frankfurt on the Main: Fischer Athenäum.

Kallmeyer, W., and Schütze, F. 1976. Konversationsanalyse. *Studium Linguistik* 1:1–29.

Kamlah, W., and Lorenzen, P. 1967. *Logische Propädeutik.* Mannheim: B. T. Hochschultaschenbächer.

Katz, J. J. 1970. *Philosophie der Sprache.* Frankfurt on the Main: Suhrkamp.

Kemper, W. (Ed.). 1971. *Psychoanalytische Gruppentherapie.* Munich: Kindler.

Kerbrat-Orecchioni, C. 1977. *La connotation.* Lyon: Presses Universitaires de Lyon.

Kintsch, W., and Dijk, T. v. Toward a Model of Text Comprehension and Production. Manuscript (n.d.).

Klann, G. 1977. Psychoanalyse und Sprachwissenschaft. In *Die Sache der Sprache.* Ed. F. Hager et al. Stuttgart: Metzler.

———. 1979. Die Rolle affektiver Prozesse in der Dialogstrukturierung. In *Therapeutische Kommunikation. Ansätze zur Erforschung der Sprache im psychoanalytischen Prozeß.* Ed. D. Flader and R. Wodak-Leodolter. Königstein/Taunus: Scriptor.

Kohn, M. L. 1962–63. Social Class and Parent-Child Relationships. An Interpretation. *American Journal of Sociology* 68:471–480.

Kolers, P. A. 1973. Some Modes of Representation. In *Communication and Affect.* Ed. P. Pliner et al. New York: Academic Press.

Komarovsky, M. 1946. Cultural Contradictions and Sex Roles. *American Journal of Sociology* 52:184–189.

Kraft, E., et al. 1977. Die Konstitution der konversationellen Erzählung. *Linguistische Arbeitsberichte* (LAB) 8:2–59.

Krappmann, L. 1972. *Soziologische Dimensionen der Identität.* Stuttgart: Klett.

Kraus, K. 1976. *Magie der Sprache.* Ein Lesebuch. Frankfurt on the Main: Suhrkamp.

Kress, G. (ed.). 1976. *Halliday: System and Function in Language.* Oxford: Oxford University Press.

Krüger, L. (ed.). 1978. *Thomas S. Kuhn.* Die Entstehung des Neuen. Frankfurt on the Main: Suhrkamp.

Kutter, P. 1970. Aspekte der Gruppentherapie. *Psyche* 10:721–738.

———. 1971. Übertragung und Prozeß in der psychoanalytischen Gruppentherapie. *Psyche* 1:856–873.

Labov, W. 1966. *The Social Stratification of English in New York City.* Washington D.C.: Center for Applied Linguistics.

———. 1972. Rules for Ritual Insults. In *Studies in Social Interaction.* Ed. D. Sudnow. New York: Macmillan.

Labov, W., and Fanshel, D. 1977. *Therapeutic Discourse.* New York: Academic Press.

Labov, W., and Waletzky, J. 1967. Narrative Analysis: Oral Versions of Personal Experience. In *Essays on the Verbal and Visual Arts.* Ed. J. Helm. Seattle, London: University of Washington Press.

Lacan, J. 1958. Les formations de l'inconscient. *Bulletin de Psychologie* 11:283–296.

———. 1975. *Schriften I.* Frankfurt on the Main: Suhrkamp.

Laing, R. D. 1969. Mystifizierung, Konfusion und Konflikt. In *Schizophrenie und Familie.* Ed. G. Bateson et al. Frankfurt on the Main: Suhrkamp.

Lakoff, R. 1975. *Language and Woman's Place.* London: Harper and Row.

Lang, P. J. 1973. Die Anwendung psychophysiologischer Methoden in Psychotherapie und Verhaltensmodifikation. In *Neuropsychologie der Angst.* Ed. N. Birbaumer. Munich: Urban und Schwarzenberg.

Van Lancker, D. 1972*a.* Language Lateralization and Grammars. UCLA *Working Papers in Phonetics* 23:24–32.

———. 1972*b.* Language Processing in the Brain. UCLA *Working Papers in Phonetics* 23:22–24.

Laplanche, J., and Pontalis, J. B. 1975. *Das Vokabular der Psychoanalyse* I, II. Frankfurt on the Main: Suhrkamp.

Lawendowski, B. 1970. Some Observations Concerning Emphasis. *Studia Anglica Posnaniensia* 2:73–83.

Lazarus, P., et al. 1973. Ansatz zu einer kognitiven Gefühlstheorie. In *Neuropsychologie der Angst*. Ed. N. Birbaumer. Munich: Urban und Schwarzenberg.

Leclaire, S. 1979. The Unconscious: Another Logic. Manuscript.

Leithäuser, T., et al. 1977. *Entwurf zu einer Empirie des Alltagsbewußtseins*. Frankfurt on the Main: Suhrkamp.

Lenga, G., and Gutwinski, J. 1979. Sprechstunden-Psychotherapie des Arztes. In *Therapeutische Kommunikation. Ansätze zur Erforschung der Sprache im psychoanalytischen Prozeß*. Ed. D. Flader and R. Wodak-Leodolter. Königstein/Taunus: Scriptor.

Leodolter, R. (Wodak). 1975a. *Das Sprachverhalten von Angeklagten bei Gericht*. Ansätze zu einer soziolinguistischen Theorie der Verbalisierung. Kronberg/Ts: Scriptor.

_____. 1975b. Die Kategorie der "Sprechsituation": Zur soziolinguistischen Theorienbildung. *Grazer Linguistische Studien* 1:142–150.

_____. 1975c. Gestörte Sprache oder Privatsprache: Kommunikation bei Schizophrenen. *Wiener Linguistische Gazette* 10/11: 75–95.

_____. 1976. Interaktion und Stilvariation. Teilaspekte einer explorativen Studie über das Sprachverhalten von Angeklagten bei Gericht. In *Sprachliches Handeln - Soziales Verhalten*. Ed. W. Viereck. Munich: Fink.

Leodolter, R., and Leodolter, M. 1976a. Kommunikative Interaktion und Sozialisation. In *Soziolinguistik*. Ed. A. Schaff. Vienna: Europa Verlag.

_____. 1976b. Sociolinguistic Considerations on Psychosocial Socialization: The Beginnings of a Theory of Verbalization. In *Language and Man*. Ed. W. McCormack and S. Wurm. The Hague: Mouton.

Levin, S. 1977. The Psychoanalysis of Shame. In *The World of Emotions*. Ed. C. W. Socarides. Bloomington: Indiana University Press.

Lévi-Strauss, C. 1958. *Anthropologie structurale*. Paris: Plon.

Levy, D. M. 1979. Communicative Goals and Strategies: Between Discourse and Syntax. In *Syntax and Semantics*. Ed. T. Givon. New York: Academic Press.

Liberman, M. I. 1978. The Intonational System of English. Bell Laboratories. *Indiana University Linguistics Club*. Bloomington, Indiana.

Litowitz, B., and Litowitz, N. 1977. The Influence of Linguistic Theory on Psychoanalysis: A Critical, Historical Survey. *International Review of Psycho-Analysis* 4:419–448.

Lobner, H. 1979. "The Unconscious" in the Soviet-Union. *Sigmund Freud House Bulletin* 3, 1:20–28.

Lord, R. 1966. *Teach Yourself Comparative Linguistics*. London: English Universities Press Ltd.

Lorenzer, A. 1970. *Kritik des psychoanalytischen Symbolbegriffs*. Frankfurt on the Main: Suhrkamp.

————. 1972. *Zur Begründung einer materialistischen Sozialisations theorie*. Frankfurt on the Main: Suhrkamp.

————. 1973. *Sprachzerstörung und Rekonstruktion*. Frankfurt on the Main: Suhrkamp.

————. 1976. *Die Wahrheit der psychoanalytischen Erkenntnis*. Frankfurt on the Main: Suhrkamp.

————. 1977. *Sprachspiel und Interaktionsformen*. Frankfurt on the Main: Suhrkamp.

Lüder, C., et al. 1970. Geschlechtserziehung und Sprache. *Schule und Psychologie* 17:113–121.

Lyons, J. 1977. *Semantics*. Cambridge: Cambridge University Press.

McCarthy, D. 1953. Some Possible Explanations of Sex Differences in Language Development and Disorders. *Journal of Psychology* 35:155–160.

Maccoby, E. 1966. *The Development of Sex Differences*. Stanford: Stanford University Press.

McCormack, W., and Wurm, S. (eds.). 1976. *Language and Man*. Anthropological Issues. The Hague: Mouton.

Maclay, M., and Osgood, C. 1959. Hesitation Phenomena in Spontaneous Speech. *Word* 15:19–44.

Mahler, M. S. 1969. *On Human Symbiosis and the Vicissitudes of Individuation*. New York: International Universities Press.

Marek, B. 1975. Derivative Character of Intonation in Polish and English. Ph.D. Dissertation. University of Massachusetts.

Martens, K. 1974. *Sprachliche Kommunikation in der Familie*. Kronberg/Taunus: Scriptor.

Mel'čuk, I. A. 1974. *Opyt teorii lingvističeskich modelej "smysl ↔ tekst"*. Moskva: Akademičesky.

————. 1976. Towards a Linguistic "Meaning ↔ Text" Model. In *Das Wort. Zwischen Inhalt und Ausdruck*. Ed. I. A. Mel'čuk. Munich: Fink.

————. (ed.). 1976. *Das Wort. Zwischen Inhalt und Ausdruck* (herausgegeben und eingeleitet von J. Riedermann). Munich: Fink.

Menne, K., et al. 1976. *Sprache, Handlung und Unbewußtes.* Kronberg/Taunus: Scriptor.

Menninger, K., and Holzman, P. 1973. *Theory of Psychoanalytic Technique.* New York: Basic Books.

Meringer, R. 1923. Die täglichen Fehler im Sprechen, Lesen und Handeln. Zu Freuds "Psychopathologie des Alltagslebens." *Wörter und Sachen* VIII:122–141.

Meringer, R., and Mayer, C. 1895. *Versprechen und Verlesen*-eine psychologisch-linguistische Studie. Stuttgart: Göschen'sche Verlagsbuchhandlung.

Meyer-Hermann, R. 1979. Zur Funktion metakommunikativer Sprechakte. Manuscript. Bielefeld.

Miller, D., and Swanson, G. 1960. *Inner Conflict and Defense.* New York: International Universities Press.

Miller, S. M., and Riesmann, H. 1961. The Working-Class Subculture: A New View. *Social Problems* 9:86–97.

Mitchell, J. 1976. *Psychoanalyse und Feminismus.* Frankfurt on the Main: Suhrkamp.

Moeller-Gambaroff, M. 1977. Emanzipation macht Angst. *Kursbuch* 47:1–26.

Moersch, E. 1976. Psychoanalytische Bemerkungen zu Lorenzers Revisionsvorschlägen. Zur Kritik des Gebrauchs Von Symbol, Repräsentanz und psychischem Primärvorgang. In *Sprache, Handlung und Unbewußtes.* Ed. K. Menne et al. Kronberg/Taunus: Scriptor.

Moore, T. E. (ed.). 1973. *Cognitive Development and the Acquisition of Language.* New York: Academic Press.

Morris, C. 1938. *Foundations of the Theory of Signs.* Chicago: University of Chicago Press.

Muschg, W. 1975. *Freud als Schriftsteller.* Munich: Kindler.

Navratil, L. 1974. *Über Schizophrenie und Die Federzeichnungen des Patienten O.T.* Munich: DTV.

Nedelmann, C., and Horn, K. 1976. Gesellschaftliche Aufgaben der Psychotherapie. *Psyche* 9:827–853.

Norman, D. and Rumelhart, D. (eds.). 1975. *Explorations in Cognition.* San Francisco: Freeman.

OBST (Osnabrücker Beiträge zur Sprachtheorie). 1979. Sprache und Geschlecht, III (Akten des Symposiums vom 29.3.–31.3.1979; herausgegeben von Aebischer, V. et al.). Osnabrück.

Ochs, E. 1979. Planned and Unplanned Discourse. In *Syntax and Semantics*. Ed. T. Givon. New York: Academic Press.

Oevermann, U. 1972. *Sprache und soziale Herkunft*. Frankfurt on the Main: Suhrkamp.

———, et al. 1979. Die Methodologie einer "objektiven Hermeneutik." In *Interpretative Verfahren in den Sozial- und Textwissenschaften*. Ed. H. G. Soeffer. Stuttgart: Metzler.

Ogden, C. K., and Richards, I. A. 1972. *The Meaning of Meaning*. London: Routledge and Kegan Paul.

Osgood, C., Suci, G., and Tannenbaum, P. 1957. *The Measurement of Meaning*. Urbana: University of Illinois Press.

Overbeck, G., et al. 1974. Über die Anwendung eines Sprachanalyseverfahrens (On-Off-Pattern) in einer laufenden Psychotherapie. *Psyche* 9/10:815–833.

Pagès, M. 1974. *Das affektive Leben der Gruppe*. Stuttgart: Klett.

Palmer, F. R. 1976. *Semantics*. A New Outline. Cambridge: Cambridge University Press.

Parker, B. 1974. *Meine Sprache bin ich*. Frankfurt on the Main: Suhrkamp.

Parsons, T. 1951. *The Social System*. New York: Free Press.

Peisach, E. C. 1965. Children's Comprehension of Teacher and Peer Speech. *Child Development* 35:467–480.

Petöfi, J. S. 1973. Towards an Empirically Motivated Grammatical Theory of Verbal Texts. In *Studies in Text Grammar*. Ed. J. S. Petöfi and H. Rieser. Dordrecht: Reidel.

Petöfi, J. S., and Rieser, H. (eds.). 1973. *Studies in Text Grammar*. Dordrecht: Reidel.

Piaget, J. 1969. *Nachahmung, Spiel und Traum*. Stuttgart: Klett.

Piro, S. 1967. *Il linguaggio schizofrenico*. Milano: Feltrinelli.

Pliner, P., et al. 1973. *Communication and Affect*. New York: Academic Press.

Pohlen, M. 1972. Versuch einer systemkritischen Analyse der Gruppenkonzepte. *Zeitschrift für Gruppenpsychotherapie und Gruppendynamik* 5:135–151.

Popitz, 1967. *Der Begriff der sozialen Rolle als Element der soziologischen Theorie*. Tübingen: Mohr and Siebeck.

Posner, R. 1972. *Theorie des Kommentierens*. Eine Grundlagenstudie zur Semantik und Pragmatik. Frankfurt on the Main: Athenäum.

Prangishvili, A. S., Scherozia, A. E., and Bassin, F. V. (eds.). 1978,

The Unconscious: Nature, Functions, Methods of Study, I, II, III. Tbilissi: Mezniereva.

Preuss, H. G. (ed.). 1960. *Analytische Gruppenpsychotherapie:* Grundlagen und Praxis. München: Urban und Schwarzenberg.

Propp, F. J. 1928. *Morfologija skazkii.* Moskva: Nauka.

Quasthoff, U. 1979. *Linguistische Studien zu Erzählungen in Gesprächen:* Eine integrierte strukturell-funktionelle Analyse. Habilitationsschrift. Berlin.

Rapaport, D. 1965. Toward a Theory of Thinking. In *Organization and Pathology of Thought.* Ed. D. Rapaport. New York: Columbia University Press.

————. (ed.). 1965 *Organization and Pathology of Thought.* New York: Columbia University Press.

Rehbein, J. 1976*a*. Planen I: Elemente des Handlungsplans. *LAUT Papier* 39. Trier.

————. 1976*b*. Planen II: Planbildung in Sprechhandlungssequenzen. *LAUT Papier* 39. Trier.

Reiter, L. 1973. Zur Bedeutung der Sprache und Sozialisation für die Psychotherapie von Patienten aus der sozialen Unterschicht. In *Psychotherapie: Grundlagen, Verfahren, Indikationen.* Ed. H. Strotzka. Munich: Urban und Schwarzenberg.

Remplein, S. 1977. *Therapieforschung in der Psychoanalyse.* Munich: Reinhart Verlag.

Richter, H. E. 1972. *Die Gruppe.* Reinbek/Hamburg: Rowohlt.

————. 1974. *Lernziel Solidarität.* Reinbek/Hamburg: Rowohlt.

Ricoeur, R. 1974. *Die Interpretation.* Frankfurt on the Main: Suhrkamp.

Rosen, H. H. 1972. Sprache und Psychoanalyse. *Psyche* 2:81–88.

Ross, R. N. 1975. Ellipsis and the Structure of Expectations. *San José State University Occasional Papers in Linguistics.* I:183–191.

Rubin, R. 1972. Sex Differences in Effects of "Kindergarten" Attendance on Development of School Readiness and Language Skills. *The Elementary School Journal* 72, 5:265–274.

Rumelhart, D., and Norman, D. 1975. The Active Structural Network. Chapter 2. In *Explorations in Cognition.* Ed. D. Norman and D. Rumelhart. San Francisco: Freeman.

Ruth, D. 1966. Language, Intelligence and Social Class: A Study of Communicative Effectiveness Within Same-Class and Cross-Class Pairs. Undergraduate honors thesis. Harvard College.

Sachs, L. 1969. *Statistische Auswertungsmethoden*. Berlin: Springer.

Sacks, H. 1966. The Search for Help: No One To Turn To. Ph.D. Dissertation, University of California, Berkeley.

————. 1972. An Initial Investigation of the Usability of Conversational Data for Doing Sociology. In *Studies in Social Interaction*. Ed. D. Sudnow. New York: Macmillan.

Sandig, B. 1978. *Stilistik*. Berlin: De Gruyter.

Schaff, A. (ed.). 1976. *Soziolinguistik*. Vienna: Europa Verlag.

Schank, R., and Abelson, R. 1977. *Scripts, Plans, Goals and Understanding*. Norwood, N.J.: Ablex.

Scheflen, A. E. 1973. *Communicational Structure:* Analysis of a Psychotherapy Transaction. Bloomington: Indiana University Press.

Scherer, K. R. 1979. Personality Markers in Speech. In *Social Markers in Speech*. Ed. K. R. Scherer and H. Giles. Cambridge: Cambridge University Press.

Scherer, K. R., and Giles, H. (eds.). 1979. *Social Markers in Speech*. Cambridge: Cambridge University Press.

Schifko, P. 1975. *Bedeutungstheorie:* Einführung in die linguistische Semantik. Stuttgart: Fromann-Holzboog.

Schindler, R. 1957/58. Grundprinzipien der Psychodynamik in der Gruppe. *Psyche* 5:308–314.

Schmitt, R. (ed.). 1977. *Etymologie*. Darmstadt: Wissenschaftliche Buchgemeinschaft.

Schnitzler, A. 1978. Der letzte Brief eines Literaten. *Gesamtausgabe Band V*. (Das erzählerische Werk). Frankfurt on the Main: Fischer.

Schröter, K. 1979. Einige formale Aspekte des psychoanalytischen Dialogs. In *Therapeutische Kommunikation. Ansätze zur Erforschung der Sprache im psychoanalytischen Prozeß*. Ed. D. Flader and R. Wodak-Leodolter. Königstein/Taunus: Scriptor.

Schütz, A. 1960. *Der sinnhafte Ausbau der sozialen Welt*. Vienna: Springer.

Searle, J. 1971. *Sprechakte*. Frankfurt on the Main: Suhrkamp.

————. 1975. A Taxonomy of Illocutionary Acts. In *Language, Mind and Knowledge*. Vol. VII. Ed. K. Gunderson. Minneapolis: University of Minnesota Press.

Skinner, B. F. 1938. *Behavior of Organisms*. New York: Appleton-Century-Crofts, Inc.

Slater, P. E. 1978. *Mikrokosmos:* Eine Studie über Gruppendynamik. Frankfurt on the Main: Fischer.

Slavson, S. R. 1960. Die historische Entwicklung der analytischen Gruppenpsychotherapie. In *Analytische Gruppenpsychotherapie*. Grundlagen und Praxis. Munich: Urban und Schwarzenberg.

Smith, P. M. 1979. Sex Markers in Speech. In *Social Markers in Speech*. Ed. K. R. Scherer and H. Giles. Cambridge: Cambridge University Press.

Socarides, C. W. (ed.). 1977. *The World of Emotions*. Bloomington: Indiana University Press.

Soeffner, H. G. (ed.). 1979. *Interpretative Verfahren in den Sozial- und Textwissenschaften*. Stuttgart: Metzler.

Sonneck, G. 1976. Krisenintervention und Suizidverhütung. *Ars Medici* 10:419–424.

Sperling, O. E. 1977. On the Mechanisms of Spacing and Crowding Emotions. In *The World of Emotions*. Ed. C. W. Socarides. Bloomington: Indiana University Press.

Spitz, R. A. 1967. *Vom Säugling zum Kleinkind*. Stuttgart: Klett.

_____. 1970. *Nein und Ja*. Die Ursprünge der menschlichen Kommunikation. Stuttgart: Klett.

Strasser, H., et al. 1979. Studien zur sozialen Ungleichheit. Manuscript. Vienna.

Strauss, F., and Sonneck, F. 1978. Statistische Untersuchungen Uber die Selbstmorde in Österreich aus den Jahren 1971–1975. *Mitteilungen der Österreichischen Sanitätsverwaltung* 4, 79:3–11.

Strotzka, H. 1972. *Psychotherapie und soziale Sicherheit*. Munich: Kindler.

_____. (ed.). 1973. *Neurose, Charakter und soziale Umwelt*. Munich: Kindler.

_____. (ed.). 1975. *Psychotherapie: Grundlagen, Verfahren, Indikationen*. Munich: Urban und Schwarzenberg.

Strupp, H. H. 1973. *Psychotherapy: Clinical Research and Theoretical Issues*. New York: Jason Aronson.

Strupp, H. H., Fox, R. E., and Lessler, K. 1969. *Patients View their Psychotherapy*. Baltimore and London: Johns Hopkins Press.

Strupp, H. H., Hadley, S., and Comes-Schwartz, B. 1977. *Psychotherapy for Better or Worse*. The Problem of Negative Effects. New York: Jason Aronson.

Sudnow, D. (ed.) 1972. *Studies in Social Interaction*. New York: Macmillan.

Tannen, D. 1979. What's in a Frame? Surface Evidence for Underlying Expectations. In *New Directions in Discourse Processing*. Ed. R. Freedle. Norwood, N.J.: Ablex.

Tausch, R. 1970. *Gesprächstherapie.* Stuttgart: Kiepenheuer und Witsch.

Thorne, B., and Henley, N. (eds.). 1975. *Language and Sex: Difference and Dominance.* Rowley: Newbury.

Tiger, L. 1972. *Men in Groups.* Harmondsworth: Penguin.

Till, W. 1977. Effizienz von Krisenintervention. Ph.D. Dissertation. Vienna.

Todorov, T. 1972. *Poétique de la prose.* Frankfurt on the Main: Suhrkamp.

Trapp, P. (ed.). 1963. *Expressions of Emotions in Man.* New York: International University Press.

Trömel-Plötz, S. 1979. "She is Just Not an Open Person." Linguistische Analyse einer restrukturierenden Intervention in der Familientherapie. In *Therapeutische Kommunikation. Ansätze zur Erforschung der Sprache im psychoanalytischen Prozeß.* Ed. D. Flader and R. Wodak-Leodolter. Königstein/Taunus: Scriptor.

Trudgill, P. 1974. *The social differentiation of English in Norwich.* Cambridge: Cambridge University Press.

Turner, R. 1972. Some Formal Properties of Therapy Talk. In *Studies in Social Interaction.* Ed. D. Sudnow. New York: Macmillan.

Vanderslice, R., and Ladefoged, P. 1972. Binary Suprasegmental Features and Transformational Word-Accentuation Rules. *Language* 48:819–839.

Vaneček, E., and Dressler, W. 1975. Bericht über psycholinguistische Experimente zur Sprechvariation. *Wiener Linguistische Gazette* 9:17–37.

Viereck, W. (ed.). 1976. *Sprachliches Handeln - Soziales Verhalten.* Munich: Fink.

Vitt, N.V. 1965. Vyraženie emocjonal'nych sostojanij v rečevoj intonacii. Ph.D. Dissertation. Moscow.

Walter, H. (ed.). 1973. *Sozialisationsforschung* I, II, III. Stuttgart: Fromann-Holzboog.

Warren, E., et al. 1979. Event Chains and Inferences in Understanding Narratives. In *New Directions in Discourse Processing.* Ed. R. Freedle. Norwood, N.J.: Ablex.

Watzlawick, P., et al. 1972. *Menschliche Kommunikation.* Bern: Huber.

Weinrich, H. 1971. *Tempus.* Besprochene und erzählte Welt. Stuttgart: Metzler.

Weiss, H. 1977. Soziale Schicht und psychiatrische Versorgung. *Österreichische Zeitschrift für Soziologie* 3/4:43–54.

Weiss, J. M. A. 1954. Suicide: An Epidemiological Analysis. *Psychological Quarterly* 28:225–252.

Werlich, E. 1975. *Typologie der Texte.* Heidelberg: UTB.

West, C., and Zimmermann, D. 1975. *Women's Place in Everyday Talk.* Santa Barbara, Calif.

Whyte, W. F. 1973. *Street Corner Society.* Chicago: University of Chicago Press.

Windhoff-Héritier, A. 1976. *Sind Frauen so, wie Freud sie sah?* Weiblichkeit und Wirklichkeit. Hamburg: Fischer.

Winitz, H. 1959. Language Skills of Male and Female Kindergarten Children. *Journal of Speech and Hearing Research* 2:377–386.

Wittgenstein, L. 1967. *Philosophische Untersuchungen.* Frankfurt on the Main: Suhrkamp.

Wodak, R. (Leodolter). 1981*a*. Geschlechtsspezifische Strategien in einer therapeutischen Gruppe. In *Das ewige Klischee.* Ed. Autorinnengruppe Uni Wien. Vienna: Böhlau.

———. 1981*b*. How Do I Put My Problem? *Text* 4/1:191–213.

———. 1981*c*. Women Relate, Men Report. *Journal of Pragmatics* 5:261–285.

———. 1983 Arguments in Favour of a Socio-Psycho-Linguistic Theory of Text Planning. *Klagenfurter Beiträge zur Sprachwissenschaft* 9:313–350.

———. 1984. *Hilflose Nähe?-Mütter und Töchter erzählen.* Vienna: Deuticke.

Wodak-Leodolter, R. 1977. Interaktion in einer therapeutischen Gruppe: eine soziolinguistische Analyse. *Wiener Linguistische Gazette* 15:33–60.

———. 1978*a*. Soziolinguistische Analyse therapeutischer Kommunikation: Gruppen- und Einzeltherapie. *Studium Linguistik* 5:99–104.

———. 1978*b*. Dialogtexte bei Schizophrenen. In *The Unconscious: Nature, Functions, Methods of Study, III.* Ed. A. S. Prangishvili, A. E. Scherozia, and F. V. Bassin. Tibilissi: Mezniereva.

———. 1979. Auf der Suche nach einer neuen Identität: Geschlechtsspezifisches Sprachverhalten in einer therapeutischen Gruppe. *Osnabrücker Beiträge zur Sprachtheorie,* Beiheft 3:36–47.

Wodak-Leodolter, R. 1980. Probleme der soziolinguistischen Feldforschung am Beispiel der Analyse spontansprachlicher Texte. *Linguistische Studien,* Reihe A, 72, 2, Berlin: 50–75.

Wodak-Leodolter, R., and Dressler, W. 1978. Phonological Variation in Colloquial Viennese. *Michigan Germanic Studies* 4, 1:30–66.

Wodak, R., and Schulz, M. 1984. *The Language of Love and Guilt.* Amsterdam: Benjamins.

Wolf, A., and Schwarz, E. K. 1962. *Psychoanalysis in Groups.* New York: Grune and Stratton.

Wolff, P. M. 1974. Überlegungen zu einer psychoanalytischen Theorie des Spracherwerbs. *Psyche* 9/10:853–899.

Wunderlich, D. 1976. *Studien zur Sprechakttheorie.* Frankfurt on the Main: Suhrkamp.

———. 1979. Was ist das für ein Sprechakt? In *Sprechakttheorie und Semantik.* Ed. G. Grewendorf. Frankfurt on the Main: Suhrkamp.

Wygotski, L. S. 1971. *Denken und Sprechen.* Stuttgart: Fischer (conditio humana).

Wynne, L. 1969. Pseudogemeinschaften in den Familienbeziehungen von Schizophrenen. In *Schizophrenie und Familie.* Ed. G. Bateson. Frankfurt on the Main: Suhrkamp.

Zetterberg, H. L. 1962. Theorie, Forschung und Praxis in der Soziologie. In *Handbuch der empirischen Sozialforschung.* Ed. R. König. Stuttgart: Enke.

Zilboorg, G. 1977. Anxiety without Affect. In *The World of Emotions.* Ed. C. W. Socarides. Bloomington: University of Indiana Press.

Žolkovskij, A. K., and Mel´čuk, I. A. 1967. O semantičeskom sinteze. *Problemy kibernetiki* 19:171–219.

Index

Designer:	U. C. Press Staff
Compositor:	Publisher's Typography
Printer:	Edwards Bros., Inc.
Binder:	Edwards Bros., Inc.
Text:	10/12 Sabon
Display:	Sabon